D0986767

CHRONICLES *of an* AFRICAN WANDERER

Nick Ngazoire Nteireho

outskirtspress
DENVER, COLORADO

The opinions expressed in this manuscript are solely the opinions of the author and do not represent the opinions or thoughts of the publisher. The author has represented and warranted full ownership and/or legal right to publish all the materials in this book.

Chronicles of an African Wanderer
All Rights Reserved.
Copyright © 2013 Nick Ngazoire Nteireho
v3.0

Cover Photo © 2013 Nick Ngazoire Nteireho. All rights reserved - used with permission.

This book may not be reproduced, transmitted, or stored in whole or in part by any means, including graphic, electronic, or mechanical without the express written consent of the publisher except in the case of brief quotations embodied in critical articles and reviews.

Outskirts Press, Inc.
http://www.outskirtspress.com

ISBN: 978-1-4787-0409-6

Outskirts Press and the "OP" logo are trademarks belonging to Outskirts Press, Inc.

PRINTED IN THE UNITED STATES OF AMERICA

One

AT THE BEGINNING of April 2004, my father, Mzee Tobi Ngazoire, had not felt well for close to a month, and I was getting worried, since his bouts of illness usually lasted for much shorter periods. My sister, Monica, an assistant physician at the famed Johns Hopkins Hospital in Baltimore, Maryland had traveled there with her husband about a month earlier, partly to parade their new baby before the patriarch. They had arranged for him to travel to Kampala, where they would also use the opportunity to take him to the better city hospitals, to treat him for the minor complaints he had.

My family had had more than its fair share of tragedies during the last decade and a half, having lost three of my brothers and a sister, all in their prime years. Then on Friday evening, I received a distress call from my sister. Her distraught voice could not betray the message behind the reason she was calling.

"Mzee is not well", she announced between restrained sobs. "He is neither talking, nor eating anything", she continued. Mzee is an affectionate title in the Kiswahili and related languages, re-served for people you love and respect, mostly applied to old men. I attempted to calm her down, to no avail. That evening, I made a hasty call to my young brother Tony, at his home in the Kampala suburbs. He, too, sounded very worried about the old man, and encouraged me to make a quick trip to Uganda. I

1 ❧

assured him that I would begin on a search for a ticket.

April is that month, when the travel industry makes a transition from the low-activity months of winter, to the high-demand travel season of the summer months, accompanied by escalating airline fares. The matter only gets worse if one has to find a seat at short notice for such out-of-the-way places like Entebbe, only served by a handful of international airlines. However, there are some things in life which cannot be put on hold, and this was one of those. I called British Airways, and told the lady at reservations that I had an emergency. Some airlines provide discounts in such situations. Her first question was, "Is the person you are trying to see already dead?" she asked. I said, "No, thank God", and immediately hang up. I didn't want a discount on Mzee's head.

I got on my computer right away, and by mid-night, thanks to the internet, I had secured a reasonable ticket on KLM, the Dutch airline. The itinerary was from Dulles Washington International Airport to Nairobi, via Amsterdam, and then connecting to Entebbe on Kenya Airways, which had recently formed a partnership with the European duo of KLM-Air France.

Not known for traveling with a lot of luggage, I did some hasty packing of the bare necessities. Among the items I included for the trip, was a Newsweek Magazine, profiling a young State-Senator from Illinois, called Barack Obama. Until then, I had only heard of this young Turk through my old buddy, Frank McCoy, who had encouraged me to explore a little more about him. And this was long before the 2004 Democratic Convention, held in the City of Boston, Massachusetts. The young legislator would later that year, give a rousing keynote address to the delegates who nominated Sen. John Kerry of Massachusetts as the flag bearer of the Democratic Party for the 2004 Presidential Elections.

It's not easy contemplating the loss of a parent. My father had always been my idol, my wise counsel, and a constant presence whether or not I could see him. I had left home for boarding school at the tender age of fifteen, but I could always count on him for advice, even long after I had matured into a man, and had children of my own.

As I was boarding the KLM flight in Amsterdam, I run into an old friend who once lived in the Washington DC metro area while he interned at Intelsat, the Global Satellite Communications Company. We exchanged some pleasantries, but my mind was meandering too much about Mzee's condition to get involved in casual conversations. Once on the plane, I fixed myself in my seat, and tried to read for the best part of the journey to Nairobi. Soon, however, I abandoned the reading and found solace striking a conversation with a fellow passenger.

Next to me, was a middle-aged lady from Scotland, named Doreen, who, as it turned out, had established a school for disadvantaged children, north of Lamu, a small town on the Kenya Coast. She told me she had retired from the Scottish Police, and had stumbled on this project, after looking for something more meaningful to do. Doreen and I found some common ground, as I told her my ailing dad had also established a fledgling school, which I was helping to support with a donated book here and there. My chat with Doreen was very refreshing, as it temporarily took away the weight off my back. I bade farewell to her at the Jomo Kenyatta International Airport in Nairobi, as we both left the transfer desk to board flights to our final destinations.

I once again run into Mr. Kazinduki, the Intelsat guy while waiting for the connecting Kenya Airways flight to Entebbe, where we finally arrived close to mid-night. Although I was exhausted and rather haggard from the long flight, my mind was full of anxiety, on whether or not I would do anything to keep the old man alive.

Fortunately, my nephew, Peter, was waiting for me at Entebbe Airport, and soon, we were maneuvering our way through the poorly-lit streets of Entebbe, on our way for the thirty-two kilometer drive to Kampala. Entebbe, (which means seat in Luganda), was named so, because the Kabaka (king) of Buganda used to hold court adjudicating over legal matters, seated on a set of boulders overlooking Lake Victoria, at a place called Bugonga. The first colonial governor, Sir Gerald Portal, adapted the peninsula as the seat of the British Protectorate in 1893, and to-date, State House, the official residence of the Ugandan president is located in Entebbe.

Earlier, on February 17, 1879, two French missionaries, Father Simeon Lourdel (also known as Mapeera by locals, from the French mon pere), and Brother Amans Delmas, had landed at Kigungu Beach on the southern part of the peninsular. They had been part of a caravan of white fathers who had left Marseilles on April 22, 1878, arriving on Zanzibar Island on May 30. The whole caravan then left the island on June 17, to explore the African hinterland by foot, and spread the word of God.

When Kabaka Muteesa I first heard of their arrival, he sent out his guards, who had them detained at Kitebi, three miles from Rubaga, for fifteen days, some days going without food, and shivering from bouts of malaria. The Kabaka later summoned them to his court, where Lourdel laid out his case regarding the purpose of their mission, asking the king for permission to set up a church on his territory. The king gave his consent on February 23, 1879, thus marking the establishment of the Catholic Church in Uganda. The church was later built on Rubaga Hill, which still serves as the headquarters of the Catholic Church in the country. Similar permission had been granted in 1877, to the Church Missionary Society of England, to set up a church on Namirembe Hill, which also still serves as the headquarters of the Anglican Church.

It was also from Entebbe, in 1952, that the young Princess Elizabeth and her husband, Prince Phillip, boarded a flight to return home as future Queen Elizabeth II of England, after learning of the death of her father, King George V. In June 1976, Entebbe made world headlines as the site of the daring raid by the Israeli Defense Forces, when Operation Thunderball was staged to rescue their nationals, held by PLO freedom fighters, after hijacking

Air France Flight #AF139 to the airport.

The road between Kampala, the Ugandan capital, and Entebbe, the location of the only International airport in the country, is as treacherous as they come. Except for a four-kilometer stretch of dual-carriage between Kibuye traffic circle on the edge of the city, and Zana, the rest is a two-lane highway, dotted with all manner of transportation, competing for space, like vultures fighting each other over a carcass. The massive gas-guzzling SUVs carrying Cabinet Ministers, Diplomats, and the nation's nouveau riche, driven at breakneck speeds, literally sweeping the boda-boda cyclists off the road, are hard to miss. And rare, is the day that passes without a fatal accident, as one unlucky rider gets sucked in by one of these monsters as he fails to yield space in time.

Upon arrival in Kampala, I threw myself in bed, only to turn around and stare at the empty ceiling. One or two mosquitoes buzzed by, ignored unimpressively, they soon left, as I had bigger problems to worry about. Across the valley, in Nateete, some loud music was blasting from one of the trans-night clubs that litter the Kampala suburbs. Finally, in the wee hours of the morning, a combination of the long flight and sleep depravation began to take their toll, and my weakened body succumbed into a deep sleep.

Two

THE MUEZZIN'S CALL pierces the air every morning at dawn, as he indulges in this age-old ritual of calling the Muslim faithful to prayer. I had been sleeping for about three hours when I heard the voice crackling on the loudspeaker from the other side of Nateete. As my internal clock adjusts fairly quickly, the short sleep had cleared my head enough to get me planning the events for the upcountry trip. Although private buses plying the Kampala-Rukungiri route have mushroomed over the last fifteen years, that mode of transport still poses a challenge to someone unfamiliar with the hustle of Ugandan roads. Luckily, my niece, Grace, had arranged transportation that would take me upcountry. She and Richard, her husband, were generous enough to provide me with their car and driver. All I had to do was buy some gas, and pay Kanyankore, the driver, a daily stipend. Grace, my eldest brother's daughter, had spent most of her early childhood years with her grandparents, and was extremely attached to them. Their welfare ranked high among her priorities.

Traffic in Kampala's narrow and pot-holed streets can be unnervingly slow. The last few years have witnessed perhaps a tenfold increase in the number of vehicles in the country. There has been a frenzy to import mostly used and reconditioned vehicles that are considered a menace in developed countries, on account of their unhealthy emissions. The bulk of these are imported from Japan, but a sizeable number also comes from Dubai. Most end up in the Kampala area, the largest city with the economic muscle to absorb them. Yet, the city's road network has hardly changed since independence, leaving drivers to fight for the little space there is to get to wherever they are going. If you live in the Ntinda-Kamwokya suburbs, east of the city, for instance, and you have a flight to catch at Entebbe International Airport, located about thirty two kilometers south-west of Kampala, budget a good three hours. Better still, carry minimal luggage, hop on a Bajaj boda-boda motor-bike, and pray that an errant kamunye driver doesn't knock you down.

I had to make a few errands around the city, to pick some basic items from a list Grace had prepared for me. Some were available from pharmacies, which usually do not open until after eight O'clock, and yet, I had planned to start the 220-mile journey to my parents' home no later than 9.00 am. Uganda's healthcare system has deteriorated to a point where the patient is expected to provide such basics as bandages, drip fluids, etc, not only in public hospitals, but private clinics as well. Expectant mothers are advised to arrive at a maternity ward with their own surgical gloves and cleaning cloths. Some unscrupulous doctors, who, officially work at public hospitals, but maintain private clinics in city suburbs, pilfer drugs from the public hospital pharmacies and use these and other materials to stock their private pharmacies. In the worst-case scenario, they replace genuine drugs with cheap imitations, whose origins have, over the years, been tracked to either India or China. I had already purchased an assortment of drugs from the US, including painkillers such as Tylenol and Advil, something that had become routine during trips to my homeland. However, the advent of September 11, 2001, had limited the liquid items passengers could carry on a plane, thus eliminating such effective cough and congestion solutions as Robitussin and Vicks Formula 44 from my carry-on luggage.

As the city pharmacies were still closed, I decided to check both Mulago and Mengo hospitals in case they had what I needed, to no avail. Hospitals in Uganda, especially public ones like Mulago, have simply become a place where patients go to die.

Mulago, a sprawling edifice, completed in 1962, just in time for Uganda's Independence that took place on October 9, 1962, was once the envy of sub-Saharan Africa. As the nation's premier medical teaching facility for Makerere University's once famed Medical School, the 1500-bed hospital and its facilities sit on about 500 acres of prime real estate, on a hill just opposite Makerere University. The crowded valley between the two institutions was dubbed "Katanga Valley" in the 60's, perhaps in solidarity with the rebellious Katanga Province of Congo Leopoldville (now Democratic Republic of the Congo). It is mostly inhabited by shady characters, such as ladies of ill-repute, who render invaluable services that soothe the tired minds of academics on both hills.

In its heyday, the Medical School attracted students from the British Commonwealth, straddled across the globe, from Canada to Jamaica in the western hemisphere, to India and Australia, for studies at the School of Tropical Medicine, whose degrees were, at the time, conferred by the University of London.

During the nation's tumultuous years of Idi Amin and Obote II, the hospital became a shell, a mere shadow of its old self. Cases were rampant during the dreaded regimes, where unruly soldiers, on mere suspicion that a physician dated a particular beautiful girl they liked, would burst into an operating theater, snatch the doctor, and drag him out screaming, never to be seen again, and leaving the unfortunate patient in the theater, to die of infections from the open wounds. It was at this same hospital, where the elderly Mrs. Dora Bloch, a hostage on the ill-fated Air France Flight AF139, hijacked by Palestinians to Entebbe in June, 1976, was taken after choking on a fish bone, only to be abducted by State Research soldiers, on the orders of Idi Amin, in retaliation for Israel's rescue of its citizens at Entebbe International Airport, in

Operation Thunderball. Such acts of brutality left a lot of people demoralized, and impacted the healthcare delivery system of the country more than any other sector of the economy, as most doctors and nurses trained in Uganda in the last thirty years, have left the country for greener pastures.

Conditions at Mulago Hospital haven't improved that much during the National Resistance Movement regime headed by President Yoweri Museveni, in power since January 1986. Nevertheless, the regime was a big relief to the long-suffering populace in the early years, instilling some discipline among the soldiers. However, given the insatiable greed with which the so-called liberators have looted the economy, this has left many people wondering if this regime change wasn't merely a case of a blackened kettle calling another cooking pot black. The regime has since lost its luster, tainted mainly by unprecedented levels of corruption, seemingly with tacit approval of the top brass. Hundreds of millions of dollars have been received from the donor community, both on a bilateral government-to-government basis, and the bulk, from multilateral institutions such as the World Bank, International Monetary Fund (IMF), and the African Development Bank (AfDB). Although a big share of these resources was targeted at priority areas of the economy, such as education, health and infrastructure, it is not surprising to encounter shelled-out structures in some streets of Kampala, thirty years after Amin was booted out. This prompted one former World Bank vice president, having just returned from the country in the 1990's, to remark that "the streets of Kampala leave a visitor with the impression that the war was fought yesterday".

Mulago Hospital, as well as Makerere University, underwent some cosmetic coats of paint, leaving some building structures crumbling underneath, in extreme cases, missing sections of the roof became conduits as mini streams whenever it rained, sending the occupants scampering for shelter elsewhere. In maternity wards, it's not uncommon for medical personnel to deliver two mothers on the same bed within minutes of each other, the only cleaning done, being the wiping of the bloody mess from the plastic sheet on top of a thin mattress. In the children wing, two or even three children may be attended to on the same bed at the same time, with the potential for the one with a contagious ailment infecting the others.

The excesses of the current regime's corruption, and its impunity, were amplified by the Justice Ogoola Commission of Inquiry into GAVI funds, conducted in 2005. The funds, originating from the Global Fund of the World Health Organization in Geneva, Switzerland, were meant to purchase drugs for the most vulnerable of Uganda s citizens inflicted with the deadly Aids virus and its related ailments such as tuberculosis. While the judge's report found the health minister and his two deputies culpable for misappropriation of the public funds, and recommended that criminal investigations should be pursued, to-date, only one of those officials has been dragged into court, prosecuted, and sentenced to jail, only to be released after one month. Many commissions of inquiry conducted under this regime, including those related to murder, such as that of Dr. Andrew Kayira, are gathering lots of dust on some shelf in the Attorney General's Chambers.

Abandoning the futility of obtaining the items at Mulago Hospital pharmacy, the driver and I headed back to the now open pharmacies at Wandegeya, a satellite city suburb of Kampala, which serves the communities of Makerere and Mulago Hills. It is mostly here, that patients, or their relatives, first make a stop for their shopping needs before going to the hospital. Sure enough, I got the catheters, gloves, and the drip water that I needed, and by ten O'clock, we were headed west towards my ancestral home in Rukungiri District.

Three

NO JOURNEY TO western Uganda is complete without a stop at Kyengera shopping center, to load up on the essential supplies of bread, sugar, etc, that the city residents almost take for granted, but which may either be in short supply upcountry, or obtainable at higher prices. This dusty little town, located on the western limits of Kampala City along Masaka Road, perhaps epitomizes what President Amin had in mind when he gave business owners of Asian origin an ultimatum to either become full Uganda citizens, or "take your British passports to your masters in London". Today, Kyengera's thriving businesses are entirely owned, run and operated by indigenous Ugandans. Before 1972, the scenario would have been one, where all the shops were owned and operated by Asians, with an occasional African as an assistant, helping only to restock the shelves, but, certainly unheard of, for him to be managing the books. All this changed, following a pronouncement, in what Amin himself described as a dream with an order from Allah, to expel the non-citizens, of mainly Indian and Pakistani ancestry, who monopolized the commercial sector. In his edict, Amin declared, what he referred to as an Economic War, or Operation Mafuta Mingi, intended to transform Ugandan peasants into overnight merchants. Of all Idi Amin's transgressions, this may be the only act over which most Ugandans sided with him, at least in principle, although not necessarily in its execution.

This single event remains controversial to this day, forty years after it happened. Many of the Asian business owners have since, been grudgingly invited back under pressure from the two Breton Woods institutions in Washington DC, supported by conservative governments in both London, and Washington, much to the chagrin of the Ugandans, who were beginning to hone their skills at running businesses.

Among the rumors doing the rounds at the time of the Asian exodus, was that President Amin, a self-declared devout Muslim, who had recently divorced three of his "official" four wives, had sought the hand of one of Muljibhai Madhvani's daughters, whereupon the family's repulsion of his humble request sealed the fate of the entire Asian community. The Indian community in Uganda at the time, constituted descendants of the Indian coolies brought in by the British colonialists around 1890, to help with the construction of the Kenya-Uganda Railway, from the coastal city of Mombasa, with a terminus at Kasese, near the base of the Mountains of the Moon in western Uganda. The Madhvanis of Kakira near Jinja, and the Mehtas of Lugazi, are the scions of the sugar industry in Uganda, but also extending their tentacles into other business interests, such as cooking oil, steel, and tourism. The Museveni regime has been considered too cozy with them, to a point where they have been perceived to be favored in business deals, over indigenous Ugandans. This relationship came to a boil in 2005, when State House (which is synonymous with Mr. Museveni), announced that a portion of one of the nation's remaining tropical rain forests, known as Mabira Forest, located about thirty miles east of Uganda's capital, Kampala, was being allocated to the Mehta family, to expand acreage for their sugar plantation.

A spontaneous reaction deploring this action arose from people of all walks of life, culminating into massive parades in Kampala. Mr.Museveni, whose grip on the country, had never been tested in such a manner, panicked, sending his police and military into the streets to break up the protests. However, this further infuriated the crowds, some of whom directed their frustration at Indian businesses, breaking windows, looting some stores, and sending the owners scampering for their safety at police stations. By the time the police took control of the situation, at least seven people were dead, two of them, Indians ambushed by the crowds. The incident sent shivers among the Indian business community, and it took a lot of diplomatic maneuvering to assure potential Indian investors that the government would not let the situation deteriorate to a point where their properties would be seized a la Mafuta Mingi era.

Following a recent report by Parliament's Public Accounts Committee, under the chairmanship of Budadiri County member of Parliament, Nathan Nandala Mafabi, Hoteliers such as Surdhir Ruparelia of Speke Resort Hotel Munyonyo, Karim Hirji of the Imperial Hotel group, and the late Joseph Behakanira of J&M Hotel, at Bwebajja, were given billions of shillings of taxpayers' funds to speed up completion and furbishing of their structures, in order to accommodate guests who were expected to attend the bi-annual Commonwealth Heads of Governments Meeting, better known by its acronym of CHOGM. More revealing, however, was how the stewards of the Ugandan economy, all the way to the president, flouted the usual procurement procedures, to award lucrative contracts to a selected few, including, those to upgrade and modernize roads to personal residences. But even more shocking, was the fact that some of these contracts were awarded without any pieces of paper signed between contracting parties!

For a brief period, following the Indian expulsion, the country was awash with merchandise, either looted from abandoned stores, or sold cheaply by new owners with no concept of how to price the items acquired freely. Cases were abound, where semi-illiterate owners simply looked at the collar-sizes of garments, and took that to be the price.

Soon, however, the chickens came home to roost, as shelves emptied without replenishment, since the new owners, lacking the requisite skills and financial wherewithal to run these operations, had taken the proceeds from the sold merchandise, and gone on a limb to acquire fancy new cars, and a retinue of concubines, forgetting that stock had to be replenished for a business to continue with its daily operations. The resulting shortages caused an inflationary spiral, akin to the Latin American versions of the same era. Government workers, slowly by slowly, began to abscond from work, spending the better part of the day lining up for a kilo of sugar here, a bar of soap there, and going from butchery to butchery, sometimes ending up with the last few bones on the butcher's chopping board.

Then, as now, resentment started setting in towards the group closely associated with the regime. Amin was from the Kakwa tribe, a minority ethnic group from the West Nile district of northwestern Uganda. Some of the tribes in this region have bloodlines linking them to the Dinka, Nuer, and Nubians of Sudan. In his quest for "Africanisation of the Ugandan economy, Amin had awarded a disproportionate share of the former Asian properties to his Kakwa and Nubian tribesmen. This had angered many people, since the Nubians were considered as foreign as the Indians they had replaced. According to regional migration movements, the Nubians were first recruited from Sudan by British colonialists, and brought in to quell down any resistance from internal tribal uprisings such as those of the anti-colonial Omukama Kabalega of Bunyoro-Kitara. Once the wars were over, these groups were rewarded with spoils of land, and they stayed to this day. The Nubians had a legendary reputation for ruthlessness, and it is this quality that Amin exploited to the maximum in recruiting them into his dreaded State Research Bureau, whose atrocities were probably, only surpassed by Pol Pot's killing fields in Cambodia.

During most of Amin's rule in the 1970's, the regime enjoyed little support, apart from Arab countries, which rewarded him for expelling Israelis from the country, in a gesture of the so-called Afro-Arab solidarity. Uganda, in the eyes of the rest of the world, remained, like present day Iran, North Korea, and Zimbabwe have been over the last few years, a pariah or rogue state. Nonetheless, Amin forged a relationship with some fringe organizations in the west, such as the Congress of Racial Equality (CORE), whose president Mr. Roy Innis, could be seen, sometimes hobnobbing with Amin in Nile Mansions Hotel. As the old saying goes, it takes years to build a fortress, but only seconds to destroy it.

Four

LEAVING THE COMMOTION of venders at Kyengera, one travels through the lush greenery of Uganda's countryside towards
Masaka Town, some eighty five miles from Kampala. The sharp
corners at Nsangi give way to a fairly straight two-lane tarmac
road that is the only link between Uganda, the small countries
of Rwanda and Burundi to the south-west, and the eastern part
of the mostly inaccessible Democratic Republic of Congo (DRC).
Besides being scenic, this stretch of highway is a roadside shop-
per's dream, especially, as far as fresh fruits and vegetables are
concerned. For the hungry, a stop at Mbizzi-nnya (meaning four
pigs), will whet the appetite, as any vehicle that stops there is ac-
costed by hawkers, peddling all manner of merchandise. These
range from mouth-watering nyama-choma (roast meat), still drip-
ping with fat, straight from a shoulder-carried sigiri, (never mind
what has been roasted-you won't necessarily get the right an-
swer-a case of don't ask, don't tell), to bottled water, soda, and
plastic totes of squeezed juices, which some locals have dubbed
"typhoid", due to the unpredictable origin of the water used in
making them.

After savoring the flavors of Uganda at Mbizzi-nnya, it's
time for the visitor to take in a quick lesson of Geography, and
hydrology at Kayabwe, where the Equator bisects the country
placing one half into the northern, and the other half into the

southern hemisphere. For a small fee, some enterprising young people are available to demonstrate how the flush of water in a toilet bowl, can change from a clockwise to a counter-clockwise movement as you cross the imaginary line from north to south. The place has become a popular tourist rest-stop, providing a distraction to curious foreigners to and from visiting the national parks. Five of these, including Queen Elizabeth, at the base of the Rwenzori Mountains, (also known as the Mountains of the Moon), Lake Mburo in Mbarara District, and the World-famous Bwindi Impenetrable Forest, home to the Mountain Gorilla, and Mgahinga on the Uganda-Rwanda boarder, are located in South-western Uganda.

A few kilometers past the Equator, the road passes through one of the country's largest wetlands, known as Lweera. This is a huge expanse of marshy flatland bordering the Mighty Lake Victoria, which, at 64,000 square kilometers (25,000 sq milies), is the world's second largest fresh water lake, dwarfed only by Lake Superior. It is shared by Tanzania to the South, and Kenya to the East. During some particularly heavy rainy seasons, such as El Nino, the entire area is transformed into another lake, forming an extension of its giant neighbor, and obstructing traffic on this major highway to the hinterlands of Rwanda and DRC. Lweera is also famous for its juicy, mouth-watering tilapia and catfish, which the local fishermen hook from the many rivulets in this swampy terrain. Drivers and passengers alike on this road cannot miss the sight of fishmongers dangling their water-dripping wares by the roadside. Although over-fishing in Lake Victoria has greatly reduced the catch, more than tripling prices for local consumers, a five pound fresh tilapia could still be purchased for between ten and fifteen thousand Uganda shillings in 2011, that's the equivalent of about five US dollars, or a dollar per pound, which is mighty cheap by international standards.

I acquired my fish-eating habits late in my adult life. As kids, my parents discouraged us from eating fish, generally describing it as food for those who lacked "real food". My village is nowhere close to a large body of water. The closest is Lake Edward, about forty miles away to the west, at the border between Uganda and DRC. During the 1960s, before the population exploded, the nation's lakes, such as Victoria, Kyoga, Albert, Edward and George, were teaming with fish, which had few consumers. Traditionally, the cattle-keeping people of western Uganda lean more towards a diet that relies on dairy products and beef, rather than fish. There was only one man in my village of Kabura, named Desiderio Beyanza, who traded in fish. He had a young brother, Severino, (whom we called Sereve) about my age, with whom we used to play. One day, after playing the hide-and-seek games that were popular with children, Sereve, my brother Marcel and I, stopped by Mr. Beyanza's fish stand. Since he had no freezer, the only way to preserve the fish was to sprinkle some salt over it, and smoke it over a log-fire.

When we got there, Mr. Beyanza pulled a smoked "ngege" from the platform above the fire, and said, "You kids can enjoy that". Sereve was, of course, already adept at eating fish, but my brother and I were not. So he took us through the ritual, making sure we extracted the needle-like bones before attempting to chew and swallow the tiny morsels of white meat. When we got home that evening, our child naivety got the better part of us as we described the experience to my parents. After listening intently to our story, my father got his cane, which he kept in his bedroom, and used to straighten any of us whenever we took a path he didn't approve of. Each of us received about five lushes, with a stern warning not to repeat the act. Later in life, however, after establishing homes of our own, we started enjoying fish like the rest of the city dwellers, but still refraining from preparing and serving fish whenever my parents were in town.

We headed straight for Mbarara town, by-passing Masaka, once an important provincial town in the coffee-growing region of Buganda. Masaka's degeneration started in the late 1970's, when it became a battleground between the invading Ugandan exiles, helped by the Tanzanian Peoples' Defence Forces (TPDF), and the retreating Amin soldiers. Earlier, in his quest to flex his muscles, Amin had provoked the President of Tanzania, the late Mwalimu Julius Nyerere, by claiming a tiny swathe of territory across the Kagera River salient, which forms the official border between Uganda and Tanzania. Mwalimu Nyerere, a pal of ousted President Milton Obote of Uganda, had never attempted to hide his disdain for the mercurial dictator, whom he had variously described in contemptible terms, including, "a snake in the grass". Amin's action of sending his soldiers to occupy what was clearly part of Tanzania territory, tickled the wrong nerve in the Tanzanian president, who immediately vowed to "smoke the snake out of the grass, and crush it". The combined invasion of TPDF and Ugandan exiles, mostly hosted by Tanzania, is what drove Idi Amin from power on April 11, 1979, despite considerable support from fellow dictator and Muslim brother, Muammar Qaddafi of Libya.

Half-way between Masaka and Mbarara, is Lyantonde town, equally devastated, not by marauding soldiers, but by an even more formidable foe, known as "slim" in this part of the world. Lyantonde is where Uganda's first cases of HIV, the virus that causes AIDS were identified back in 1983, marking this, as one of the epicenters of the dreaded disease in the world. The small shopping center, dating perhaps back to the 1940s, had thrived well as a major rest stop for long-haul truck drivers, prowling the only route that links the land-locked countries of Rwanda, Burundi and eastern DRC to the major port of Mombasa, Kenya, on the Indian Ocean. Its proximity to the Bukoba region of northern Tanzania, also allows truckers from the alternate port of Dar-es-Salaam, Tanzania, to converge at Lyantonde.

Today, Rakai district where Lyantonde is located, has been littered with graves of once heads of families, who passed on, leaving kids, sometimes as young as nine years, as the only "adults" in the family, responsible for their even younger siblings. On the flip side, the town has perhaps singled-handedly supplied most of the World's research data on HIV to-date, through such major research organizations as the Johns-Hopkins Hospital, Harvard Medical School, the Centers for Disease Control (CDC) in the United States, and the Pasteur Institute in Paris, France.

Lyantonde also forms the official southern boundary of the Kingdom of Buganda, the central region of the country, from which the name B(Uganda) was derived by the colonialists. Driving thirteen kilometers further down, on the Masaka-Mbarara highway, we reach Sanga Gate, the entrance to Lake Mburo National Park, one of the five major parks scattered in western Uganda. There is another entrance gate, located five kilometers down at Nshara. This park is one of the best places to see gigantic eland antelope, zebra, topi, sitatunga, and a variety of birds. An occasional lion has been spotted, but the ranchers in the surrounding area, have almost exterminated this species. During the infamous Obote II regime of the early 1980's, an over-zealous man called Chris Rwakatsiisi, who served as President Obote's Security Minister, was said to have introduced vicious man-eating lions from Tanzania, in order to quell down over-grazing by Rwandese cattle-keepers. However, like many rumors making the rounds at that time, no one could prove or disprove it until it died with the regime itself.

The Obote regime was viewed by many, as anti-immigrant, and therefore, unfriendly to the Rwandese refugees, concentrated in the Oruchinga valley of nearby Lake Nakivale. It was this animosity against them that Yoweri Museveni exploited to his advantage in recruiting a large group of Banyarwanda refugees into his National Resistance Army, when he launched a rebellion against the Obote regime in January 1981.

Five

AT BIHARWE, A sprawling roadside market, I ask the driver to stop. It has become more of a ritual to meander around, and haggle with market women over prices for their agricultural merchandise. I have, over a period of years of traversing this route, got friendly with a few of these women, who will try to lure me to their particular stall. And in my own way, I practice some "customer democracy", spreading a few shillings to as many vendors as possible. This market, located about four kilometers from Mbarara town, got its start in the early 1980's, when the country was still a wasteland, left behind by the devastating wars, beginning with the Amin and Obote wars.

Drivers traveling to Kampala in those days, needed to stock up on supplies of staples such as beans, groundnuts (peanuts) and onions, which were hard to find in Kampala's popular markets like Nakasero, Wandegeya or Kamwokya. As time went by, however, enterprising business-minded people began buying more than they could consume, and selling the surplus. As demand shot through the roof, prices began to rise, creating rival setups along the same route, such as Biharwe II, just a few kilometers away. Meanwhile, the country set on the road to recovery, boosting agricultural production in most areas, except northern Uganda, where the rag-tag Lord's Resistance Army led by a reclusive former catechist called Joseph Kony, bled the countryside to death, through abductions of children, rape and maiming of innocent citizens. Biharwe market began to lose its luster, since commodities could almost be obtained anywhere. But it's still a popular place with people like me, if only for old time's sake.

Close by, is an army barracks, once known as Simba Barracks, a dreaded place during the Idi Amin regime. Simba is the Swahili word for lion. The first attempt to overthrow the regime in 1972, by Ugandan exiles, based in Tanzania, unsuccessfully tried to overrun the barracks with disastrous consequences. When Amin got wind of trouble here, he quickly mobilized reinforcements from Masaka Mechanized battalion a little over one hour away, crushing the invaders, and sending them scampering for cover all over Mbarara town and its environs. That invasion was partly led by Yoweri Museveni, the current president.

In September 1972, about one week after the attempted invasion, two of my brothers (Matia & Marcel) (both now deceased), Matia's wife, Jane, and her brother, Byarugaba, and I, were packed in Matia's Toyota Corolla, heading towards our home near Rukungiri town. The country was very tense, with Amin suspicious of people from western Uganda, whom he alleged were in cahoots with his predecessor, Milton Obote. Road blocks could be mounted by the military anywhere in unexpected places. We had been warned about the looming danger at roadblocks, but then again, the Uganda of that period had almost come to accept them as normal. From the time we left Kampala, we had encountered no less than ten or fifteen. Some soldiers would simply extort a few shillings for cigarettes and wave you off. Besides Matia, who worked for National Insurance Corporation at the time, and Mr. Byarugaba, a medical assistant with Kampala City Council, the rest of us were students in various institutions of higher learning. None of us was engaged in politics, which Amin hated with a passion, so we didn't expect to be considered guilty by association.

The first salvo was fired when one of the three soldiers manning the roadblock asked us to produce "our densities", as the semi-illiterate soldiers called identity cards. Everything was alright until Jane, then a second year student at Makerere University, produced hers. The university was known for its radicalism, and opposition to Amin's regime.

"Wewe muyizi ya university kweli?" said one of them, asking whether she was really a university student.

"Lakini tuwoneshe degree yako", meaning, "show us your degree". Jane began to be agitated.

"If I had one, I would have left the university already", she said.

At this point, they ordered us out of the car, and did what they had perfected as an art.

"Lara chini", meaning, "hit the ground", which we did.

Unknown to us, was the fact that the three soldiers were part of a detachment assigned to guard this area. Once they heard their colleagues raising voices, more soldiers appeared out of the blue, and surrounded us, with their machine guns at the ready.

Two of them asked for the "pilot", to show them the registration. Matia, who was by now shaking like a palm tree in the middle of a hurricane, produced the registration as they ordered him to open the hood door and read out the engine number (VIN). One by one, he read the digits while one of the soldiers matched them on the registration, as the rest of us held our breath, praying that there wouldn't be an error. Once that was finished, the inquisitor for Jane returned to her.

"Where are the letters you've been writing to Tanzania?" he asked.

"I don't have any letters, and I've never written any letters to Tanzania", she said. The reference to Tanzania was because the recent invasion had originated from there. Jane was wearing an Afro wig on her head at the time, and the soldier, who was smoking a cigarette, put it to her head, burning a few strands as we all looked on timidly.

As luck would have it, one soldier, who had stayed at their

makeshift thatched hut a few meters from the road, but who had apparently been tuning in to the conversation, emerged. He started asking her about a girl that stayed in Mary-Stuart Hall, the same hall she stayed in. When she started saying she didn't know her, her brother had the quick sense of mind to whisper into her ear, and tell her to acknowledge that she knew the girl. That seemed to distract the attention of the inquisitor, as his friend turned to the more friendly matters of the heart. After a few minutes of what had seemed like an eternity, they ordered us back into the car and told us to proceed. For the first few meters, we couldn't dare look back, as we suspected that they could change their minds and shoot us in the car. Finally, as we cleared the ground and put some distance between the soldiers and ourselves, we all heaved a big sigh of relief, knowing that in those days, many motorists met their fate at roadblocks like these, and that we were among the lucky ones who lived to tell the tale.

Among the ones who didn't make it beyond Simba Barracks, were two Americans, journalist Nicholas Stroh from the family of the founders of Stroh Beer Brewing Company, and his colleague Robert Siedle, a sociology professor at Makerere University. In July 1971, barely six months after Idi Amin's January coup, the two set off to investigate some rumors about a mutiny within Simba Battalion. Information remains sketchy as to what exactly transpired, except that a few days later, their car was found, a mangled heap, having been pushed over a cliff in the mountainous terrain of Omunkombe on the Ishaka-Kasese Road. No bodies were ever recovered, and a commission of inquiry into their disappearance never yielded any conclusive results.

Mbarara town's prominence grew with the current National Resistance Movement, partly because the top leadership of the regime, including the president himself hail from this region. And, following in the African tradition of the "big man", the resources of the nation tend to follow the big man right to his village. The name Mbarara itself is meaningless, and was corrupted by colonial administrators who could not pronounce 'emburara", a type of grass favored by cattle, and commonly found in surrounding hills. Until the late 1960's, the town doubled as the headquarters of Ankole District and kingdom, whose palace or Kikaari was at nearby Kamukuzi. When the kingdoms were abolished by the Obote regime in 1966, Mbarara remained an administrative center for the district. With the ascendance of native son Yoweri Museveni to the presidency in 1986, however, the town's fortunes multiplied overnight.

When the traditional rulers such as the Kabaka of Buganda, the Omukama of Tooro, that of Bunyoro, and the Kyabazinga of Busoga, were restored in the mid-1990s, Museveni deliberately left out the Omugabe of his native Ankole, preferring, perhaps to defray some competition, and retain pecking order supremacy. He declared himself "Ssabagabe", or king of kings. Even today, at the time of writing this, nearly twenty years later, Ankole still has no king recognized by the government. Prince John Barigye, the heir to Sir Charles Gasyonga, the last Omugabe, died about two years ago. Some Ankole monarchists took the trouble of installing his son Prince Rwebishengye, as a mere ritual that went unrecognized. The custodians of the kingdom are still agitating for their royal drums, known as Bagyendanwa. The drums, along with other regalia, have been stashed away for safe custody in the national museum in Kampala since the dethronement of the late Sir Charles Gasyonga, in 1966.

Mbarara University of Science and Technology was added quickly with the help of Cuba's Fidel Castro, transforming institutions such as Mbarara Hospital into a regional referral facility. The population, which had been stagnant for a long time, more than doubled, and now numbers in the hundreds of thousands. Before the university's establishment, the town's most famous institution was Ntare Secondary school, a boys- only secondary school, which boasts of Presidents Museveni of Uganda and Paul Kagame of Rwanda as alumni. There was also Maryhill Girls

Secondary School, just across the Rwizi River. These two schools were, for a long time, among the top performing schools in the country. Today, the town has added a few industries, such as the Sameer Milk processing plant, a Coca-cola plant, a Bank of Uganda regional headquarters, other banks, and hotels serving the thriving tourism in the region, and has leapfrogged Jinja in eastern Uganda, to become the second largest city in the nation, after Kampala City.

Past Mbarara, we had a choice between taking the Mbarara-Kabale road, branching off at Ntungamo, onto a newly constructed tarmac road to Rukungiri, or following an alternative route that goes through Bushenyi towards Fort Portal, and diverting from it at Ishaka. The Ishaka route was favored until about 2005, when the Ntungamo-Rukungiri road was finally given a tarmac coating. Now, the entire journey from Kampala to Rukungiri, takes about five hours, instead of nearly a whole day. However, the whole stretch from Kampala, all the way to Kigali the capital of Rwanda, is narrow, and seriously congested with traffic. And now that Rwanda and Burundi have joined the regional economic grouping of the East African Community, the congestion problems are expected to get worse.

The liberalization of the transportation sector in Uganda gave birth to a thriving, albeit unregulated, private sector, which poured all kinds of vehicles on the typical two-lane roads in the country. The road is teaming with fast-driven buses and heavy trucks, the latter hauling tonnage of merchandise beyond their designated capacity, to and from such remote cities as Bujumbura, Burundi, and Goma in eastern DRC. This theater of activities is repeated along the entire stretch, all the way to Mombasa on the Indian Ocean. Over-stretched national budgets leave little money allocated for road maintenance, resulting in fast-deteriorating surfaces. This creates giant potholes, which force hapless drivers to compete for space around the scanty smooth surfaces. For an outsider, watching drivers maneuver through this process, which sometimes gets within a hair's breadth of a fatal crush, or worse, is a feat in itself. It has created an unwritten code among drivers, known as "okutegelegana", a Luganda word literally meaning "internal understanding".

Ntungamo, which is both the name of a district, and the administrative town within it, only gained prominence as a result of being home to the first lady, Mrs. Janet Kataha Museveni. For the last few years, since immersing herself into the local politics of the area, she has represented her constituency of Ruhama in Ntungamo District, as a member of Uganda's Parliament. More recently, her husband, the president, appointed her to his cabinet, as a minister responsible for the least developed region of the country, known as Karamoja. Janet's burst on the political landscape was laced with fundamentalist overtones, telling her constituents, that "God had told her in a dream, to wake up and deliver her people from abject poverty". In her promotion to cabinet minister, her husband cited "her eagerness to serve", unlike the bulk of the population who would rather pass on the buck. Uganda must be blessed with leaders who communicate with the Mighty one in their dreams. Amin too, cited a dream, and a command from God, when he woke up one day in 1972, and gave orders to Ugandans of Asian ancestry, to leave the country within ninety days.

The pillow-talk cabinet meetings appear to have yielded some positive results for Ruhama, because areas surrounding the first lady's village of Bwongyera, which used the kerosene tadooba for their lighting before her ascendency to the parliamentary seat, have since been added to the national electricity power grid.

About one mile out of Ntungamo town, we come to the junction for the newly-tarmarcked Rukungiri Road. Twelve miles west, along this road, is a smaller town called Rwashameire, whose most prominent citizen, Major-General Mugisha Muntu, was Mr. Museveni's army commander for nine years during the 1990's, but is now firmly in the opposition camp as president of the main opposition party, FDC. In 2012, he finally replaced Dr. Kiiza Besigye, the main opposition leader, and is expected to vie for his one-time mentor's job of President of the country, as the face of the main opposition party. Drive on for another five miles or so, and you come to a tiny place called Nyamunuka. The non-decrepit town has always been a sort of cultural island. Unlike people in the surrounding villages who speak the Runyankore dialect, and are mainly Christian, the residents here tend to use Luganda, and are predominantly Muslim.

During the Idi Amin regime, Nyamunuka was sometimes depicted on national television, with Hajjis and Hajjats in their flowing Islamic gabs celebrating one mauledi after another, often-times, having invited one of Amin's ministers to attend. However, as the regime began to crumble, this close association became a millstone, hanging around the necks of the local citizens. When Amin and his henchmen were finally driven out of power, former associates from the area were targeted, rightly or wrongly, making it more of a burden on the local people to identify themselves with the town. Some prominent citizens from the area disappeared without a trace, not unlike the manner that had characterized the abhorred Amin regime itself. Even today, more than thirty years since the regime's fall, one still sees signs that remind him or her, of the destruction epoch of that period, manifested in abandoned homes that resemble the ruins of Pompei.

At the bottom of the valley, we come to Kahengye, mark-ing the border between Ntungamo and Rukungir districts. If ever there was one place former US vice president, Al Gore, needed to study the effects of environmental degradation, this would be it. As a kid, I used to hear many frightening tales about this place, narrated by travelers from our area. Until about the early 1970's, the river here, locally known as Kyambu, used to flood in the rainy season, creating a mini lake for several days, until the water re-ceded on its own, flowing down to the natural catchment of Lake Edward. The narrow steel and concrete bridge over the river was, even at the best of times, very dangerous, especially for heavy or long vehicles such as buses. The hilly terrain on both sides of the valley, had forced the constructors to locate the bridge in a sharp corner, making it difficult for an unfamiliar driver to slow down enough before getting too close. This resulted in many lives of motorists and their passengers perishing, as inattentive drivers lost control, their vehicles plunging into the swift waters of the river down below.

The river valley, once covered with thick vegetation, was also home to various types of fauna and fowl, including the indomitable hippo. However, today, after the mushrooming population upstream has cleared the natural bushes, especially papyrus, in order to access more farmland, the river has been reduced to a mere creek. The hippos and fish are gone too. And, with the new tarmac road and bridge which straightened the road, eliminating the sharp corner, if you miss the signpost pronouncing it, it's very easy for someone to bypass the spot without even recognizing it.

Rukungiri District beckons us as soon as we cross the bridge. There is always a sense of relief as one approaches home, but not this time for me. We are in Kebisoni sub-county, which, together with Buyanja, further ahead, are to Rukungiri, District, what Dallas County is to the Lone Star state of Texas. The long-horn cattle reign supreme here too. This breed is the same as the famed Ankole longhorns, valued for their lean and low choles-terol beef. Lately, however, there has been significant dilution by cross-breeding these local animals with foreign breeds such as Friesians, in an attempt to increase milk production. The neat-ly-fenced ranches sprawling over the undulating hills of Kitojo, all the way to Kabahirayo swamp near the Nyakishenyi border, would arouse a twitch of envy in a Texas rancher.

The roadside view is constantly interrupted by the broad leaves of the abundant banana trees. Bananas form a staple diet in this, and many other parts of the country, especially the west-ern and central regions. Globally, it is estimated that Uganda produces as much as ten million tons of green bananas a year, only surpassed by India and Brazil. But Ugandans love their matooke, as bananas are called in the Luganda language. Matooke is to a Muganda, what the tortilla is to a Mexican. Some inroads have been made recently, exporting the surplus to as far-flung areas as Europe and the Middle-East. The country has also had to contend with the black sigatoka fungus which attacks the banana tree, destroying the fruit and stem. Any reduction in banana production has grave food security implications for the country. Researchers at the National Agricultural Research Organization (NARO), based at Kawanda, a few miles outside Kampala, have come up with a genetically modified banana. Although the GM version is resistant to the fungus, and yields faster than its older cousin, the taste is said to be different, and this has limited its wide acceptability among local consumers.

Whizzing past Nyamayenje, now, a collection of old and rusty iron-roofed shops lined up along the road, reminded me of the role this place once played as a popular open market, known as "ekikomera". Farmers used to haul all manner of merchandise to this open market every third Tuesday of the month. As kids, we loved visiting different food stalls, where we'd get free samples. If you visited enough stalls, you ended up going home with a full stomach. Costco Super markets remind me of this by-gone era, with their free food samples throughout the giant store. But the roaming in the kikomera was usually limited by the responsibility one carried while at the market. If the parent had taken a goat or a cow to sell, the kid was expected to stay with it all the time, until it sold. And, if it didn't sell, you were expected to shepherd it back home.

We stop briefly at Nyakibale, just opposite the hospital. The missionary hospital, built by the Mill-Hill Fathers sect of the Catholic Church during the 1960's, was, for all intents and purposes, a fine facility, ranking among the best in the region. Nyakibale mission was established in 1929 by white missionaries, continuing their quest of spreading Christianity to the hinterland of the African continent. It was at this church, that my parents were converted to Christianity, and were later married in 1942.

I attended part of my primary and later, junior school here between 1963 and 1965 when the Headmaster was a vivacious man called Joseph Macumu. He was a tough nut to crack, this Macumu. He had attended the elite St. Mary's College, Kisubi, the leading Catholic high school near Entebbe, for his Ordinary level secondary school, but had not done well enough to advance to the higher school certificate, which is the pre-requisite for entering university. This seems to have created some sort of resentment within him, about the entire education system, which he carried around, and occasionally manifested itself through his actions. He spared no rod on us the students, sometimes using the sjambok, which is a whip made from the tail of a cow. When used, it leaves permanent scars on the body of the victim.

He was also known to occasionally use his high-handedness on his wife, Restatuta, a fine woman who taught at Nyakibale Immaculate Heart Girls School on the opposite hill. One day, during a heated meeting in his office with his school board, which included the Father Superior of Nyakibale Catholic Church, he was challenged to elaborate on some student-related issues and school finances. He excused himself, pretending to go to the loo outside. Upon reaching the door, he grabbed the handle at lightning speed, reached for a padlock from his pocket, slammed it on the door from outside, and disappeared for the rest of the day leaving his tormentors captive. It wasn't until a passerby heard them yelling, that he informed the commander of the local police post in Rukungiri town, to come and rescue them from their ordeal.

Among those he locked up, was a veteran school headmaster called Balthazar Rwemisisiro, whose son Louis, was a classmate of mine. Unlike some of us who commuted to the school every day, Louis, together with a few others, resided at the school as boarders. The fees they paid were supposed to cover, among other things, their lodging and meals. But the kids were always complaining about how inadequate their meals were. One week-end, the kids made a bonfire, and as excitement got the better part of them, they raided Mr. Macumu's cornfield nearby, each kid extracting a few ears of corn which they roasted on the fire, and ate, mostly to supplement the meager diet they were receiving at school. When the news about the bonfire feast reached Mr. Macumu, he went ballistic, and immediately suspended all the kids who participated, with a note to their parents, to pay Ush 50 (about US$7, a hefty sum in those days), before the children could be re-admitted. This act infuriated the parents, especially Mr. Rwemisisiro, who burst out in his Rukiga dialect,

"Abaana orabeisa enjara, kyonka hati orenda kubashashuza otuchori tubariire. Nanye ndahinga obuchori, ndabasa kukuha ekibo, kyonka empiha tindazikuha!" meaning,

"First you starve the kids, and now you want to extort a lot of money for a few ears of corn. I also grow some corn, if you wish, I'll give you a whole basket, but I won't give you even one shilling for the ear of corn my son supposedly ate!" Other parents took a similar stand until Mr. Macumu relented.

At the time I attended Junior School, Mr. Macumu was building his private residence. If a student got to school late, Mr. Macumu levied on him a punishment to make several trips from the brick-yard to his house carrying a load of bricks. Despite parent protests regarding this practice, the stubborn headmaster stood his ground to the end, until the house was completed.

He later resigned from teaching, took some law courses at Makerere University's Law Development Center, and became a magistrate. Then, one day, during the torturous Idi Amin Regime, some soldiers stopped him at one of the road blocks they had mounted at a moment's notice. When he failed to come up with the cash they wanted, one of the soldiers slapped him, and he began pleading with them, saying, "Basebo mundeke ndi omulamuzi", meaning, "Please, leave me alone, I am a judge", to which another soldier replied,

"Kwori omulamuzi noramura owa Ruhanga?" meaning, "Whether or not you are a judge, do you adjudicate cases before God?"

Mr. Macumu survived the regime, but later died of complications from diabetes during the 1990's.

Six

ARRIVING IN RUKUNGIRI around one O'clock, the driver and I, headed straight to Dr Ndyomugyenyi's clinic on Karegyesa Rd. My brother Tony had already alerted him that I was on my way, and since he'd been at our home to see Mzee, I had very little explanation to do. The doctor briefed me about the old man's condition, and told me he would be coming in later in the evening. Aware of the fact that there would probably be a crowd gathered at home to see Mzee, I decided that it was best to eat something in town before proceeding. Luckily, we bumped into my childhood friend, Matsiko, who used to run a lodge called Nkore Eribwa, and he took us to a new establishment he had just started running.

Rukungiri town sits on a saddle that joins two hills, Rwakabengo to the south, and Kagunga to the north. Until Idi Amin's expulsion of the Indian community in 1972, the northern part formed the bulk of the town, with a mixture of indigenous Ugandan, and Arab shops. The Indians had setup shop around Rwakabengo area, located about one mile to the south. The town started as a small settlement, probably in the 1930's, when colonial administrators initially used it as the headquarters of what would be called Rujumbura County. Rujumbura itself was part of Mpororo Kingdom, a loose association of pastoral chiefs unified under the Bashambu clan, whose headquarters was at a place called Kagunga, in Nyakagyeme sub-county, just about three miles west of present day Rukungiri town.

The Bashambu of Rujumbura, are distant cousins of the Bahinda ruling class of Ankole Kingdom, the former having separated from the latter sometime in the 1800's following sibbling rivalry within the ruling household. The last person to hold the substantive title of Omwami/Omukama in Rujumbura, was Karegyesa, who died around 1958. His sons, Kamu Karekaho, and Filimoni Kitaburaza, played major roles in the early administration of the county. Mr. Karekaho was the first Member of Parliament, representing Rujumbura County immediately after Uganda's independence in 1962. His brother Kitaburaza served as a district commissioner for the larger Kigezi district, before it was subdivided into present Rukungiri, Kanungu, Kabale, and Kisoro districts, beginning in the late 1970's.

Although subject to a lot of interpretation, written accounts of the history of Rujumbura, such as works by the late Patrick Kakwenzire (son of Kitaburaza), and Simeon Beitwababo, would suggest that Karegyesa's reign was marked by a more lackluster performance than his father Makobore, perhaps, setting the stage for the kingdom's eventual demise well before kingdoms were officially abolished by the Obote regime in 1966.

Among the Bahororo, an ethnic group, almost culturally indistinguishable from their Banyankole cousins, there are two major distinctions, namely the Bahima pastoralists, and the Beiru, who have adapted to agriculture. These groupings are also to a great extent, physically and culturally similar to the Tutsi and Hutu in Rwanda and Burundi, linguistic dialects notwithstanding. For centuries, their symbiotic relationships have tended to thrive and exploit a master-servant relationship, interspersed by periods of mild forms of violence. Extreme cases such as Michel Micombero's pogroms of the early 1970's in Burundi, or the mother of all violence, which culminated into the 1994 genocide in Rwanda were extremely rare.

Although inter-marriages and more enlightenment with education have bridged the gap between these groups, the pace of integration has not been fast enough as to eliminate the age-old suspicions that have existed among them.

The Bashambu hereditary rulers in Mpororo, like their Bahinda and Tutsi counterparts in Ankole, Rwanda, and Burundi, respectively, were more feared than loved or admired by the ruled. Stories abound regarding the nature of brutality they administered on their subjects, even for mere mishaps. A man could, for instance, easily lose his life through spearing by the chief, for staggering and causing the team carrying the chief to lose their step. Among the stories of these inhumanities I heard as a kid, was how one of the cousins of Karegyesa, a man called Rwabambari once amused himself by ordering his servants to hold a young woman astride, while he applied a red-hot iron rod to see if "rwata nayo nesya", or if her genitals could burn like any other object. Needless to say, the woman died in the process, and such crimes went unpunished.

Such acts are long gone now, and only confined to the history books. Rukungiri District, which was curved out of the original Rujumbura county, and a small portion of Rukiga county called Nyakishenyi, has become a connercorpia of different ethnicities, bound together with a common destiny. My high school classmate, Zedekia Karokora-Katono, until recently, sat at the helm as the District Chairman of Local Council V, the highest level in the administrative hierarchy, akin to the County executive in the United States.

Boasting of a tarmac road on Main Street today, the town used to be a dusty backwater until the 1970's when a group of citizens, including my late father, approached President Idi Amin and demanded for district status for Rujumbura County. When first granted this status, it was known as North Kigezi. Until then, the region was part of Kigezi district, with its headquarters in Kabale, some seventy miles away. But Rujumbura, later Rukungiri District, was always a distinct entity, separated from Rukiga county by one of the most mountainous terrains in the country. The town itself was composed of two rows of plain-looking rusty corrugated-iron sheet shops, anchored by a general store owned by a plump Arab called Shariff. The locals called him "Rubondo", a reference to his potbelly. There was also a post office, run by a man called Katombozi, who later died under mysterious circumstances arising out of rivalry with a local businessman called Obadiah, who immediately took over the role of postmaster. The only gas station was run by a man called Moses Kifeefe, the father of President Museveni's arch-rival, three-time opposition presidential candidate, a retired Colonel called Dr. Kiiza Besigye.

North of the main town, was the seat of the "Saza chief", the chief administrator of the county, a prison, and a dispensary at Rwamahwa. When the town acquired its first thermal generator in the late 1970's, a coffee-processing plant was added, followed later, by a milk-cooling plant. The town also had its "unofficial" mayor, in a mentally-deranged man called Buherezo, who developed a passion for chasing out shabbily dressed boys and men. One of my classmates, a boy called Pascal Behweera, whose poor father, Yowana Baryeija, couldn't afford him decent clothing, was continually chased around by "Mayor Buherezo." My two brothers, Marcel (RIP), Jerome and I, together with other kids from my village, crisscrossed the town every day on our way to Nyakibale, where we all attended primary and junior secondary school. Those days, we walked this five-mile journey twice a day, once in the morning, and making the return trip in the evening. On top of that, we were expected to perform such domestic chores as fetching water and gathering firewood to cook the evening meal when we got home. On weekends, we spent long days helping the old man and the few farm hands we had, weeding, harvesting or transporting coffee beans to the nearest cooperative outlet at our small town of Kasoroza, located four miles west of Rukungiri. If the cooperative officers couldn't make it to receive the crop, we either had to carry the bulky stuff back home, or take it to Rukungiri, all on our heads.

Preparing coffee beans for sale is one of the most laborious chores a farmer can go through, because all the tasks are performed manually. Harvesting involves climbing wobbly ladders, balancing a basket with one hand, while reaching and selecting the ripe berries with the other, all performed under the hot tropical sun. Once in a while, a deadly snake crosses your path, and you have to move fast enough to avoid a possible fatal confrontation. Once the harvesting is done, drying the beans is another chore that sucks the energy out of you, as they have to be moved, sometimes at short notice, to avoid getting them soggy in a downpour. Finally, transporting the coffee to the market without the use of any mechanical equipment is no task for the uninitiated. There was very limited use of animal power in this part of the world, although cattle were abundant, and bulls could easily have been adapted and utilized for this purpose.

Mzee was one of the pioneer coffee farmers in our area, having copied the skill from the Buganda region, where most young men of the era used to go in search of work. Oftentimes, as a kid in the 1960's, I'd watch him, leave home, after putting in a full day in his own shamba (field), take around a bunch of newly-germinated seeds to demonstrate to neighbors, near and far, who had not yet taken up to growing this cash crop. Sometimes he would ask me or one of my brothers to carry the seeds for him as he did the demonstrations. As coffee growing caught on, it soon dawned on the farmers that they needed someplace to sell their crop. Once again, Mzee, along with a few other pioneers such as the late Kigorogoro, hit the road, promoting the concept of a cooperative union, where farmers could take their crop, and expect to receive a predictable price, but none more passionately than my dad.

At my primary school of Kahoko, I recall many times, when Mzee would show up, gather the teachers around, and implore

them to join "Ekibiina kya Society", because some of these teachers also doubled as farmers. Once they got people on board,
they started religiously selling their coffee to the cooperative.
Unfortunately, the cooperative didn't always pay the farmers on
time. The officials only handed them IOU slips with promises to
pay them "very soon", which sometimes extended into weeks
of waiting. Some officials became unscrupulous, and would take
advantage of the poor, often illiterate farmers, who could not even
read the weight on the scale, of the crop they'd just delivered for
sale.

One such fellow was Obadiah, the same man that had taken
over the post office from the dying Katombozi, and run it from his
own building, eliciting endless complaints by parents, about missing letters containing school fees, especially at the beginning of
the school year. It did not take him long to cast his net wider, and
pretend to become savior to the poor farmers. On one occasion,
the farmers delivered their coffee, and received the usual IOU's
that they'd come to expect. However, since some of these farmers
couldn't read, the canning Obadiah had pre-selected some of the
slips and endorsed them with a"Paid" stamp. When payday was
finally announced, the poor farmers showed up, only to be told
that they had already collected their pay! One of the victims was
an old man called Bujoka from Katobo. When the irate old man
confronted Obadiah, the latter asked him,

"Iwe Bujoka, nomanya kushoma, torikureba ngu bakushash-
wire", meaning,

"Bujoka, do you know how to read? Can't you see that your
receipt says you've already been paid?"

The old man, who knew Obadiah and his father Muheru, pro-
nounced what amounted to a curse on the crafty businessman.

He told Obadiah that, if he cheated him of the little money
meant to send his children back to school, it would bring him no
peace at all, and with that, the old man walked away.

Indeed, by the time he died in the 1980's, Obadiah, once

a seemingly successful businessman by Rukungiri standards, had lost most of what he once had. At one time, he was hounded by the Obote Regime, taken to the infamous Luwero triangle, beaten, tortured, and abandoned for dead, until rescued by a soldier from Rukungiri who recognized him and hid him, providing him the chance to escape. He died a few years later, a humbled and despondent man.

My father was a disciplinarian of the old school, who strictly believed in the concept of "spare the rod and spoil the child". Like every father, he wanted his children to succeed and live a better life than what he had experienced. A first-born son, especially in Africa's patriarchal society, is always seen as a beacon, the shining light that will propagate the father's hopes and aspirations. He will often get the lion's share of the meager resources, with the expectation that this generosity will rub off on his siblings long after the father has passed on.

Mzee held my eldest brother Matia to such standards, and never tired of reminding him of his role. Matia was generally a good student, and often came home with a beaming smile at the end of the school term, waving his report card, which my father quickly grabbed from him and scrutinized it as if he was a doctor reading a patient's bedside record. But every kid makes a misstep at one point. My dad was an ardent believer in education, and he made every effort to put his money where his mouth was. However, our village, and most families in the surroundings, couldn't afford sending their children to school. As kids, we couldn't escape interacting with the group that didn't go to school. We met them at the village water well, at the local church, and in many other places where children meet and play. I have no idea who might have influenced Matia, because his age group was much older than mine, and therefore did not interact with them that much. All I remember, is that, one day, I overheard that a few boys from our village (including Matia), wanted to run away to Mbarara town, nearly seventy-five miles away, to work for wealthy Indian shopkeepers, looking after their children. News spread very quickly, and Mzee soon got wind of it.

As usual, he kept his cool and methodical approach, until he had gathered enough incriminating evidence. Then one evening, he stayed home waiting for Matia to come home from school. He asked all of us to sit before him, and after casually asking each one of us how we liked school, he turned and focused on Matia.

"Is everything alright at school?" he asked

"Yes, tata" Matia answered.

"Has anybody fought you or chased you away? Mzee persisted

"No one has chased me from school" said Matia

"Then why do you want to run away to Mbarara?" asked Mzee

Matia looked stunned by the question. He had all along assumed that he was acting in complete secrecy. No doubt someone had betrayed him.

But Mzee insisted that he gives him a straight answer, as Matia began to quibble around the issue, telling Mzee that, in fact it was not him, but rather the other boys, who wanted to go earn themselves some "easy money". The old man was clearly not amused by these vague answers. Before Matia could utter another word, Mzee grabbed him by the arm, dragged him through the door, and straight to the mushebeya tree around the corner. We followed them, and stood watch as Mzee used the goat's tether to tie him to the tree. Nearby, was a pile of bishansha (dry banana leaves), gathered earlier for a more mundane purpose. But the old man picked and put them under the now wide-eyed Matia, threatening to light them up if he didn't tell him the truth. My mother tried to open her mouth in objection, but Mzee shouted her down. We had never seen such fury in him.

Unsure where this was going, my mother asked my other brother Marcel, to run and fetch Ruzabeti, one of the respected old women around Kabura, who lived nearby. She took a little while showing up, but finally, we all turned around as we heard the tapping of her walking cane. She said something in rebuke, and went straight to the tree, pushing the flammable bishansha away with her stick. Mzee retreated back inside the house, while my mother and the old lady struggled to untangle the knots in the rope.

Matia, and all of us learned a vital lesson from this incident, one we would never forget, and later applied to our own kids whenever they showed signs of slackening from their school responsibilities.

While Mzee was a good people-mobilizer, he was not an astute businessman. In fact, my mother used to keep all the money, especially after dad received payment from the local coffee cooperative. Since my father's generosity knew no bounds, she feared that leaving him with all the hard-earned funds was tantamount to a carte blanche to giving it all away.

My dad loved bread, and on Sunday morning, which was the only day during the week, when the family gathered for breakfast together, he made sure we had some. If he had not been to Rukungiri, the closest town, four miles away, where Arab bakeries flourished, he insisted that one of us go there early in the morning, to fetch some and be back in time for breakfast.

Then in the late 1960's, he put his money where his mouth was. Like Victor Kiam who loved the Remington micro shaver so much, that he bought the company, my dad too, loved his bread so much, he started a bakery. But you can't run a business like a charity, giving away most of your products to non-paying customers. Many people took advantage of his giving spirit, especially female relatives, who would stop by with hungry kids in tow. A hungry child was anathema to my dad, and they knew it. So when a kid saw the bread, and insisted that the mother give him some, the mother pretended to pull the kid away, which made him cry even more, until the old man called them back and offered the kid a scones, locally known as "mwana akaba", or "the kid is crying".

Naturally, the business didn't last long although my dad's giving spirit never wavered, often manifesting itself in food donations to less fortunate families like Tibiruho and his wife Perepetwa. It was not unusual for me, to go on my "home leaves", and while discerning the crowd of people who may have come to see me, notice one donning a shirt I had carried home for my father on a previous visit.

Questioned on why he'd given away his present, the answer was almost always the same,

"He needed it more than I did".

Seven

THERE WAS VERY little activity, by way of entertainment, to keep young people busy in a place as remote as Rukungiri those days. Makerere University Department of Music Dance and Drama (MDD), whose short form, some had caricatured as"Musiru Dala Dala, which means "stupidest of the stupid", had come up with an innovation called Makerere Traveling Theater, to introduce up-country people to this form of entertainment. But the scheme was constrained by the supply of resources and actors the university could make available.

At about the same time, the Ministry of Information and Broadcasting, had also introduced a form of entertainment called the Traveling Cinema, which showed a few movies at Gombolora headquarters, while at the same time educating the locals about such issues as vaccinations, agricultural techniques, etc. But these forms of entertainment took place late in the evening, when the farming communities were expected to have returned from their fields.

One day, on our way back from school, our traveling pals convinced us to stay in Rukungiri and watch this traveling cinema movie. The guys showing the movie would mount a projector on top of their Volkswagen Combi, connect it to the car battery, and project the picture onto a screen several meters away. After watching, what to most of us, was our first movie experience, we started walking back home in a hurry. A few months earlier, following the first ethnic disturbances in Rwanda, an endless stream of refugees had started crossing into Uganda, some camping just about anywhere they could find space. The Uganda government had designated two special places, one known as Oruchinga Valley, and the second near Lake Nakivale, to settle the refugees, while at the same time, encouraging churches and private families to absorb some of the displaced families. We had watched the daily processions, as children our own age, but with spindly legs, swerved on the narrow road behind their equally starved parents, bearing weights on their little necks, some of us couldn't fathom lifting.

One gentleman by the name of Mbarara, his wife Ndeti, their children Kalori and Maria, and his mother-in-law, Mukarutamu, were settled at our small church in Kabura. But having only arrived with just about the clothes on their back, and little else, the community was expected to feed and look after them, until they could get on their feet. As it turned out, not many people seemed ready to fulfill this commitment, except for my father. Every day of the week, we took them some raw food, occasionally, inviting them over to share a meal with us. As the children were about my age, my brothers and I, got fond of them, sometimes spending time playing with them.

So, on that fateful evening, when we arrived home from the movie, my father, who usually took time to check on their welfare, was already at home waiting, as my mother served the evening meal. As we said our good evening to them, he posed to ask us why we were so late. We tried to concoct all kinds of excuses, to no avail. Then, he asked us whether we had delivered any food to the Mbararas, to which he was met by silence.

"Who fetched water and firewood for tonight's meal?" Silence again.

Mzee kept a cane near his pillow, which he once in a while, used to straighten any of us whenever he felt someone had gone astray. And if it was your turn, he sent you to bring it yourself. I was the youngest among that night's culprits, so he sent me to bring the gadget. He told us to lie down, and took turns giving each one of us five lashes, then told us to proceed to bed "to learn what an empty stomach feels like" I've never forgotten the lesson. Forty years later, I continue to remind my own kids about showing a little compassion to others, especially those who have less than we do.

After a lunch of chapatti, matooke and beef stew, we embarked on the home stretch. The tarmac road ended on Rwabanyambu, just a few meters from Main Street. At the bottom of the hill, we pass the late Tiberondwa's home. During the first Obote Regime, he was one of the sycophant UPC party supporters, ready to kill for his boss. He was once a primary school teacher, who abandoned teaching for politics, and got rewarded as a Gombolora chief of Kebisoni for his loyalty. His wife, Freda, was the daughter of Kezekia and Kezia Barungira, our neighbors to the east, just across the valley. Freda was also a primary school teacher when she married him, but left teaching to raise a family.

Tiberondwa had another brother, Kabegambire, a teacher at Makobore High School, Kinyasano, right next door to their home. They had a sister, Esther, who had briefly visited the United States in the late 60's, and returned a transformed woman. Not only had she changed her accent, she pioneered the moon walk, long before Michael Jackson, all in the short space of the two years she was away. Upon her return, she had fallen for a stocky British businessman called Douglas, who abused her at every chance he got. First, they lived in Lusaka, Zambia, before settling in Kampala, where Douglas run Makerere University's student canteen. Once a vivacious young woman, years of relentless abuse had transformed her once shapely figure into the amorphous features of a babushka.

Makobore High School was established at Kinyasano in 1965, along with another thirty or so other secondary schools nationwide. It was the first secondary school set up in Rujumbura County. Before that, male students had to travel to Kabale, to study at Kigezi College Butobere, or to Mbarara, to enroll at Ntare School. Girls had a choice between Mary Hill High School in Mbarara, or Bweranyangyi Girls Secondary School near Bushenyi. Although Makobore's establishment was a relief to some parents, its performance remained lackluster for a longtime, forcing parents who valued a quality education, to continue sending their children to the better performers.

Before Makobore, there was the Junior Secondary School, headed by Eliya Biryabarema who run the school like a tight ship. His penchant for corruption was legendary. He never made his solicitations directly, instead wrapping them within some parable. If he wanted to squeeze a goat out of a parent before admitting his son to school, for instance, he might say,

"Your son seems to have a lot of goat hair around his clothes, does he look after goats?"

The Anglican Church had established its first mission here back in the 1920's, in direct competition with the catholic mission at Nyakibale. After the initial squabbling by the pioneering missionaries, religious institutions in Uganda in general, though competitive, never developed the kind of rivalry that erupted into open violence. That might have been because many families were often likely to have members of different faiths under one roof. Although party politics tried to exploit the religious differences, they did not register quite the success they had hoped for.

On special occasions such as Christmas and Easter, neighbors of different faiths, met, greeted one another on the way to their respective places of worship, and came home to share meals together. My school days at Nyakibale, for instance, were characterized by an early morning walk to school with kids, such as Matsiko, who attended school at Kinyasano. Matsiko, Gershom Mishambi (RIP), and other kids from Kinyasano, would wait for us for the return journey home in the evening. Although missionary schools played a vital role in the nation's education system in the early part of the twentieth century, their role is getting diminished as private entrepreneurs build schools that emphasize the secular aspect of education.

The drive to Kasoroza, takes about twenty minutes, past Kinyasano. We pass Katobo, where a man called Rwamutojo used to live. His son, Rwabugarame, once worked in the copper mines at Kilembe, near Kasese, at the foot of the Rwenzori Mountains. When he retired from there, he got some gratuity package in a lump sum. Out of this, he bought himself a beat-up Volkswagen Beetle, which in the 1960's, was a tremendous achievement. Rwamutojo used to wake up early in the morning, ask his son to open the car, and the old man would sit in the back for the better part of the day, telling anybody who cared to listen, that he was enjoying the results of his sweat. The same road continues towards Bwindi Gorilla National Park, home of the World famous mountain gorillas, about forty miles to the west. These creatures, perhaps, man's closest relatives number around 750, and roam the forests around the borders of Uganda, Rwanda and the Democratic Republic of Congo. Conservation groups such as the WWF have put in a lot of money, in collaboration with the host governments, to try and save the species. During Uganda's chaotic period of the 1970's and 80's, and the period leading to Rwanda's genocide, marauding soldiers almost reduced them to extinction. Since then, however, governments have realized that they are a valuable tourism resource which generates vital foreign exchange for the countries. As a result, the three countries now even go to the extent of deploying contingencies of their national armies to protect them.

Eight

KASOROZA, IS MY boyhood town which hasn't changed much in more than sixty years of its existence. Of late, however, it has been boosted by a connection to the national electricity grid, on a line that will eventually extend to Kanungu district, and Bwindi Impenetrable Forest, home to the World-famous mountain gorillas, near the DRC boarder. Life has begun to change with the arrival of electric power. Entrepreneurs such as Filipo Begumisa, my primary school music teacher, have set up flour mills in as far-flung places as Rwerere, once considered hard to reach. Night owls have also sampled their first taste of night-club life, where music was once played on the gramophone, and later, on the ubiquitous radiogram. The narrow gravel one-lane road connecting Kasoroza to my parents' home was constructed by us, following the Buganda tradition of "bulungi bwansi", a community-based effort. The local government has never made any effort to service it, let alone, expand it, despite many pleas from the local people.

Back then, frustrated by lack of a road, my brother Matia, led the mobilization effort to link our village "to civilization". Some people in the village refused to join us, arguing that neither they, nor their children had any vehicles to use on the road, and that they were just simply further glorifying Tobi's (my father's) family, whose children had the means to purchase the vehicles. But we persisted, and slowly, won over some of them, convincing them that in case of an emergency in their own families, it would be better if their homes were easily accessible. In the end, we connected the one-mile or so to the Rukungiri-Kambuga road, and this tiny rural road has since been extended further. However, the bridge at the bottom of the hill, past the late Mr. Kaharuza's home had posed a challenge. We had attempted constructing one using heavy logs of wood. But since there were no firm structures, such as concrete bases anchoring them firmly to the ground, the bridge kept being washed away in major rainy seasons, which carried both water and debris downstream.

Then one day, on our way back from school, we came across what we envisaged would be a permanent solution. The road maintenance division of the Public Works Department, known locally as Pida, had piled several concrete culverts near the junction, where our little road joined the main road. About ten of us, including my brother Jerome, along with another fellow, Tibananuka, whom we called Banana, got excited, and decided to roll at least two of those heavy culverts to use on our bridge. We had obviously no idea what effort it would take to get the monsters down to the valley, nor had we any inkling of the estimated risk to life it could pose if it got out of control. In the heat of the moment, we slowly started rolling them with our bare hands, first on the gentle slope, until the gradient of the slope got steeper. Then, they got completely out of control, gathering momentum and speed, and heading uncontrollably towards Kafumu's home, crushing everything in their path, until they hit a boulder further down, and disintegrated into dozens of pieces. We all watched in awe as this happened, only managing to raise an alarm for the people below to immediately get out of the way. One more effort lost on a good cause. It took close to twenty years and a lot of cajoling before this bridge was fixed more firmly.

Kanyankole turned right at the junction, moving slowly, careful not to hit some of the large stones that still dot this road, mostly exposed by rainwater washing away the top soil. He was familiar with the terrain, as he often drove Grace or other family members to Kabura whenever there was some function requiring them to attend. Along the way, a few kids waved to us, as they always do to every passing car. Near Nyansio's home, a scrawny dog burst into life, barking incessantly, as it chased the car, almost getting run-over by the rear tires. As we passed the late Musa's home, I looked around for signs of Nkyereme, his wife, who had become a constant feature, always seated near the entrance to the door. This time she was not there, perhaps a bad back, or some other old age ailment had afflicted her, preventing her from absorbing a few rays of sunlight that morning.

Finally, that familiar sight as we arrived home. All eyes focused on me as I alighted from the car in our compound. I had called my brother Dominic before leaving Washington, and told him to go whisper into Mzee's ear, that I was on my way. The somber crowd gathered at the house, some, I was told, for more than a week, seemed to get some temporary relief from my arrival, as if I'd perform some miracles. The home is a one-story brick rambler, with additions in the back forming a quadrangle of open space in between. The front also, has an open space that can accommodate a sizeable crowd of a few hundred. We built the structure in the mid-1980's, as a gathering place for the present, and future descendants of Mzee Tobi and Solome Ngazoire, the patriarch and matriarch of the clan. Many happy, as well as sad occasions, have taken place here since it was built. The original mud brick home in which I was born and raised, used to be located maybe two hundred yards below the current home, and was demolished as soon as this was completed.

Discerning the crowd, my eyes could pick out the faces of some long-lost relatives, especially those who frequented our home when I was a kid, before going to boarding school in Kabale. Most were old now, their faces having been reworked by nature's craftsmanship over a forty-year period. Also, quite a few were conspicuous by their absence, having left for the nether world, to join their ancestors, in line with Darwin's process of natural selection. Mzee's home had always been open, to friend and foe alike. He had consoled many bereaved families in his time on this earth, and helped to extend a helping hand to many in need. It was very gratifying to look in the eyes of that crowd, and take comfort in the fact that they were sharing the same sorrow with me. It made me proud to realize how many lives he had touched.

I shook a few hands, then maneuvered through the crowd to my parents' bedroom, where the closest relatives covered whatever little space there was, surrounding the bed on which Mzee lay in a semi-comatose state. I embraced my mother, Solome, who sat on a high chair, to allow her stretch her left leg, which had been incapacitated following hip replacement surgery about ten years earlier. Everyone's eyes were fixed on Mzee, who was hooked on some drip fluids because he could no longer take in anything on his own. His eyes could move a little, but it was clear, they were out of focus, and could hardly recognize anyone.

I had carried some cans of the energy-giving "Ensure", which I hoped the doctor could administer to the patient, to raise his energy level.

I stretched my hand and squeezed Mzee's, careful not to pull it from the needle delivering the life-giving fluids. I clung on to it for a while, though there was hardly any movement at all. Many people kept coming, some standing in the doorway, looking at his face, some becoming overwhelmed with emotions, and withdrawing to rejoin the crowd outside. Although I felt exhausted from nearly three days of traveling, there was hardly any place to take refugee for some sleep. After sitting in the room for a while, I decided to go out and work the crowd. Aunt Flora, Mzee's only sibling was there too, looking rather frozen in time. But other relatives and family friends, from near and far, were chatting, and expressed their happiness that I could show up at a moment's notice, even though I lived so far away. Aunt Flora, a tiny woman in stature, standing no more than five-foot-four, loomed large in our lives as we grew up. She was the only woman, as far as I can remember, who could stop my father from using a cane on any of us if she was around.

On one such occasion, she faced a rather berated Mzee, and told him the story of how a leopard, after giving birth to several cubs, hid around the nearby bushes and tried to scare them, in order to see which of them had the right stuff. Those of them that got too timid and run away, turned into "emondo" or cheetahs, while those that yelled back and stood their ground, grew up to be real leopards. During my primary school days at Kahoko, there were times I stayed at her home in Kahenda, on the other side of the giant Mashure hill, waking up early to join other kids who commuted to Kahoko. The only thing I dreaded about my stay was the food. Aunt Flora grew all kinds of pumpkins, and whenever they were in season, she hardly served anything else. Some days, she cooked the yellow ones with hard skin as the main course, accompanied by the tender green ones as source. And for snacks, she would roast the sun-dried seeds. Her husband, Shiringyi, a stout man with bulging eyes, was still alive, and used to amuse us with a few stories.

When I had just arrived in the US, I was awe-struck by the giant sizes of the yellow pumpkins the stores stocked for Halloween. Equally shocking, was how few of those were actually eaten, except for pumpkin pies around Thanksgiving. Although I eventually caught up with the American tradition of curving a pumpkin for the kids around Halloween, I still refrained from consuming the pies at Thanksgiving, telling them that my body absorbed enough pumpkins in my youth, to last me a lifetime.

The doctor called and said he could not come in that evening, but assured me that the nurse would come and check the vital signs and make sure the drips were working alright. I had wanted either the doctor or the nurse to administer the patient with the Ensure formula, but when the nurse finally came that evening, she could not get a vein that could dilate enough to allow for the flow of the thick solution. We had to wait for the doctor to come in the following day, and try the force-feeding option through the throat. People took turns to watch him overnight. I went back to the room and sat there, until my eyes couldn't take it anymore, then I sneaked into one of the adjoining rooms outside and managed to catch a few hours of sleep.

The following day, people started streaming into our living room as early as seven O'clock in the morning. Some, like Bamutooza and Kapiira, distant nephews of Mzee, were coming for the second time in a week. They told me, that after seeing the old man's condition the last time they were here, they went home, only to remain so restless that they felt they had to come back and update themselves about his condition. Although my father had been baptized catholic, his secular nature meant that he treated people from other religious faiths equally as those of his own. They, in turn, paid equal respect to him. During his campaigns to introduce and encourage local farmers to grow coffee, for instance, my father used to attend church services at different denominations, seizing a chance to talk to the congregations afterwards.

This reciprocity was shown by the nature of people who turned up to see him and wish him well. In mid-morning, the pastor of Kabura Church, built mostly with funds raised from my extended family, showed up, said a few prayers with those present and left. That afternoon, Father Banyenzaki, a priest from Nyakibale, a friend of the family, arrived, and conducted a bedside mass. And later in the evening, my maternal uncle, Rev. Kahiriita, from the Anglican Church of Uganda, also showed up, and held yet, another prayer session. The people gathered around would join in regardless of their religious affiliation.

Finally, at sunset, Dr Ndyomugenyi arrived. The nurse briefed him about her failure to administer the Ensure solution through the nearly collapsed veins. He asked most of the people in the bedroom to leave and give him and the nurse some space to work. He then checked the flow of the drip solution which was, itself going very slowly, and determined that a thicker fluid wouldn't go through. He decided to use the forced-feeding option as the last resort. I stood a few feet away, watching with a lot of indignation, as the doctor forced a long tube through my father's throat, while they held him down as he apparently resisted the act. The hero to many, who once downed an African buffalo with a single shot, lying on his back after the beast had knocked him down, now had to be fed like a baby. It was surreal, a truly pathetic sight, especially to those of us who had known him all our lives.

With the tube far enough beyond the throat, the doctor introduced the pinkish-brown Ensure solution, first very slowly, then gradually increasing the flow. He stopped after a few minutes, so he could watch the effect. Within a few minutes, the stuff began coming back, some through the nose. Apparently, the body was getting too fragile to handle anything other than pure liquid. They cleaned him up, and tried to re-connect the lighter mineral salt solution, but this too, was being rejected. Miraculously, however, the starved body seemed to have absorbed a few of Ensure solution drops, energizing the body a little bit. I had been around for two days now, and Mzee had not shown any sign that he recognized my presence. Now in a seated position, I approached him and stroked his hand. He slowly moved his head, and gave a little nod. Among his male children I am the only one who developed a bald head, a resemblance he referred to with fond memories of his uncle Kibihena. He often teased me about it, sometimes running his hand through my head. I tilted my head so he could touch it with his weakened hand, and as I did so, I noticed a gentle smile on his face. I leaned closer to his ear, and whispered to him that I had flown in to see him. He tried to touch my head, but his arm was too weak to move. Instead, still bearing the same smile on his face, he moved his hand in a gentle wave, a clear sign that he was waving his last farewell to me.

At that point, I became too emotional, and burst out of the room, a stream of tears running down my cheeks. It was one of those eternal moments cut in stone, which one cannot erase from memory, no matter how hard you tried. It was a precious moment, which I knew might not repeat itself, given the weakened condition my father was in. The doctor and nurse left, after promising to try performing the same exercise the following day. Deep inside, however, I knew that this might be the last I would ever communicate with my father.

I went back and sat among the crowd in the living room. Some, especially the elderly, had their usual demands of "a little tobacco here, and a little soap there". Nevertheless, I used this occasion to explore as much oral history about the family as I could. They were the only channel of communication about my past left, now that Mzee was no longer able to pass on his side of the story. Kezia Komumbibo had, over a period of years, shed more light about my father's side of the family than anyone else. But this gathering included aunts and other close family relatives who could collaborate on the stories she had told me. Some, like Aunt Kibatenga were, themselves literally on their last leg, and might not be around much longer. I found a lot of solace chatting with distant cousins like Bamutooza of Rukondo, and Kapiira of Katonya, despite the wide age difference. They poured their hearts out in deference of Mzee, who had been the dominant male figure in their lives, having lost their own fathers at a young age.

Nine

THE PRECISE DATE of Mzee Tobi Ngazoire's birth is unknown, but according to events that took place around that time, he was born sometime around 1920, in a small village called Rwanyanja, Bugangari, in Rujumbura County, bordering present day Queen Elizabeth National Park. His father, Kabunu, was, according to the late Kezia Barungira, and other elders who knew the family, a fairly well-to-do farmer and cattle-keeper, who had easy access to the "Kikaari", or palace of the ruling Bashambu of Kagunga. My paternal grandmother mother was called Kayirebwa, a tall and beautiful woman of Rwandese Tutsi origin, who spoke very little of the Ruhororo/Runyankole dialect. It is said that she, and her sister, had been given out as "appeasement" for an earlier cattle raid by Rwandese warriors that had resulted in the death of Nkobererwa, Mzee's great grandfather. Cattle raids between neighboring tribes were common those days. From conversations I had with elders in the area, it would appear that most people who eventually settled here, originally migrated from the Karagwe area of northern Tanzania. That would explain the incursions between them and their Rwandese neighbors.

Although the exact nature of the relationship between my grandfather and the ruling clan of the Bashambu remains cloudy, what's apparent is that the rulers used to take some of their herds to graze alongside my grandfather's, often spending a few days at his compound, drinking and making merry. And, from what's known of the social structures of the period, people considered to be of a lower social class could not have freely mixed with the rulers, making one suspect that he must have occupied a high place in the society of the period. Indeed, the way Mzee schmoozed with the Karekahos, the Kitaburazas, as well as the Kabonero families, showed a level of interaction that was more than skin deep. But my father never ventured into discussing this area of social structures, preferring to let other people throw all kinds of labels around him instead.

My father had only one sibling, a half sister called Flora. A tiny woman, standing no higher than about five-foot-two, in sharp contrast to my father's towering figure of about six feet, she exercised a lot of influence over him. We all loved Aunt Flora, and she in turn returned the favor ten-fold. One could always count on Aunt Flora to intervene and protect him from an impending stroke of the cane if she was around when my father wanted to administer some punishment for errant behavior. Aunt Flora was married to a man called Shilingi, who died fairly young, probably in his early forties, or even thirties. They lived about three miles away in Ruteete. To get there, one had to cross the saddle over Mashure, the giant hill that separates Kabura village from Ruteete. In the valley below Mashure, known as Rwamashunju, is where, as kids, we often went to gather firewood, eat matunguru, a reddish, sweet, onion-like fruit for which we competed with birds, and monkeys, depending on who got there first.

We also watched, as Barimbanza, a boy from the neighborhood, displayed his dexterity at extracting honey from the giant tall mitooma trees with his gloveless hands. First he antagonized the bees by blowing a plume of smoke inside the groove where they had settled. The smoke immediately caused some disturbance to the colony, which then emerged and chased everyone around, injecting a few stings into whoever happened to meander in their path. The giant trees that were once native to the valley, have almost been cut to extinction today, to create more land for farming, in order to feed the ever-burgeoning population, leaving a desolate brown landscapes, where once one only saw a lush greenery.

Since Mzee never had any male siblings, as kids, there was really only one man we could truly call Uncle. His name was Petero Mugyeru, a muhima from Kitojo in Buyanja sub-county. He was a devout protestant, known as a mulokore (born-again), which would have been at odds with my family, which was catholic. My mother was very devout about her faith. My dad, though a regular churchgoer, was more secular. He once refused to address an insisting Father superior of Nyakibale Diocese, as "father", telling him "tala akafa" meaning, "my father died".

It didn't matter what faith you believed in whenever Petero and his wife Melabu were around, and that was quite often. The Mugyerus belonged to the Anglican Church, later re-named Church of Uganda. But in our home, religious matters were inconsequential, since most of our relatives were almost equally divided among the two predominant religions, Catholics and Anglicans. If dinner was about to be served, Petero led the prayer, and we had to pray with him, even if this sometimes stretched for an hour or more, until the food literally grew cold. He prayed for fishermen in the middle of lakes, people climbing trees, those in planes, the sick in hospital, and the healthy alike. There were no shortcuts until he himself said "Amen". By the end of the prayer, everybody looked exhausted, but certainly much relieved that it was, at last over. I never heard any objections from my parents about this, though my mother sometimes displayed some anxiety if this went on too long.

According to my mother, Petero's and my father's families were so close, that when my father was ready to get married, following his father's death, Petero's family provided the cattle that my father used as bride-price or lobola as it's known in southern African cultures. During the divisive politics of the 1960's, the late President Milton Obote, a protestant was favored by the

Anglican Church of Uganda, with connivance from the British Government, against Benedicto Kiwanuka, a charismatic catholic lawyer from Buganda. Most clergymen of the two predominant religious denominations drew their lines in the sand as to which candidate they would support. At that time, fellow balokole (saved ones), approached Mr. Mugyeru, and advised him to refrain from frequenting our home, telling him that,

"Abasaselidoti nibeija kuha Tobi obutwa amwite", meaning, that my father would receive poison from catholic priests, which he would administer to him.

These allegations infuriated Petero so much, that he reacted like Winston Churchill, when castigated by Lady Astor about his incessant carousing habits:

Lady Astor, "Winston, if you were my husband, I'd flavor your coffee with poison"

Churchill: "Madam, if I were your husband, I'd gladly take it!"

Petero told his detractors, that if any poison targeting him was to ever come out of Tobi's home, he would be more than glad to drink it. Instead, he advised them to keep their distance away from him least they tried to poison him. Mzee Petero passed away around 2002, two years before my father. His wife Melabu joined him in the yonder world more recently, at the beginning of 2010.

Mzee lost his father while he was still very young, forcing him to fend for himself at a relatively early age. His Uncle, Kibihena, bundled his own family, his nephew and niece (my father, his sister Flora), and their mothers, around 1940, from Rwanyanja to Rweibare, close to the current location of my parents' home. My father later struck up a friendship with a local Mutongole chief called Yakobo Rubinduka, who gave him the piece of land in Kabura on which he built the home where we were born and raised. Land was still very abundant and the country's population relatively scanty. Yakobo, who was a polygamist, sired a lot of offsprings from his three wives, Biisa, Bwisho and Katima, the children spreading around the vast piece of land their father once held. Although Yakobo himself passed away more than twenty years ago, and most of his older children have since joined him in the yonder world, the clan continues to thrive and have a presence in Kabura village. Over the years, intermarriages such as those between Mirembe, Aunt Flora's daughter, to Leo Makiga, Yakobo's grandson, have made family relationships inextricably interlocked.

The Kabura of my youth offered quite a pleasant experience in child upbringing. People didn't have much money then (and now), but then again, they didn't seem to need it, because most of the basic needs of food and shelter, were obtainable at very little cost. For instance, every family was located on land, either bequeathed from their ancestors, or acquired from the existing stock of unoccupied land which was still relatively abundant. On this, they built what qualified as average shelter at that time, typically, a mud-brick hut with either grass thatch, or banana fiber. All the food they consumed was grown on their piece of land, with hardly any need to purchase any food beyond what they produced. With very little exchanged in the market place, people lived a complete agrarian lifestyle, occasionally buying meat for the family, or slaughtering a goat or chicken from their own stock. With little money to play with, purchases were limited to, may be a dress for the wife around Christmas, and school uniform for the kids.

Unlike the scenes of African emaciated bodies flashed on TV screens all over the world today, our villages were teaming with surplus produce then. The mutongole chief was the government's first line of contact, going around the villages every day, to ensure that each family had filled up a grain store for food security, and maintained a latrine away from the living quarters, for hygienic purposes. The mutongole, in turn reported to the muluka chief, who in turn reported to the gombola chief, who finally, reported to the county chief, the highest level of local administration. These positions were filled with people of considerable stature and integrity, unlike today's partisan administrators, who seem to march only to the tune of the appointing authority, and show very little interest in the people they supposedly represent.

Most people in my village seemed to be either related by blood or marriage. Although most folks belonged to the domineering Bahinda clan, my father, who belonged to the Bashambu clan was well respected, partly because his natural demeanor was such that he avoided open clashes with anyone, but also since the Bashambu were the ruling clan, the lesser clans had to tread rather carefully. Moreover, some of his cousins, like the late Nyandira, were married to Bahinda, making him an in-law.

People got along well, to a point where parents didn't have to worry about their kids, if they knew that the kids had crossed over to a neighbor's home to play with other kids. Good and bad times alike were shared by all. A neighbor's wife, who gave birth, was visited by women from the neighborhood, and assisted in the performance of various chores, including, harvesting ripe crops such as millet or beans, depending on what was in season. Neighbors also ensured that the other kids of the new mother didn't go without a meal. Weddings and funerals were a joint effort, everyone pitching in as much as they could. Weddings were particularly festive occasions. There was no need to extend invitations, anybody who wanted to be there just showed up. Food was not a problem, as every family in the village contributed towards the feeding of the masses, including the preparation of the food. Christmas too, was a festive period, to the extent that people had dubbed it "kulisamani", meaning over-eating in the Runyankole dialect. Kids went from house to house, sampling food, long after they had filled up from their homes. People welcomed you to share a meal with them on an occasion like Christmas. A wedding was also an occasion where old traditions met western culture. Men of the cross were particularly treated in high esteem, no matter which side of the valley they came from. The catholics referred to their pastor as "omusomesa", while the Anglicans called theirs "omwahure".

One mwahure, called Muhindi, stood above the rest when it came to presiding over wedding ceremonies. As there were hardly any vehicles in the village, he walked most of the time, often arriving a little late, sweating profusely all over his generous body. His crimpled jacket and trousers, hanging over dusty shoes, whose soles had, over the years, curved themselves in line with his bow-legs, made him quite a sight to behold.

His arrival was usually announced by the master of ceremony. And, the mwahure didn't disappoint. With his old bible carefully tucked under his left arm, he shook hands with just about everyone in sight, and bellowed out some greeting in his baritone voice. The hosts always ensured that he was well catered for, beginning with a large tea kettle and several slices of bread before his sermon, followed by a sumptuous meal of kalo (millet bread), accompanied by a large bowl of stew.

The other colorful character of the day was Ntungwa, the rain-maker (omwamuzi), who would usually be at the same occasion, to ensure that he held the rain clouds at bay. He was a small man, afflicted with polio, which left him with one leg thinner and shorter than the other, rendering walking impossible, except by hopping around using a long wooden stave. His was a rather tricky business. If all went well, and it didn't rain, he was treated like royalty, which usually involved a basketful of kalo, and rwabya (clay pot) filled to the brim with chunks of beef, washed down with a gourd of tonto and, as a bonus, he might carry home with him, a head of one of the slaughtered goats to share with his family.

However, if on the other hand, his concoctions couldn't defeat nature, and the rain came down over the guests, then the poor man became a subject of ridicule, harassed and harangued to a point, where in the extreme case, he was tied to a tree at the edge of the compound, so that he could be thoroughly drenched by the downpour he failed to prevent.

Just about the time my parents got married in 1942, the British Colonial Administration began establishing national parks in the country, some would say, mostly for their own enjoyment, since the natives couldn't afford such a luxury. Among other things, they needed to recruit young men to work as game rangers. One of the reasons, I was told, Mzee's uncle had moved the family from Rwanyanja, a small village in present day Bugangari sub-county, was to avoid the frequent attacks by wild animals on their flocks. The 1940s and 50s was also the period when a visionary Mukiga administrator called Paulo Ngorogoza, confronted with a population explosion in the Kabale area of Kigezi, came up with the idea of migrating some Bakiga to other less populated areas. Both Rujumbura and Kinkizi counties in north Kigezi, were still relatively virgin territory with scattered populations. The only problem with them was that they were too close to the area forming natural habitats for wild animals, later designated as Queen Elizabeth National Park.

My father had been spared recruitment into the King's African Rifles regiment, (K.A.R or Keyala) at the start of the 2nd World War, because he was the only boy in his family. However, when recruiters came knocking again, looking for young men to serve as game rangers, he readily answered the call, making him one of the pioneers in his area to work for the newly-created national park service. He set out on his new career, with a zeal that soon got him noticed by both park authorities, and other prominent administrators of the era. It did not take long before he was the most sought out hunter who schmoozed with the likes of Paulo Ngorogoza, then District Commissioner of Kigezi, Kamu Karekaho, first Rujumbura Member of Parliament, and Kesi Nganwa and Kasapuri, the last two, prominent members of the Ankole Kingdom Administration.

When Paulo Ngorogoza needed someone to help with the resettlement of Bakiga from Kabale to areas of Kayonza, and Bwambara in Kinkiizi and Rujumbura counties, respectively, my father was one of the people called upon to assist. His experience with the national park service was an asset, because, the new locations chosen for immigrants were too close to Queen Elizabeth

National Park, and therefore, prone to frequent invasions by park animals. My father would be called at short notice, to go, hunt down, and shoot a stray animal, such as a buffalo, or lion, which would have found its way to the new settlement, destroying some crops, or in the case of the big cats, having killed a cow or a goat, leaving panic in its wake.

Most of these incidents passed without a lot of fanfare. If an invading buffalo was gunned down, most of the meat was distributed among the settlers, an action for which my dad was revered in star-like fashion. Nevertheless, there were times when confronting these wild beasts posed grave danger. As my mother tells it, about three years into the job, long before most of us were born, my dad was away on one of these hunting safaris, when one day, two messengers from the park service showed up at her home, and delivered an urgent message for her to go with them to Bugangari Dispensary, where my dad was being hospitalized after having been seriously wounded by a charging buffalo. Most people associate ferociousness with the king of the jungle, the lion. However, few people know, that, among Africa's Big Five attractions, namely, the elephant, the buffalo, the rhino, the lion and the leopard, the female buffalo ranks top in its viciousness, particularly when defending its young. More evidence of this was captured on a widely circulated video, played on You tube in 2008. The video showed a herd of buffalo visiting their vengeance on a pack of lions which had attempted to snatch a baby buffalo from its mother as the animals gathered at a drinking hole in the Kruger National Game Park in South Africa. The victory belonged to the buffalo, which sent the lions scampering for dear life, leaving their intended victim in the safe custody of its mom.

Some of the dignitaries my father escorted on their hunting expeditions, had developed a special taste of keeping exotic animals such as baby buffalos, as pets. But getting these pets was no cake-walk. It involved either chasing the mother away to a point of exhaustion, or in the worst case scenario, wounding it, and snatching the young. On one such mission, my dad shot the mother in the leg, whereby the beast temporarily got shocked and fell down. Meanwhile, my dad, and two aids proceeded to catch the young and tie it up, ready for transporting to a waiting vehicle. Oblivious to the hunting party, the mother-buffalo awoke from its shock and charged. As my dad was the only one with a gun, he stood his ground, and squeezed the trigger, hopping that the slugger would stop the animal in its tracks. The bullet hit the buffalo alright, but not where the impact was hard enough to stop it. Within seconds, it had knocked my dad down, and was going for the jugular. His companions, who had fled for dear life, were just shouting at the top of their lungs from tree branches. The rifle in my father's possession almost became an impediment, as the animal's giant body was too close to allow for maneuverability.

Then, as my dad's desperation was beginning to set in, having been battered into submission, the buffalo turned around, heading towards its calf, which was all but bundled up with rope. With the little energy and quick survival wits left in him, he aimed the rifle at the beast, and squeezed the trigger. This bullet sent the animal flying into the air, only to crush in a big thump right next to him. That's when the rest of the party came out running to the rescue. By that time, my dad was almost unconscious, the beast having stuck the edge of one of its horns in his lower abdomen, and broken part of his lower jaw. My dad was evacuated to the only medical facility in the area, located at Bugangari Gombolora headquarters. The dispensary had been set up to provide medical services to the factory workers of the Campbell Tobacco company. My mother, with two toddlers in tow, spent the best part of two months nursing and caring for her husband, until he got on his feet again. As for my dad, he remained passionate about animals, and his respect for the buffalo never left him from that incident, as he kept a wooden curving of it by his bedside until the day he joined his victim in the nether world, more than fifty years later.

Ten

EDUCATION WAS SOMETHING else my father paid attention to with a passion. It was partly, a compensatory mechanism, to make up for a chance he missed as a kid. Although, as a kid, he had missed the benefit of attending formal education, he later learned to read and write through informal courses offered through the church. What he missed as a kid, he decided to compensate for, by educating all his children, and even extend this privilege to those, whose station in life did not offer them the opportunity. For instance, Mzee brought in my cousin, Philip, whose father could not afford to pay for him in school. My brothers and I had our first exposure of reading and writing from my dad. He had purchased some slates, which is akin to a miniaturized chalk board. On this, he would patiently sit with you, while crafting those letters of the alphabet on the slate, and then watching you repeat them, one after another, till you got them right. He also read the local newspaper of the day, called Agetereine, a predecessor to today's Orumuri, both written in the Runyankole language.

His interest extended beyond the home coaching, to a close collaboration with the headmasters and teachers who taught us. For instance, my dad used to attend the functions at the end of the school term, to cheer and clap for you, if you were one of the top students who got a prize. The pressure was always on for us to excel and get that prize, knowing very well that Mzee would be there. And if you didn't get one, you loathed answering the questions that would follow from him why you didn't get that prize.

When my brother Matia, somewhat rebellious in his youth, expressed his intention to quit school and go to Mbarara to find a job, probably in an Indian shop, my dad expressed his anger by tying him to a mushebeya tree outside our home, gathering bisanja (dry banana leaves) under him, and threatening to light them up, unless he could recant his silly ideas for good. It wasn't until Aunt Flora, and the Elderly Ruzabeti, sat there, and implored my dad to let Matia off, with a few lashes of the cane. Matia never looked back after that, and in fact went on to set a good example to us, by attending such elite schools as Butobere, and the School of Science and Mathematics at Uganda Technical College, Kyambogo, and later, Makerere University.

There were no kindergartens then, and for all I know, they are still non-existent in villages like Kabura, where I grew up. Most schools at the time, had been founded by missionaries, and depending on your religious affiliation, you almost certainly ended up at a school associated with your religion. The closest thing to kindergarten that I attended was a one-room school, located under the same roof as our local church at Kabura. Our teacher was a middle-aged man called Yowana Kagurutsi. He was not a real trained teacher. Those were reserved for more established schools like Kahoko, which offered a full primary school curriculum. However, Mr. Kagurutsi turned out to be a wonderful teacher, and an even more excellent story-teller. On reckoning now, except for lack of facilities, he would have given the hosts on Sesame Street, a run for their money.

He read to us, and then dramatized the stories from 'Ninshoma", which means "I can read" in the Runyankole language. Ninshoma was a classic children reader, written by a white missionary, called Father Spandock, who had lived in the area for so long, and had mastered the local language. Kagurutsi flavored the stories with his own words, and mimicked facial expressions, making them more believable and memorable. To this day, I still remember some of his versions more than the stories I read much later. Among my all time favorites, was how the canning Wakame, the hare, tricked Warugwe, the leopard, into carrying a food basket full of his own cubs, to his in-laws, who had been stricken by a disastrous famine. Wakame, always wary of his carnivorous friend's intentions, knew that getting rid of Warugwe's off-springs would effectively be saving his own species. So, when Warugwe, in a casual conversation, broke the news that his in-laws in a far off village were facing famine, Wakame, never short of survival tricks, concocted one, where the two would deliver some needed help to the deprived in-laws. Wakame would obtain the food, package it, but since the basket may be too heavy for his small body, his friend would carry it all the way. Warugwe was very delighted about the idea, After all, who wouldn't want to save his inlaws? On the appointed day, Warugwe checked on his cubs, fed them, and then left for his usual hunting expedition, leaving the nuances of journey preparation to his lazy friend.

Wakame knew the times his friend left and returned home. He had hidden a large raffia basket, complete with a lid, in a thicket of bushes near Warugwe's home, and this time, he had sat there watching, and waiting for Warugwe to leave. As soon as the latter left, Wakame run to where the cubs were, lifting one at a time, and placing them in the basket. Once all the four cubs were inside, he placed the tightly-fitting lid on top, and then hurried to find his friend, intercepting him, even before he got his kill for the day. Since Warugwe had fed the cubs over night, Wakame assured him that they would be ok until the two returned from their trip later that evening.

Leading Warugwe to the basket, he helped him lift it to his head, and then Wakame led the way, as he seemed to know his way to just about any place in the jungle. Along the way, they kept running into friends, who curiously gazed at the odd combination, with Warugwe swaying with a heavy basket on his head, while Wakame puffed at his pipe, and walked leisurely with a walking stick in one hand, while he freely swang the other. Wakame also greeted their friends with a rather strange greeting,

"Mureiregye abagyenda bekoreire ebibatamanyire", meaning "Are you well my friends, who travel laden with unknown luggage?"

When they finally arrived at their destination, the in-laws welcomed them, and since they had very little to offer, Wakame told them to go ahead and prepare a meal out of the food they had brought for them. Upon opening the basket, the food preparer came running, with a bewildered expression and said to Wakame,

"Hona ebyokurya bimwaturetera, omutwe ka ni Warugwe, namatu ka ni Warugwe", meaning, "But the food you brought us, from head to ears, the cub resembles Warugwe"

Wakame, who doubled as an entertainer, had pulled out his flute, and was by now blowing out some lovely lyrics that made his hosts swing their heads and clap their hands.

"Otafayo, nikwe bigyenda oweitu", meaning, "Don't worry, that's how we do things in our home" he whispered into the food preparer's ear, making sure that Warugwe wouldn't hear. The food preparer went back to the kitchen, removed a second cub, stared at it, then came back running at top speed. He turned to Wakame again, and said,

"Ayi bambe, byona, hona nameisho, namatu, nerangyi ka ni Warugwe", He let out a curse, meaning, "All of them, including the eyes, the ears, and even the color resemble Warugwe"

To which Wakame quickly replied, "Mumare agachwagach-wagura muteeke", meaning, "Simply go ahead, chop and cook".

Later, when the meal was brought, a large bowl of succulent meat was given to Warugwe, who, upon tasting, declared it the most delicious meal he had eaten in a long time.

But Wakame as usual, had found yet another trick. He feigned a full stomach, and told his hosts that there was plenty of food where this came from, and that it was better to leave this to the hungry.

On their way back, Wakame found an excuse to take another route back home, leaving Warugwe to return to an empty home. That's when it dawned on Warugwe, that Wakame had tricked him into eating his own cubs. From that time on, Warugwe vowed that Wakame would never be his friend again.

That's why leopards hunt and eat rabbits!

In another story, a man called Rushaju, tries to convince his friend Rwahurutu, to buy the skin of a lion, which Rushaju plans to hunt and kill. Rwahurutu, knowing about his friend's cowardice, remains skeptical as his friend pitches about the sale, but remains mum. While all this talk was going on, Warucuncu, the lion, was listening in. Finally, after the handshake over the deal was made, Warucuncu rushes out from under the bushes, headed straight towards Rushaju. Fortunately, Rwahurutu sees the menacing look on Warucuncu's face, and takes flight into the nearest tree, shouting at the top of his lungs for Rushaju to follow suit, and flee for his life. The lion misses both of them narrowly, but stands at the bottom of the tree, spitting fire with fury, and gives them a stern warning," Otariguza oruhu rwekicuncu otakakisire", meaning, Never sell the skin of a lion before you kill it". Equally amusing, were "Kanyonza egamba nk'abantu", referring to the morning lark, emulating people's voices, or how "Frog lost his tail" in his attempt to visit his good friend Kihangare, the Gecko.

Makes the title of the book, "All I know, I learned in kindergarten", sound so true.

My dad's home-schooling was so effective, that, like my elder brothers before me, we skipped the first grade at Kahoko, and went straight into the second grade. There, the headmaster, Mr. Francis Nkorenta, impressed with my performance, offered me scholarships for the time he was headmaster of the school, which took me to the fifth grade. He had developed such confidence in my abilities, that one day, while I was in fourth grade, he put it to test. He was teaching a class of nature study (today's biology), to sixth-graders when he paused this question to them: "What do you call an animal that feeds on land during the day, but spends most of its night time in water?" None of them could answer it, and he threatened to punish them, especially, if he could get a kid from the lower grades to answer it. The sixth graders didn't believe that any lower graders knew the answer either. So, Mr. Nkorenta burst into our classroom, and asked me to come with him to his class. He provided me with no clue about the question, only that there was a question he wanted me to answer before his class. Once inside, he made me stand in front facing the class, then he paused the same question to me.

"Amphibian", I thundered out, much to the delight of the older kids. "See what I told you?" he retorted, as he pulled out a shilling coin and handed it to me.

"You can buy yourself some samosa later", he said as he waved me off to return to my class.

Mr. Nkorenta remained headmaster until I finished fifth grade, after which he was transferred back to his native Rushasha Primary School. (Update:) I run into Mr. Nkorenta during my mother's funeral on August 3 2012. Now a frail old man walking with the aid of a stick, he approached me, and with an infectious smile, extended his hand, while asking me at the same time, "Hona wamanya?", meaning do you know who I am? I hesitated a moment, not too sure who this familiar face was. There were tens of faces I hadn't run into for thirty, even forty years, who had come to pay their last respects to the fallen matriarch. Finally, he broke the ice, "I am Francis Nkoreta…" I couldn't let him finish the sentence. I gathered my strength and lifted him off the ground.

"I am so very happy to see you again", I told him. Then I confessed to him that I believed he had passed on a long time ago. He was standing there with another icon of the family, Peter Kagumaho, who had been Matia's mentor when he was the Headmaster of Nyakibale Boys Primary School.

Mr Nkorenta's replacement was Peter Mwemeire, a man with

a giant ego about his self-worth. He was rather brisk, with a sharp tongue which he used readily to slice his subordinates down to size. He liked to comb his hair with a parting, which, combined with the gap in his upper teeth, gave the impression that someone had once tried to saw his head in half. He seemed to harbor some disdain for my father, because of the influence my dad appeared to command over some of the teachers in the school. When the cooperative movement was introduced in our area, to aid farmers with the marketing of their coffee, my dad embraced it with zeal, and spent countless days preaching about the advantages of joining "ekibiina kya Society", at schools and churches. Some of the teachers at Kahoko, it appears, were more willing to listen to him than their boss, which did not augur well with Mr. Mwemeire.

In my younger days, I used to spot a big afro on my head, typical of the era of the rebellious look. One day, the headmaster called me to his office, and told me to cut my hair short. When I got home, I told my parents what had transpired, and my father simply told me to ignore the order. The following day, I went to school, and attended classes until mid-morning break, when everybody went outside to play in the school playground. I had just gotten out when I run into Mr. Mwemeire, who stopped and asked,

"Did I not tell you to chop that hair of yours off?" I stood there staring at him, without talking. After a brief moment, he left, but soon returned with three big boys from the sixth grade.

"Get a basin of water, soak his hair and shave it off with a razor blade", he ordered them. I tried to run, but was soon subdued and restrained by two of the boys. The third one immediately went to work, carrying out the orders of his omnipotent boss. And, while this indignity was taking place, the headmaster came by, watched me as I struggled to free myself, then sarcastically said, "Gyenda ogambire sho, oti nankiza omwani kwonka nimukiza amagezi", meaning, "Go tell your father, that he may have more coffee, but I am more intelligent than him!"

By this time, I was extremely upset, and did not go to class afterwards. Instead, I cried all the way home. When I told my dad what the headmaster had said, my father simply shook his head and did not say much. However, the following day, he told my brothers and I not to go back to Mr. Mwemeire's school. That same day, my dad went to Nyakibale Primary School and negotiated with the headmaster there for our transfer. That fateful day in the 1960s, was the last time I stepped on Kahoko's grounds, although the school is only about three miles from my parents' home. Mwemeire, who never grew beyond his primary school headmaster status, didn't seem to make a big deal out of the incident, let alone remember it. Decades after its occurrence, I used to meet and even chat with him, sometimes at my father's home, and outwardly showing no ill will towards him. However, in my soul of souls, until his death around 2005, he remained someone I deeply despised.

Life at Nyakibale was better, considering that this was a more urban environment than Kahoko. It also exuded more status, being located at the regional headquarters of the Catholic Church. But Nyakibale was five miles away from my home, compared with about three miles for Kahoko. Then, as now, there were no school buses to shuttle students around, and hardly any parents owned vehicles to drop their children at school. We therefore had to get up very early in the morning, and start the commute to school, where we were expected to attend roll call every morning by eight o'clock. One year later, I entered junior secondary school, where the headmaster was Mr. Joseph Macumu.

Mr. Macumu ran his school like a tight ship. His highhanded ways extended to his immediate family, where it was said, he didn't spare the rod even when dealing with his wife, Restatuta, or his young brother Bampomwanya, my classmate. But he challenged us to succeed in what we were doing, although it was said, that he himself had not passed his Ordinary Level School certificate well enough at the elite St Mary's College, Kisubi. This was the very reason he had branched off to a teacher training college, eventually qualifying as a grade three teacher at Shimoni Teachers' College. As in the case of Mr. Nkorenta, my good performance in class soon endeared me to the headmaster, who in turn, showed his soft side by offering me free tuition for the two years of junior school. This was quite a relief to my father's finances, since at the time, three of us, including my brothers Jerome and Marcel, were in junior school. For all his cruelty I was lucky to escape Nyakibale without as much as a scratch from his infamous sjambok.

However, he might have single-handedly, determined the course of my professional destiny, when, during the course of filling out an application for my high school, he forced me to fill in Kigezi College Butobere, as first choice, instead of his alma mater of St. Mary's College Kisubi, insisting that the latter was too far, and that it would put a strain on my father's meager finances. My cousin, Francis Kasura, who, like Macumu, had attended St. Mary's, and proceeded to go to Makerere Univerity, had encouraged me to make St. Mary's my first choice. I had performed exceptionally well during my primary leaving exams, and could have been admitted to just about any school I chose, if not for Mr. Macumu's hand.

Fotunately, Butobere at the time, ranked among the top ten high schools in the country, the others being Ntare school, in Mbarara, Nyakasura School in Fort Portal, St Mary's Kisubi, King's College Budo, Uganda Technical College, Kyambogo, Namilyango College, Gayaza High School for girls, Mount St. Mary's Girls school, Namagunga, Teso College Aleot, and Busoga College, Mwiri near Jinja. These became the lingering positive legacies of colonialism, along with institutions like Mulago Hospital, and Uganda Hotels, the latter being setup with a selfish element, since the posh hotels of the time only served expatriates, as the indigenous Ugandans couldn't afford the exorbitant prices.

My elder brother, Matia, had attended Butobere Secondary

School, locally known as "Siniya", so I already had some familiarity with it. I had also developed a liking for science, which Butobere had a reputation for. Back at Nyakibale, I had scratched the top of my desk with my name, followed by the title (B. Sc). Butobere Secondary school was one of those built by the colonial government between 1956 and 1959, to serve the rural districts upcountry. Located on the outskirts of the town of Kabale, in Kigezi district, the school soon grew to prominence as a favorite for European expatriates, who were drawn to the area by its temperate weather conditions. Its mountainous terrain, and the azure blue Lake Bunyonyi, the second deepest lake in Africa, after Lake Tanganyika, had earned the Kabale area, the title of "Switzerland of Africa." The White Horse Inn, overlooking Kabale town, was the playground of the expatriate community in Kabale. Here, they gathered to reminisce and spoil themselves over martin lunches. Service was provided by well-trained Ugandan waiters and waitresses in impeccably clean white uniforms, complete with white gloves, all hotel furniture and crockery embossed with the Uh logo of Uganda Hotels.

During my stay at Butobere, our Headmaster was Mr. W. H. Lamplough, an English, archetypal colonial-era pompous septuagenarian. He, and his equally egotistic wife Minnie, probably never ate a single meal at their sprawling home over the weekends, despite retaining a fulltime chef. They preferred instead, to have their meals at White Horse Inn, in the company of their fellow Brits, where they would either play golf on the sprawling 18-hole greens, or simply catch up on the latest news, from British newspapers, delivered weekly by the British Council in Kampala. Mr. Lamplough, who never ceased to remind the whole school at each assembly he addressed, how he was the best physicist around, once gave every student in the school, a paper version of the slide rule. He then spent the best part of the next hour struggling to instruct his bored audience, how to use it.

Mrs. Lamplough had earned herself another title "Gagool",

drawn from the ancient old woman in the best-selling novel, King Solomon's Mines. Minnie was rather obnoxious with her tiny Chihuahua called Judy, which she carried with her everywhere, to the annoyance of many people. Her main nemesis was our physics teacher, a Scotsman called Mr. Gemmel, who scolded her each time she burst into the staffroom, literally expecting the generally young Englishmen to stand up for her as a sign of respect. Some of the English men returned the favor to Mr. Gemmel, referring to him as "that barbarian from the north".

Besides carrying Judy, or tagging at the miserable little creature, whose short legs bounced up-and-down about four times for every step Minnie took, Gagool appointed herself school nurse extraordinaire. She carried aspirins in her purse, which she would dispense from just about anywhere, including classrooms, and the school dining hall.

Nevertheless, despite his eccentricity, Mr. Lamplough, along with other pioneering headmasters such as Mr. Gower, his predecessor at Butobere, Mr. Chrighton at Ntare, Sister Cephas at Mt. St Mary's Namagunga, Father Grimes at Namasagali, Miss Cox at Gayaza High School, and others, were a breed apart in as far as their dedication to education was concerned. They laid the foundations at the schools they started and led them to great heights more than half a century ago. One would struggle to find an alumnus of those schools who, today, would dare vilify, rather than praise the actions of those gallant men and women of the day.

Eleven

I ARRIVED AT Butobere Secondary School in 1966, as the only student from Nyakibale. My elder brother Matia had attended Butobere from 1963 to 1964, before transferring to Namilyango College. This made my transition a little easier, since some of the students and teachers still remembered him. Nevertheless, it was still quite a stiff acclimatization for a fifteen year-old, that had never been away from under his parents' grip, to go through. Kabale, which is located about seventy miles south of Rukungiri town, not only offered a different weather pattern, but also a different cultural atmosphere than I was used to. It's a common misconception among people from other continents, who have never visited Africa, to ask you in the summer months, "if it's hot enough for you." The same people would be shocked beyond their wits, if they spent a July night in Kabale, or found themselves around Timboroa, at 3.00 am in the morning. Timboroa (altitude 9,001 ft), is the highest point on the Kenya-Uganda Railway.

During the time I worked at the World Bank, I once advised my division Chief, Mr. Paul Armington, to include a warm sweater in packing for a safari vacation trip he was planning on taking to Nairobi, Kenya in July during the 1980's.

"Are you crazy?" he scoffed at me. "I can't find enough shorts to wear while I'll be there" he retorted. It took a little time convincing him to finally include some warm gear in his luggage.

When he returned from the trip, he couldn't thank me enough. He told me, that even with the sweaters he carried with him, he still felt quite chilly at night. If only he had researched a little, he would have learned that the name Nairobi was derived from the Masai word, "nyrobi", meaning "a stream of cold waters".

Today's modern city of Nairobi got its humble beginnings in 1898, only three years after the British colonialists took on Kenya as a protectorate. It began as a wayward railway terminal on the Mombasa-Kampala railway which was under construction at the time. The place was nothing more than an expansive bush and swampy area, inhabited by wild animals and frogs. A young Englishman by the name of John Ainsworth, then working for the Imperial British East African Company (IBEAC), at Machakos, a town located about 35 miles east of Nairobi, was tasked with making a settlement out of this swamp.

To dry up the swamp, he brought in large quantities of eucalyptus seeds, a tree species known to require massive volumes of water, which he planted at the edge of the swamp. In his effort to delineate the city for settlement, however, he only catered for Europeans and Indians, entirely leaving out the Africans, not unlike the apartheid system that was instituted in South Africa. Although today, Nairobi's posh neighborhoods such as Muthaiga, Kabete, Ngong Hills and Karen, boast of hosting the nation's well-heeled African elite, it wasn't until after Kenya's Independence in 1963 that, such people began to call these places home. Nairobi's temperatures, like Kabale's in Uganda, can drop rather precipitously, especially during the months of July and August. Woe to the European or American tourist, who forgets to throw a warm sweater in his or her luggage, expecting a tan in the tropical African sun.

Kabale's altitude is like Denver's in the United States, or La Paz in Bolivia, all three being located at about a mile above sea level. Among the items we were given as part of school uniform at Butobere, were a woolen sweater and a cape. For July nights, those who could afford tucked themselves under two blankets, while the rest put on an extra shirt before covering themselves. Despite those frigid temperatures, we had to endure taking cold showers. I do not remember whether or not the school had a hot water system at all. But if there was one, then someone must have been rising much earlier than I did and using up all the hot water for the entire four-year period I stayed there.

Most of our academic staff at that time were British citizens, with a sprinkling of young Ugandans, newly graduated from Makerere University. By and large, they were, as a whole, a dedicated lot, mostly upright in character, although there was a smattering of idiosyncratic ones as well. The latter category consisted of mostly young graduates on holiday, and in search of adventure, before settling down on a career path. The British Council screened all their staff before posting them on these overseas assignments, to ensure that the young men and women they sent out exuded only the best traits of the British character. The students created pseudo names for each one of the teachers, depending on his or her character. They coined names like Kagongo, a reference to Mr. Georgeson, the biology teacher with a hunched back. Mr Hamid, our technical drawing teacher, with looks akin to the incredible hulk character, was dubbed "caterpillar", the giant earth-moving equipment that were constructing the Ntungamo-Kabale road at the time. Mrs. Jacqueline Wilson, a shapely beautiful woman with auburn-hair, caused a stir whenever she sat on top of a table in front of the all-boys class, reading aloud to us from Jane Austin's Pride and Prejudice. The boys had nicknamed her "Bunuzi", the sweet one, a name she seemed to relish. A few whispers were making the rounds regarding her becoming a little too cozy with a French-Canadian priest named Fr. Brunnet, who was the chaplain of the school at the time. There was even an unsavory name for a young British girl on a temporary assignment, whose careless sitting in front of the class, turned the sessions into voyeur adventures.

One of the most intriguing of our teachers, was Richard White, nicknamed "Mutale", the Rukiga word for white. Richard was an affable young man from Bristol, who headed the Geography department. He was a true explorer in every sense of the word. Some days, mostly weekends, he would instruct the school truck driver, to take one of his classes some ten or fifteen miles from the school, and drop them there, letting him know that we would find our way back. From there, we would then meander across the terraced hills, where Bakiga women grew Irish potatoes, locally known as emondi, and cow peas, called amashaza. The men indulged in growing sorghum, known as omugusha, used in the production of omulamba, a thick nutritious brew. A more potent version of omulamba, mixed with honey, is called entulire, and has legendary stories about it.

In one such story, a woman and her young daughter were enticed by some men with other ulterior motives, to over-indulge with the deceivingly sweet entulire. The men kept filling their bishare (gourds) each time they noticed them getting empty. Soon after, the two women couldn't tell where they were, and they were led into a hut, where they were gang-raped by the men, almost without their knowledge. The younger woman was the first to wake up in the morning, and noticed she was wet all over. She shook her mother to wake her up, and asked her rather innocently,

"Mama, abanywaga entulire bajubaga amayasha?"she asked, meaning, "Does drinking this stuff cause one to wet herself?"

The mother, realizing that, she too, was in the same condition, let out an expletive, "Batushweire ninkahorwe!" implying that the men had had a good time at their expense.

Once in a while, we went to Lake Bunyonyi, the second deepest lake in Africa, after Lake Tanganyika. Shaped like an octopus, and stretching all the way from below the hills of Kachwekano, home to the District Farm Institute, to Rubaya, near the Rwandan border. The azure blue lake was formed from the same volcanic action that created twelve volcanoes, that include Muhavura,

Mugahinga, Sabinyo, Nyiragongo and other volcanoes lining the Uganda, Rwanda, and DRC border, only about thirty miles west of here. Nyiragongo is the only active volcano among them. As recently as 2000, volcanic activity from this mountain caused a stampede in the region's population, filling part of Lake Kivu with molten lava, while destroying everything else in its way. As a kid, I remember how we used to climb to the top of Kabwoma, the tall hill above our village of Kabura, to simply marvel at nature's wonders, as we watched red plumes of lava being spewed from the top of Nyiragongo, perhaps a hundred miles to the south-west, as the crow flies. From the same vantage point, facing north, we could discern the shinny glaciers and some smoke rising from forests half-way up the Rwenzori Mountains, the same Mountains of the Moon, whose tropical ice top captivated ancient Greek writers like Ptolemy. At the end of the trek, we would arrive back at school, thoroughly exhausted, but at the same time carrying with us, that sense of discovery and accomplishment. Mutale's out-going style instilled in some of us, a permanent love of nature and travel, which has continued to this day. It was this energy I tapped into, for instance, when I competed, and won a chance to climb Mt. Kilimanjaro, Africa's tallest mountain, just a year after leaving Butobere.

Richard had a way of interacting with students, which allowed him to be very close with them, to the extent that he was welcomed to students' homes, embracing, and sharing their humble surroundings. He made geography, one of the most popular subjects in the school, despite the school's hardcore science bias. His extensive travels around East Africa, later allowed him to write books and contribute some excellent material for the national school curriculum. A Danish astronomer named Karl Jorgensen who was on extended leave, introduced us to basic astronomy, teaching us about the planets in the solar system, and with some help from us, constructed a horizontal sun dial, outside the staff-room building. This instrument measures time by the position of the sun. The sun's position is captured by a shadow from a straight rod called a gnomon, on to the horizontal surface, marked with lines representing the time of the day.

George Lamb, or Katama as the students had nicknamed him, was the head of the history department. His father had been one of the British settlers who arrived in Kenya, beginning in the 1920s, through the 1940s. Led by an aristocrat called Lord Delamere, they quickly pushed off the indigenous ethnic groups such as the Kikuyu, Luo, Kamba, Masai and Kalenjin, off the best arable lands, creating large tea, sugar and coffee plantations which in turn drew their labor from the new concentration camps. As early as 1921, Harry Thuku, a prominent Kikuyu leader, representing the East African Association, had written to the Governor, reminding him of the promises his administration had made to those going to fight on behalf of the British Crown. These pleas were ignored time and time again, instead given promises that were never fulfilled. By 1945, the Africans had realized that nothing would be handed freely to them without fighting for it. A group called Anake a Forty, or warriors of the 1940s, formed with the sole purpose of fighting for their rights. The Kikuyu co-opted other tribes, swearing a secret oath that they were prepared to die for the cause. When the Mau Mau rebellion broke out in Kenya in 1952, in opposition to this settler invasion, the British Colonial Administration launched a vicious attack, jailing, and hanging some of the leaders they managed to apprehend. Prominent among those arrested, and incarcerated at Kamiti Prison, were Jomo Kenyatta, Achieng Aneko, Fred Kubai, Bildadi Kaggia, Paul Ngei, and Kung'u Karumba. In 1953, they were convicted and charged with leading the Mau Mau movement, an organization which had previously been banned.

With their arrest, the Mau Mau rebellion declared war against the government in earnest. The war was mainly a guerrilla war, conducted underground in Central Province, Aberdares (Nyandarua), Kirinyaga (Mt Kenya), and Nakuru District. Police stations and other government installations, as well as settler farms, were attacked randomly, and other forms of sabotage conducted. While the war was raging on, the colonial government put maximum restrictions on local civilian movement, who were essentially confined into concentration camps. The government did not regain the upper hand until after 1955. Even after that year, intermittent fighting continued. Up to this day, it is said, that, former Mau Mau fighters still emerge from the forests surrounding Mt Kenya, unaware that the war ended decades ago. After his release from jail, Mzee Jomo Kenyatta spearheaded his Kenya African National Union (KANU) party to lead Kenya to Independence on December 12, 1963.

Unknown to most students at Butobere, was the fact that Mr. Lamb's father had been hanged by Mau Mau freedom fighers in Kenya. Our classroom was adjacent to the Assembly Hall stage, and one could easily stretch the strings used to draw or close the curtains, as far as the chalkboard. There were three particularly naughty boys in my class, called Safari, Senzira and Benda, who used to play all kinds of tricks in class, and the teachers knew about them. One day, before Katama was due to arrive for his history class, I unintentionally stretched one of the loose strings to the blackboard, tied a noose, and wrote the words,

"This is the rope with which an unworthy man shall hang himself". I was just playing with words, but what happened next, shook the class like a hurricane.

As soon as the teacher got in class and saw the rope, he went ballistic, and burst into an uncontrollable rage.

"Who did this?" he inquired, but was met with blank stares. Fortunately, nobody had seen me do it, and witnessing the demeanor of the teacher, I, too, kept mum like the rest. Katama stated to us there and then, that unless we produced the culprit, he wouldn't be teaching our class anymore. He then went flying to the headmaster's office to immediately demand for action. There was an Indian boy called Chandarana, whom the "three musketeers", as we called the stubborn trio, used to bully around. He saw this incident as his chance to exact his revenge on them, so he went quietly, and told Katama, that the usual suspects had done it.

Katama immediately relayed the information to Mr. Lamplough, who in turn called a school assembly at short notice, at which he announced the suspension of the three students for two weeks. I did not like history as a subject then, and therefore, Katama's personal circumstances were of little interest to me.

I was keener on studying the physical sciences, especially physics and chemistry, where the school had a well-earned reputation. Mr. Roger Wilkins, who doubled as the deputy headmaster, was a fabulous chemistry teacher. To inculcate the love of science among students, the school had created two groups of students, categorized by performance abilities. The first group, which we jokingly called "pure", was composed of about thirty five students, while the "impure" group comprised twice that number.

Within the pure group, we had sharp-minded kids like Bazirake, and Magician, who alternated in occupying first and second place in the exams. But there was also a lineup of other bright kids from Rubaya, a village near the Rwandese border, who were equally academically capable. I still don't have a clue why those boys from Rubaya were exceptionally talented. May be it was in the water they drunk as kids. If so, I'd have liked to swallow the same fluids as a toddler, before my cerebral cortex hardened to what it is today. That group went on to produce doctors, engineers and architects for the country.

The global events of the 1960s didn't entirely leave the school untouched. Although communication was not as instantaneous as it is today, we were aware of the major events of the day. We sang Beatle melodies, much to the delight of our British teachers, some of whom, like Mr. White, were from Bristol, where it all began. And, there was the hippie-style culture of keeping unkempt hair. The one thing I do not recall happening at Butobere, was the consumption of mind-altering substances, apart from alcohol. Bakiga boys loved their mulamba, a thick brew from sorghum, and sometimes they over-indulged, especially on weekends. There was a bar, located just outside the school gate, owned by a bearded man called Bigandura. The older boys literally spent their weekends indulging themselves on the stuff. Some took in so much of it, only to throw up as soon as they hit their beds in the dorms. As only the dorm prefects had separate rooms, some of the street smart boys negotiated with the prefects, who allowed them to sneak in pimps they picked from the bar. One of these pimps, whom the students had dubbed "kiguru", had a prosthetic leg. The boys used to joke about how one needed a spanner to detach her leg for a smooth operation.

It was, also, while I was at Butobere in 1967, that the seven-day Arab-Israael war broke out. As there was no television at the school, we would crowd in the student recreation room for the BBC program, listening, as the narrator relayed the dramatic events as they unfolded. Later, we would see pictures of destroyed war materiel, printed in papers like the Uganda Argus. Some of our British teachers were of Jewish descent, and showed a lot more anxiety regarding the fate of Israel.

Closer to home, two years earlier, Ian Smith of Southern Rhodesia (now Zimbabwe), had caused a stir by breaking away from Britain in a Unilateral Declaration of Independence (UDI). However, his close collaboration with the apartheid regime in South Africa, had earned his country pariah status, especially among other African countries, in what was supposed to be Africa's independence decade. Meanwhile, at Butobere, while students debated these issues in high sounding words like imperialist blood-suckers, Zionists and communists, some calling each other comrades, one young man named Tibemanya, took this a step further. He declared that he would never wear shoes until Zimbabwe gained its independence. I did not follow up on whether or not he lived up to his promise more than a decade later, when Zimbabwe finally received its independence, with Robert Gabriel Mugabe at its helm. Recently, however, I learned that his revolutionary spirit was cut short in the 1970's, when Idi Amin's soldiers captured him and executed him as one of the regime's opponents.

In Uganda itself, President Milton Obote, had declared a republic in 1966, with his infamous pigeon-hole constitution, authored by Attorney General Godfrey Binaisa, QC, who later became president in 1979, after the overthrow of President Yusuf Lule. President Obote's actions were prompted by bitter rivalry between then Prime Minister Obote, and Sir Edward Muteesa, who was the country's non-executive president, while at the same time, the hereditary Kabaka of Buganda.

The two men had been an odd couple right from the be-ginning, with very little in common, except their religious faith. During the 1961 elections prior to Uganda's independence the fol-lowing year, a stalwart and flamboyant lawyer named Benedicto Kiwanuka, had led his Democratic Party (DP) to victory, becom-ing chief minister in the interim period. However, he had not had the backing of the Kabaka's administration at Mengo, the latter considering him disrespectful of the monarchy, even though he himself was a Muganda. This had denied him a majority in parlia-ment. Meanwhile, his rival, Apollo Milton Obote, a Langi from the northern region, had steered his Uganda Peoples Congress (UPC), into second place finish at the polls. This gave Obote, a window of opportunity to open up negotiations with Kabaka Yekka (KY), a party affiliated with maintaining Buganda as a federal state. The resulting coalition between UPC and KY, was clearly a marriage of convenience, as the two protagonists couldn't have been more different. Obote, the son of peasant farmers, had dropped out of Makerere University in the late 1940's and later joined the labor union movement in Kenya, where he honed his skills in organiz-ing people.

Sir Edward on the other hand, was born into privilege to

Kabaka Daudi Chwa II, and had attended Magdalene College, Cambridge in the United Kingdom, with a brief stint at the elite Military Academy at Sandhurst, entering the officer's corps at the rank of captain. With only their Anglican faith in common, the British, in their infinite wisdom, were not just about to let one of their prized colonies, Uganda, be led by a non-Anglican like Benedicto Kiwanuka, a catholic by faith. So, they maneuvered behind the scenes to make sure that the UPC-KY coalition would deny DP the leadership it would have enjoyed if both UPC and KY had pushed forward independently.

On October 9, 1962, Prime Minister Obote was handed the instruments of power for the newly independent state by the last British Colonial Governor, Sir Walter Fleming Coutts. Mr. Obote went on to reward Sir Edward with the mainly ceremonial position of non-executive President of Uganda.

Twelve

UGANDA'S ROAD TO independence had been a relatively smooth one, unlike many countries on the continent, whose path had been paved with blood. The colonial administration had left behind a relatively well-trained civil service, and a functioning infrastructure. This, coupled with fertile soils, and adequate supplies of water, would have provided its people with a steady economic development. But the political honeymoon turned out to be a very short one. The British had handed over the powers of a central government with a weak foundation. While they had enlisted Buganda's support in suppressing uprisings from rival kingdoms such as Bunyoro-Kitara under the recalcitrant Omukama Kabalega, this had been achieved as a quid-pro-quo. The colonialists had promised a federal status to Buganda, even after Uganda gained its independence.

Obote soon realized that, the elevation of Kabaka Muteesa to President, came with extra demands for Buganda, which were at odds with running the country as a *unified* republic. Although Uganda's economy was enjoying steady growth, there was heavy concentration of resources, first, in favor of a small business class, of mostly Indians in the commercial sector. Regionally, Buganda, in which Kampala, the nation's capital is located, constituted the lion's share, leaving the rest of the regions to fight for crumbs. As a native of the northern region, the poorest among all regions,

Obote was inclined to see the other regions increase the sharing of the nation's resources.

In the mid-1960s, Obote had forged a close friendship with Tanzania's Mwalimu Julius Nyerere, and began flirting with socialist ideas, probably influenced by the latter's Ujamaa concept. The Baganda, who, as an ethnic group, constituted about one quarter of the nation's population, tend to be capitalistic in nature. Therefore, a collision between Kabaka Muteesa and Prime Minister Obote, was almost inevitable. Tensions between the two began building in late 1965, and by 1966, push had come to shove. Then in the wee hours of May 24, 1966, Obote ordered his Army Commander, Major-General Idi Amin, to attack the Kabaka's palace at Mengo, known as Lubiri. Suspicions by Obote, about the Kabaka's intentions, plus intelligence reports which purportedly, had intercepted a letter from the President, to a certain foreign embassy (suspected to be the British High Commission) requesting for arms, had convinced Obote, that coup plans were in the offing.

The Kabaka miraculously escaped, perhaps using his military skills, and sought asylum in the United Kingdom. However, his kingdom did not survive with him. Following the raid on the Lubiri, Obote hastily ordered his Attorney General, Mr. Godfrey Binaisa, QC, a British-trained barrister, to draft a new constitution, which would elevate Obote from Prime Minister, to executive President, with a concentration of power to the new office. Copies of the new constitution were distributed overnight, into pigeon holes belonging to all members of Parliament. This "Pigeon-hole constitution", as it has been known ever since, abolished all kingdoms in the country, declaring Uganda, a republic.

Following the assault on Lubiri, the President declared marshal law in Buganda, dubbed "biseela bya kabenge", in the Luganda language, or dangerous times. People deemed to be sympathetic to Buganda, particularly the monarchy, including Grace Ibingira, at the time, Secretary General of UPC, the ruling party, were incarcerated in Luzira Prison, or the "university" at the shores of Lake Victoria. Five members of his own cabinet, including Abubakar Mayanja, a Cambridge-educated lawyer, and rising stars like John Kakonge, Baraka Kirya, and Dr. Lumu, were to languish in jail for the next five years. Obote turned increasingly autocratic as more opposition mounted against his move-to-the-left strategy, following his Nakivubo Pronouncements, referred to as "the Common Man's Charter".

Meanwhile, reduced from a king to a jack, Sir Edward Muteesa or King Freddie as he was popularly known, settled into despondency in London, taking residence in a public housing flat, and surviving on occasional handouts from a retinue of friends and royalist aficionados. Depressed, and lonely, he took to the bottle for solace. Although circumstances surrounding his death in 1969 remain hazy at best, including unsubstantiated allegations of a female assassin sent by his nemesis, alcohol would have eventually accelerated his demise sooner, rather than later. To most Baganda, royalists, Obote symbolizes the evil that desecrated their 900-year kingdom, leaving their beloved Kabaka to perish in shame and abject poverty.

President Obote presented two types of personalities. On the one hand, he enjoyed debate, and once in a while, participated in the popular sessions at Makerere University between Professor Ali Mazrui, Mr. Abu Mayanja, Dr. Yash Tandon, and Professor Mahmood Mamdani of the Faculty of Political Science. However, deep inside, he seemed to harbor some resentment towards those people he considered intellectually superior to himself. It was, under such pretext, that he promoted a semi-illiterate lieutenant named Idi Amin, on a fast track, to Major-General, and commander of the Uganda Army.

Obote believed that, a man like Amin, with intellectual limitations, would be seriously inhibited in the ambition towards accumulating more power. He was therefore, considered a safe bet as a commander of the armed forces. The President even went to the extent of boasting,

"I am the only African leader, not afraid of a military coup". Some would say, he spoke too soon, and that the devil was listening.

The British, Uganda's former colonial masters, were beginning to get wary of Obote's socialist policies. They feared that a domino effect might take place in the East African region, affecting both Kenya and Uganda, since Tanzania had already taken the socialist route. Britain had a lot of investments in Kenya, which could be nationalized, perhaps without compensation. Moreover, Presidents Julius Nyerere of Tanzania, Kenneth Kaunda of Zambia, and Milton Obote of Uganda, through their Mulungushi Club, were becoming increasingly vocal on matters regarding the apartheid regime in South Africa, and Ian Smith's UDI in Rhodesia (Zimbabwe). President Kaunda, at one time vexed British Premier Edward Heath, pronouncing that,

"Britain is a toothless bulldog wagging its tail in front of Rhodesia". The 1960s decade had raised the hopes and aspirations of the African people, as many countries gained independence, shading off their colonial yoke. The creation of the Organization of African Unity (OAU) in 1963, with headquarters in the Ethiopian capital of Addis Ababa, was testament that, Africa too, was capable of showing maturity in governing itself. But the independence honeymoon was proving to be short-lived. In Ghana, which had been the first country to attain independence in 1957, President Kwame Nkrumah, was overthrown in 1966 by the military. Next door, in Nigeria, by 1967, the military had not only overthrown the Abubakar Tafawa-Balewa government, but a civil war was raging on. The oil-rich south-eastern region, home to the Igbo people, was fighting to secede from the Federal Republic. General Yakubu Gowon, military head of the federal government, was playing Abraham Lincoln's role of holding the union together, against the ambitions of General Odumegwu Ojukwu, who, like Robert Lee, wanted to curve out a new country called Biafra.

Independence had been no panacea for the milliard of problems afflicting the African continent.

I had passed my ordinary level school certificate well enough to be admitted to higher school certificate, (HSC). But I had narrowed my choices of schools so much, that when I missed my first choice of Uganda Technical College, where I had hoped to pursue courses leading to engineering, my mind was thrown into confusion. I had spent the holidays with my elder brother Matia, who was then an Assistant Superintendent of the Uganda Prison at Kirinya, Jinja. When I left his home for Kampala, he was sure I was going to join HSC. However, instead of reporting directly to school, I spent the night at my cousin, Francis Kasura's home. His brother, also called Francis Salezi, then a student at the National Teachers' College at Kyambogo, convinced me, that if I didn't like the HSC schools like Kololo, or Makerere College School being offered to me, I could easily change course, and join him at Kyambogo. I really didn't have that much interest in becoming a teacher.

When we got to Kyambogo, Francis took me to Mr. John Dowsett, the head of the Math Department, and introduced me as someone good in math, and interested in becoming a teacher. Francis left me with Mr. Dowsett, who administered a very simple quiz involving Pythagoras' theorem, and a physics question on Newton's laws of motion. These were still fresh in my mind, having taken my final exams hardly two months before. At the end of the interview, Mr. Dowsett told me that I had passed, and that I should go to the custodian's office to get my dorm assignment. It was that simple.

I didn't immediately inform my brother about the change. He only found out two weeks later when he visited Kampala, to see how I had settled down. By that time, however, I was already beginning to realize that I had made a mistake. When I told him I wanted to switch again and take my HSC place, he said it was too late, because those offers could not be held for individuals for too long. He advised me, to concentrate on my newly-chosen vocation and do it well. A few months went by, but each day that passed, seemed to confirm to me that I was not cut out to be a teacher.

As my frustrations began to mount, I drew on my earlier strengths to keep going. I had developed an interest in some outdoor activities such as hiking and mountaineering from my days at Butobere. So, when an opportunity availed itself to go to the Outward Bound Mountain School at Loitokitok, near the foot of Mt. Kilimanjaro, I seized it. At first, the organizers brushed me off, since I was a skinny, lanky individual, aspiring to undertake a project that required a lot of muscle. But slowly, the doctor's physicals, as well as other activities that required a high degree of endurance, eliminated most of those that only looked fit on the outside, leaving a few of us to be declared "fit for duty". The grueling course at Loitokitok was initially designed for the military in the region. But, after a little while, it began to attract the interest of those who wanted to ready themselves for the climb of the giant mountain next door. Some of the instructors were actually military men, mainly from the Tanzanian People Defense Forces (TPDF).

For the first two weeks at the camp, the entire group of us, numbering about 200, and drawn from schools around East Africa, participated in military-style exercises. We rose up at 6.00 am, made our beds for inspection, and performed quick drills around the camp, all before gathering in the dining hall for a mandatory breakfast. This might be followed by a two mile run, before we went for rock-climbing, obstacle course runs and numerous other maneuvers. We also covered a lot of mileage in the Masai Mara savannah, sometimes getting dangerously close to wild animals such as buffalo and elephants, against which a team was armed with only a machete and a whistle. We even participated in a marathon during the second week. The emphasis in all these activities was on team work. New groups were formed, and individuals rotated all the time, to assess how well one fitted with diverse groups.

The last week was reserved for the assault on Mt. Kilimanjaro. For this, each of us was provided with climbing gear, including heavy boots, sleeping bags, head gear, gloves, and canned food. At the altitude of about 10,000 feet, we camped for our "solo night", during which individuals were assigned a spot on which they were required to construct a shelter out of twigs, and cook a meal. The distance between these huts was at least two hundred feet, and this part of the mountain was well-covered with vegetation, where some wild animals roamed freely. That night, a handful of kids raised alarms, some screaming at the top of their voices, others blowing their whistles to signal some emergency. Those of us who had managed to put our heads down in our shelters, remained rooted to the ground. The instructors were well aware that a few of the kids would be terrified by darkness, and sounds of wild animals in the nearby forest, but this was part of the overall experience the course was supposed to impart on us. Whether justifiable or not, the objective of the course, of creating, and dealing with fear of the unknown seems to have been achieved.

By around five-thirty in the morning, we were awakened to get ready for the ascent towards Mawenzi peak, one of the two crests connected by a saddle-like terrain. Mawenzi lies on the eastern side, and is a little lower than Kibo, the highest point on the African continent. An early start is essential, because climbers gain a lot of traction in the crisp, early morning air, before the sun hits them with a double whammy of heat and blinding sunlight, reflected on the snow. Unlike today, Kilimanjaro's top was well blanketed with snow then. In fact, while we were on our way up, a small dusting of snow fell, causing temperatures to plummet even further.

We arrived on Mawenzi peak at dusk, tired and haggard from the sheer exhaustion of the climb. As one gets higher, the air becomes thinner, with less oxygen, forcing the lungs to do even more dilations and contractions for the same amount of air. Some within the team had developed nausea and light-headedness, making it almost impossible for them to continue climbing without relieving them of the loads they carried. The camp has several aluminum huts for shelter, into which we crowded in groups of about ten a piece. There was hardly any room to move around, but the crowding itself generated the heat we so badly needed at that altitude. Anybody whose sleeping position touched the metallic walls of the hut, shivered through the night, despite being stuffed inside a sleeping bag.

By the first rays of light, we were clamoring by the kerosene stove, attempting to boil cups of coffee, in order to warm up our bodies before embarking on the final leg of the climb. As the water boiled, all of us watched in amazement, as the temperature only remained low, to a point of dipping one's finger, in it, without getting it scalded. A few years later, I would emphasize this point to my physics class, trying to convince a bunch of non-believing kids that water boils at a lower temperature, the higher you go.

We left our Mawenzi shelter around 5.30 am, and walked in a single file following our guide. None of us had ever experienced the extreme conditions of winter, so, a combination of gusty winds bombarding us with snow flurries in the face at such a high altitude, was, to say the least, a frightening adventure. We soldiered on, but within a few hours, more members of our team began to buckle under the severe weather conditions. By about 11.00 am, we were close to the base of Kibo peak, which, at 19,320 feet, stands about three thousand feet higher than Mawenzi peak. Another group had approached the climb from the north, heading towards Kibo directly. During the time it took us to cross the saddle, they had got to the "roof of Africa", and by the time we met them, were on their way down. The instructor for the other group met with our own, and for reasons best known to them, decided there and then, that we should turn around and join the other team for the decent. There were protestations among us, but these were quickly squashed, with instructors struggling to convince us, that the main objective of the exercise was not just getting to the peak, but rather, testing one's endurance on tackling a problem of this giant proportion.

Although by now we had accumulated a number of people who had been sickened by the mountain, including Mr. Amama Mbabazi, the current Prime Minister of Uganda at the time of writing this book, also a graduate of my Butobere almer mater, we were all anxious to get back to camp, and subsequently, head back home, marking the end of Course #127.

The late Director of National Teachers College, Mr. Adonia Tiberondwa, used to give weekly lectures to us in the assembly hall, in which he admonished those who felt the urge to pursue further education beyond what Kyambogo could offer, to do so, without any inhibition. The college was a co-ed institution, and for most of us, it was the first time we were learning in such an environment. Many young men and women were meeting, rubbing shoulders on a daily basis, some falling in love, and getting married. Every month or so, the Director would announce a couple who had decided to form a merger. Then one day, I showed up at Mr. Tiberondwa's office, and asked his secretary if I could see him. When the secretary announced my presence, the Director himself came out of his office, ushered me in, and with a smile, asked me, expecting what was becoming rather routine to him.

"Who is the lucky girl this time?" he asked me. I said it had nothing to do with girls, but rather about my future career. He listened attentively as I narrated how I had unintentionally joined the teaching profession in the first place, and at the end, he asked me what I wished to do.

"Can you arrange for me to take HSC courses at Uganda Technical College?" I asked.

The National Teachers College (now Kyambogo University), and Uganda Technical College, (now Institute of Technical

Education) are located on the same hill. As Mr. Tiberondwa strongly believed in education, I felt confident, after talking to him, that he would deliver his end of the bargain, and he did. He promised to talk to Dr. Shapiro, who was the Principal of UTC, and within a few days, I was a student at both places. Although I was already studying physics and math at the National Teachers College, Kyambogo, it was not of the same complexity as that undertaken at UTC, where almost all the graduates ended up in engineering or science-related fields. So, I had to play a lot of catch up, using every moment of my spare time perusing over fluid mechanics, advanced calculus etc. My busy schedule spared me from participating in the wild night life that other students enjoyed, especially during the weekends. It was not unusual for my roommate Erisa Byakora, to return from his escapades during the wee hours, only to find me still bent over a bunch of formulas, spread on my desk.

As a close Obote associate, Mr. Tiberondwa was carefully watched, and even trailed by Amin's henchmen. While he was at Kyambogo, he participated in a Uganda Television program called "Brain Trust", with such other luminaries of the day as James Bwogi, Tucker Lwanga, Dr. Kalibala and Prof. A.B.C Kweri. The show aired at around 8.00 pm every Wednesday for one hour, and as his students, we used to follow it religiously. But since he knew he was being followed, he used to ask at least two male students to escort him to the studio, and wait in his car while he participated.

Things went from bad to worse for him, especially after the 1972 Mutukula invasion, in which pro-Obote exiles based in Tanzania conducted an incursion into Uganda. The bulk of the invaders involved people from western Uganda, including the current president, Yoweri Museveni. From that moment on, Amin had no love lost for Banyankole. Mr. Tiberondwa held on under that cloud of suspicion, until he got a chance to escape while attending a conference in Nairobi. Upon reaching Nairobi, he sent for his family who travelled by road in his Mercedes. The soldiers at the border were assured that the family was only visiting Nairobi, and would return in about a week. They didn't know that Mr. Tiberondwa had already crossed into safety. When the week passed, however, the driver turned up alone in the car. He was seriously beaten up until he confessed that his passengers were not coming back.

Mr Tiberondwa was by no means, the only one who had a run-in with Amin's vicious regime. My roommate Erisa and I had friend named James Karuhanga who had just graduated from NTC, and had been posted to teach next door at Kyambogo College School. Mr. Karuhanga was a young brother to UPC stalwart Edward Rurangaranga of Kitagata, Bushenyi District. We used to walk and spend time at his house, playing and listening to music as most young people often do. For weekends, we used to hop on the college bus and go downtown Kampala, mostly for window shopping, since we didn't have a lot of money to spend. The bus driver, a middle-aged man named Ssentamu, knew almost everyone, and he had designated places in town to pick students. One Saturday in December 1972, Erisa and I boarded the bus to town as usual. But we intended to come back and visit Mr. Karuhanga later in the day.

Up to now, I'll never know if it was divine intervention that made us miss the bus back to Kyambogo that day, but we did miss it. My late brother Matia, and his wife Jane, stayed in an apartment at Bakuli, on the west side of town. I told Erisa, that since we had missed the bus, I'd go visit my folks, and that if he wished, he could come with me, but he declined. He hang around town for a few more hours, after which he took a taxi to Banda, and thereafter walked back to our dorm room, He too, decided not to go to Karuhanga's house. Uganda didn't yet have color TV. That came later in 1975, as Amin prepared to host the OAU conference in Kampala. My brother had a black and white set, 12 or 16 inches at most. I had arrived at the apartment no more than two hours earlier when we turned the TV on to watch the 5 O'clock English news. The first news headline made my heart jump into my mouth.

"Mr. James Karuhanga, a teacher at Kyambogo College School, has been arrested along with other men, suspected to be guerillas", the headline read. Matia and Jane noticed me sweating profusely, and asked if I was alright.

"Good God", I said, "I was supposed to be at Karuhanga's house this afternoon, had I not missed the bus!" They both stared at me in disbelief. I told them that my roommate Erisa must be one of those other men found in the house. I had planned on going back to the campus, but I was too shaken up to even contemplate the action. Successive news bulletins that night mentioned the same incident without elaborating on how James was connected to the regime's enemies. Since there were no telephones in our dorm rooms, I could not ascertain whether or not my roommate had been rounded up. But I got some relief the next day when I returned, to learn that he too had been saved by the bell.

James Karuhanga was tortured like all Amin's perceived enemies, tried by court martial, tied to a tree near Kampala's Clock Tower, and shot by firing squad. I had internalized this sad episode in Uganda's checkered history, until I saw an article in the Sunday Monitor of February 10, 2013, entitled "How Museveni survived public execution". The article, for the first time, connected the dots for me. It mentions one Fronasa fighter called Kangire. After being captured and tortured by Amin's operatives, he mentioned a few of his collaborators, and their contact addresses. Among those mentioned was James Karuhanga of Kyambogo College School. Although I didn't know about this collaboration at the time, I nevertheless applaud James for having been part of the fight against the evil that prevailed. Thanks James, and R.I.P.

All the hard work and persistence on my part paid off, because, just as we were graduating with our diplomas in Education, and everybody else was being posted by the Ministry of Education to schools across the country, I found myself with a different kind of problem.

I had done my last teaching practice at Mengo High School, where the Deputy Headmaster, Mr. Gita, had been offered a job in the Academic Registrar's office at Makerere University. The Ministry of Education was still pinning him down, refusing to let him off so that he could take up his new appointment. Now, I found myself facing more or less similar circumstances, having been admitted at Makerere University's Institute of Statistics and Applied Economics, but the Ministry insisting that I should stay in the teaching service, since I had just qualified as a teacher. When I approached Mr. Gita, he advised me to simply ignore the Ministry, and quietly go take my place at the university. I did just that, settling in Mitchell Hall in 1973, and pursuing a bachelor's degree in statistics and economics.

Mr. Gita also made the decision to join Makerere University. But the Uganda of the 1970s was a very violent and unpredictable place. About one year into his new job, he was way-laid by a group of thugs, probably Amin's rag-tag soldiers, who shot him dead to take his old and battered Volkswagen car. Like most murders of that period, nobody was apprehended, and it remains a cold case to this day.

Years later, my wife Christine's father, Kosea Kalebu, a mathematics lecturer at Uganda Technical College, Kyambogo, met a similar, albeit more traumatic fate on March 1st,1979, at around 9.00 a.m. in the morning. This was a particularly tumultuous period, as a joint force of Tanzanian troops and Ugandan exiles were closing in to topple Idi Amin's regime. Conditions were so treacherous, that ordinary people had chosen to stay home, rather than risk their lives going to work. That fateful morning, an army truck with several men armed to the teeth arrived at Mr. Kalebu's home at Kamuli, off Namugongo Road. No one will ever know the motive for their action, because Ssalongo Kalebu was a deeply religious man, not involved in the politics of the day. However, those who witnessed the event, including, my wife, concluded that someone might have been stalking him to snatch his Volvo station wagon from him. The door was open, as my future wife's mom, Nnalongo Kasalina Kalebu,(R.I.P) had just stepped outside.

Three men in army uniform, whom my wife describes as fitting in with Amin's Kakwa tribesmen, burst into the home, wielding their AK47s. Scared, the children, Christine, her brother Kosea Jr, and young sister Julia (R.I.P), run to hide in the closet of a small bedroom, from which they could peep into the living room. As Ssalongo Kalebu heard the commotion, he came out of his bedroom and confronted them on what it was they wanted. There was a little argument in Kiswahili (most army men at that time were from the north, and northern Ugandans in general, do not speak the Luganda language). Mr. Kalebu pleaded with them to spare his life, beseeching them that, if it was his car they fancied and anything else in the home, they could have it. He even pulled the car keys from his pocket and threw them on the table for them to take. But, it seems, no amount of pleading could soften the hearts of these beasts.

From their hiding place in the closet, the children were traumatized as they watched one of the men cock his gun, first towards the ceiling, then aimed it at their father, as he attempted to retreat towards his bedroom. Three shots later, and the poor man crumbled to the ground in a pool of blood. The thugs grabbed the keys, exited as fast as they'd entered, and drove the car in the direction of Namugongo, a small town about six kilometers east of Kampala, off Jinja Road. An attempt was made to rush him to Rubaga Hospital using a neighbor's dump truck where efforts were made to remove the bullets at the hospital, without success. As in Mr. Gita's case, and thousands of victims of that vicious regime, no one was apprehended for the heinous crime. And, like equally traumatized families of the day, his children, and those of people such as Ben Kiwanuka, Jolly Joe Kiwanuka,

Shaban Nkutu, Mayor Walugembe, Bitature, Oryema, and others too many to mention, this incident marked the disintegration of the family unit, as children began to scatter around the world in different directions. My wife and I met about three years after this had happened, and for a long period of time, she kept re-living its ugly memories.

Thirteen

IN JANUARY 1971, the biannual Commonwealth Heads of Government (CHOGM) was to be hosted by Singapore. Like all heads of state united under the British Commonwealth, President Milton Obote flew to the City-State for the conference, which is usually graced by Her Majesty, the Queen of England, the titular head of the Commonwealth. From the surface, there were no tell-tale signs that anything was wrong in the country. However, opposition to Obote's rule was growing, both from inside and outside. In 1969, an assassination attempt on his life had occurred at Lugogo indoor stadium, where he had just finished delivering a speech to his party faithful. After this incident that caused him to have an operation on his lower jaw, security around the president had been tightened to such an extent, that it was virtually impossible to see the president, even when his motorcade was cruising through the streets of Kampala, with sirens blasting all other motorists off the road.

The declaration of martial law in Buganda, after the assault on the Kabaka's Lubiri, leading to his exile in London, had irredeemably damaged whatever relationship there was with Buganda, if any at all. In his book, entitled "The Desecration of My Kingdom", King Freddie had blamed all his troubles, and by extension, Buganda's, on Obote's intransigence. Then in 1969, the Kabaka had died under mysterious circumstances in his London flat, following a rendezvous with a woman, some sources called an assassin sent by Obote's intelligence. From this point on, the one-time marriage between Obote's UPC and Kabaka Yekka, became a divorce gone wild. Obote refused to allow the body of the monarch to be returned to the country for a decent burial at Kasubi Royal Tombs, alongside those of his father and forefathers.

By all accounts, Obote had bitten the hand that fed him, having tampered with the region that was the heartbeat of the nation. At one time, the Lukiiko, Buganda's Parliament, had told him in no uncertain terms, to "move the capital of his central government" from Kampala, and re-locate it elsewhere outside Buganda territory. Although the Uganda Army of the period was dominated by officers and men from the northern region, from which Obote hailed, that appeared to be the only institution the north controlled, and as the saying goes, man does not live on bread alone. Buganda, which constituted about a quarter of the nation's population, had a disproportionate concentration of the wealth within its borders. Clearly, no government in Uganda could function without the cooperation and full participation of Buganda.

On the external front, Obote was getting increasingly vocal on the Rhodesian UDI and the South African apartheid issues, adding his voice to Mwalimu Nyerere's, and Kenneth Kaunda's, as the trio within the Mulungushi Club. The British had referred to him as "one of their most implacable enemies on matters affecting Southern Africa". While the British could have brushed off criticism from Obote, his move-to-the-left strategy on the economy was a direct threat to their interests which they couldn't ignore. So, as he joined his colleagues in Singapore for the CHOGM conference, London gave a nod to his military commander, Major-General Idi Amin, to replace him as head of state.

The morning of January 25, 1971 was very foggy in Kampala. As we went for breakfast early in the morning on the Kyambogo campus, we noticed that vehicles on Jinja Road, between Banda and Nakawa, were moving at snail speed. This was unusual for this stretch of the road, notorious for speeding motorists, especially taxi drivers who plowed it between Kampala and Jinja. By the time we finished breakfast, news had spread that a military coup was under way. Radio Uganda, the only station on the airwaves at the time, was playing martial music rather than the usual programs. As the fog began to clear, we climbed on top of buildings to gain a vantage view across the valley towards Nakawa. From here, we could see shadowy figures running away from Mbuya Army barracks towards the Uganda College of Commerce at Nakawa. We later learned that some of the deserting Acholi soldiers borrowed clothing from students at the college, dumped their uniforms, and walked out of the campus, disguised as students.

By around 3.30 pm in the afternoon Amin, in the company of a Captain Valentine Ocima, drove himself in a jeep to Malire Army Barracks, next to the Army headquarters at Bulange. While there, he picked some soldiers who quickly assembled the reasons for the coup into his so-called 18-points statement. Then they dispatched a junior Warrant Officer named Sam Wilfred Aswa, to the state-run Radio Uganda to announce a coup d'etat. The announcer's adulterated English was to become the trade mark of the Amin regime. Many Ugandans were taken aback, after listening to a half-baked soldier struggling to read a statement of only a few paragraphs on the airwaves, considering the country's pride in its education. Unlike some countries in Africa, which had attained independence with hardly any trained manpower to run the system, Uganda had gotten off on a relatively sound basis. Makerere University, established in 1922, boasts of having trained at least six regional presidents, including Obote (Uganda), Nyerere and Mkapa (Tanzania), Moi and Kibaki (Kenya), and Paul Kagame of Rwanda.

As the day unfolded, many people who had stayed away from traveling to the city summoned enough courage to do so. In downtown Kampala, jubilation was under way, with many Baganda celebrating the ouster of Milton Obote, whom they seemed to hate with a passion. As nightfall approached, Idi Amin was shown on Uganda Television, being sworn in by the Chief Justice. His brief speech, delivered in kindergarten-style English, in which he tooted himself as "a man of a few words, but many actions", is still remembered clearly by anyone alive today, who heard it nearly forty years ago.

Initially, most people laughed off the buffoonery of the semi-illiterate military government, hoping it would not hold its own, and would collapse sooner rather than later. To polish up its image, and compensate for what the regime lacked, Amin assembled a retinue of professors and other academicians to serve in his cabinet, and give it a shot in the arm. However, it soon dawned on him, that such caliber of men and women are free thinkers, who cannot be turned on or off like a tap. Even more, they are not always ready to act on every command from the top, and ask questions later, a la military chain of command. Within a few months of forming his star-studded cabinet some of that incompatibility began to manifest itself in Amin's frustrations with the highly educated. Slowly by slowly, they began to abandon him, as some, like Professor Rugumayo put it, left on moral grounds.

Amin then turned full circle, and started filling these cabinet positions with semi-illiterate soldiers of his ilk, a good number in worse shape than himself. But since he had suspended the constitution, and there was no functioning legislature, his autocratic style began to show in every aspect of life. The term "military spokesman" became part and parcel of household lingua franca, as everyone understood what Amin wanted to communicate to the nation.

The year 1971 passed as one of the most peaceful in the country. Among the first major actions of his presidency, was to appease Buganda Kingdom by returning the body of the Kabaka, Sir Edward Muteesa II, which had lain in a London morgue for nearly two years, as Obote refused to grant Mengo the permission to bring it home. This particular action ingratiated Amin to the Baganda, but also, to other well-meaning citizens, who had considered Obote's obstinacy towards a dead man, as mean and un-African. The second action was the release of high profile politicians, including Grace Ibingira and Abu Mayanja, two of the lawyers who had refused to be party to Obote's abrogation of the 1962 constitution, which had turned Uganda into a republic, and some would say, inculcated the nation's violence culture that has plagued the nation ever since. At the height of his popularity, Amin was as likely to be seen driving solo on Kampala's streets, or even turn up at some wedding or funeral in one of Kampala's sprawling suburbs. As a student at Makerere University, I owned a small Suzuki motorbike which I rode everywhere in Kampala. I can recall on several occasions, seeing Amin driving his open army Jeep on Kampala Road, right in the heart of the city.

But anyone attempting to waylay Amin would have been deceiving himself. Close by, there was always a retinue of State Research escorts mainly, Kakwa and Nubian ethnic groups hailing from his home district of West Nile. These were usually men of strong physique, the kind one normally associates with bouncers at night clubs, and were above all, trigger-happy. As Amin began to consolidate his power, these same security men who had been dubbed "111" due to a tribal custom that tattooed their faces with a pattern resembling the number 111, came to be dreaded. Their arrival in a gathering place such as a bar, restaurant or hotel lobby began to spell out a bad omen, signifying that there was trouble looming around, and people would react by leaving functions prematurely.

Opposition to Amin's rule started almost immediately. His predecessor, President Obote, was a close friend of the Tanzanian leader, Julius Nyerere, who had given him asylum, and continued to treat him as a sitting president. This had caused a fracas in the relatively new East African Community, an organization created in 1967, and embracing Uganda, Kenya and Tanzania. The heads of state of the three countries, referred to as the Authority, were expected to have a rotational summit each year, to be held alternately in the three capitals of Kampala, Nairobi and Dar-es-Salaam. But now, the coup in Uganda had created an awkward situation for Mwalimu Nyerere, whose support for the deposed Obote put him at loggerheads with Amin.

Besides Obote, a number of ex-ministers that served in his cabinet, together with other high level UPC party functionaries, had followed Obote in self-imposed exile to Dar-es-Salaam. The group was allowed to use such facilities as Radio Tanzania, to broadcast anti-Amin propaganda, and to train militia groups with the help of the Tanzanian Peoples Defense Forces. These actions, rather than cementing relationships between the two countries, were causing them to drift further apart every day. The situation got so bad between Amin and Nyerere, that the latter started re-ferring to Amin as a "snake in the grass", which had to be smoked out. At the OAU summit held in the Ethiopian capital of Addis Ababa in 1971, Nyerere had refused to shake Amin's hand, until Amin rose from his seat, crossed over to where Mwalimu Nyerere was sitting, grabbed his hand, and shook it, to the applause of all the dignitaries present.

With relentless pressure from outside, especially the exiles in Tanzania, Amin started hardening his style. Anybody suspected to be a collaborator with the exiles, was immediately arrested and taken either to Makindye military barracks, or Nakasero Presidential lodge, where the vicious state research agents would subject the victim to a battery of gruesome torture experiences. Among the first victims were Frank Kalimuzo, the Vice Chancellor of Makerere University, Joseph Mubiru, the Governor of Bank of Uganda (Central Bank), and Ben Kiwanuka, who was the nation's first Prime Minister, and later, Chief Justice at the time of his ab-duction. These honorable men, like many others who suffered a similar fate under Amin's reign of terror, were snatched from their jobs by armed agents, and their whereabouts have never been traced to this day.

Chief Justice Ben Kiwanuka's fate was sealed on Thursday, September 21, 1972, following his refusal to sanction Amin's expulsion of Ugandans of Asian descent. Two days earlier, Governor Joseph Mubiru, the head of the country's central bank, had been abducted by armed men in civilian clothes, apparently for his opposition to the same issue. Typical of those times, everything started with a rumor in one part of town, which would cause a stampede in the whole city, with people running in deer-like fashion, simply following the crowd without necessarily knowing what caused the problem in the first place.

I was still a student at Kyambogo in 1972. At one point, there was a function that the president was expected to attend. The Director mobilized everybody, students and lecturers alike, and urged us to put on a good show. We were even instructed to prepare some simple science experiments to demonstrate what we were studying. For all I remember, Amin whizzed through the building I was in, shook hands with those of us who were demonstrating experiments, and was out in no time. Up to now, I can still picture his broad hand grabbing mine, and giving me a firm handshake, as he smiled and uttered the words, "soma nnyo", meaning read hard.

Earlier in August, a Christian group headed by a preacher from Mbale, named Nicholas Wafula, in collaboration with other Evangelical preachers from Kenya, came to the college and staged a prayer session. It was a lively event, with singing, and lots of food and drinks. During the session, they announced that they would be sponsoring another prayer session in Mombasa, Kenya later that month, and that anyone interested should register with them right away. I had never been to Mombasa, and so, the idea of traveling to the East African coast, all expenses paid, became immediately appealing. I was later to learn that this evangelization was courtesy of the Billy Graham Worldwide Ministries. A group of students, numbering about two hundred, who had been selected from schools around Kampala, got on the

Kampala-Mombasa train for the 18-hour journey. Most were like me, just there for the ride. Nevertheless, we had to fulfill minimum requirements from our sponsors in order to qualify for the boarding and lodging in Mombasa. We were accommodated in Mama Ngina Hostel, named for the wife of Mzee Jomo Kenyatta, who was the President of Kenya at the time.

We were still in Mombasa, when the news reached us that, President Amin had given the non-citizen Asians in Uganda, a 90-day notice, to either establish Ugandan citizenship, or leave the country. The majority of those non-citizens held dual citizenship of India and United Kingdom. Nobody believed that Indians could be expelled from the country. Most were second or third generation Ugandans, whose ancestors had been shipped in by the British colonial administration, to help with the construction of the very same railway line I had taken to Mombasa. But if anybody could pull off such a stint, Amin was that man. For a whole week, we enjoyed pilaf rice, endured the sweltering heat, roamed the streets of Mombasa, and played on the beaches of Kilindini, oblivious to the fact that Uganda had been turned topsy turvy by the expulsion of the Asian community. We did not get the real sense of the enormity of the problem until we reached Malaba border post at the Uganda-Kenya border. Here, the train was delayed for about six hours as Immigration agents were busy trying to cope with the exodus of Asian families, some of whom had decided to leave the country before the deadline.

The way Amin explained his decision to the nation, and the rest of the World, he had recently had a dream, in which Allah told him to expel the "blood-suckers" of the Ugandan economy, by whom, he meant Indians. At the time of his dream in August 1972,, the Asian community, which constituted no more than one percent of the population, controlled close to three quarters of the commercial sector. Although President Obote had addressed this lopsidedness in the ownership and control of the Ugandan economy, he had not had the guts to face the problem squarely like Amin. Later, as the reality began to settle in, there was no shortage of stories making the rounds, as to why Amin kicked out the Indians. Among them, was a wild tale of how Amin, a Moslem by faith, had approached the most prominent of the Indian families, the Madhvanis of Kakira, Jinja, for their daughter's hand in marriage. When this request was rejected, this sealed the fate of the entire Asian community.

I had witnessed the exodus of Rwandese refugees flock into south-western Uganda as a kid in the early 1960's, but this had been viewed through the eyes of a child. The Indian expulsion and its prospective impact on the country's socio-political path, was without any parallel incident. Britain, to which the majority would eventually settle, was once the colonial power, and no matter how much the newly independent African nations wished to shake off their colonial yoke, these European powers still held the trump card.

Amin's coup had been carried out with some tacit help from Col Bar-Lev, the Military Attache at the Israel Embassy in Kampala. This was before the Yom Kippur War of 1973, in which the Egyptian Army nearly vanquished the Israeli Defense Forces. By helping Uganda, the Israelis hoped to use the country as a proxy to control the head waters of the mighty River Nile, which forms the lifeblood of their arch enemy. However, the mere fact that Britain was the first major power to recognize Big Daddy's regime, betrayed the implicit nod they must have given in the planning and execution of the operation. So, by antagonizing Britain with the Indian expulsion, Amin was essentially, biting the hand that fed him.

Initially, people cheered him on, based on the false illusion that, by turning over the businesses formerly owned by Indians to indigenous Ugandans, an African merchant class would emerge overnight to continue running the economy. The first mistake was to allocate some key businesses to a group of mostly illiterate Kakwa and Nubians from the president's West Nile district. Although a few of them had run mom and pop stores, none had the experience to run more sophisticated operations such as a sugar manufacturing plant requiring a structured set of operations. Within a few months, as the stocks the new owners had inherited began to dwindle, they soon found out that they could not replenish the stock, and that it took more than just posing behind the counter, and drinking chai all day.

Indians are very adept at forming closely-knit networks that work together towards achieving a common goal. Coupled with the fact that generations of Indians have been involved in trade, it was almost foolhardy of Amin, or anyone else, to imagine that such specialization could be duplicated overnight. For instance, an Indian merchant in Kampala, with family ties in Mumbai, could easily obtain merchandise on credit, which he could import, sell, and repay the loan.

The newly anointed mafuta mingi, as the shop owners were christened, took to ostentatious consumption, buying the latest models of fancy cars, and chasing after any beautiful woman on the street. The undisciplined nature, and lack of frugality among the new class was a harbinger for financial disaster, which was about to befall the nation. Soon, the once well-stocked shops on Kampala Road stood with empty shelves, some going to the extreme of selling chapatti and bogoya, both local foodstuffs. In fact, even chapatti became a rarity, as wheat flour disappeared due to lack of milling equipment.

These shortages were followed by galloping inflation, the like of which the country had never seen. At the peak of the inflationary cycle, prices were doubling at least once every fortnight. As the situation started to get out of hand, Amin declared an economic war, and turned to price control, which ultimately made things worse. He threatened to shoot any economic saboteurs, alleging that the shortages were artificially created by merchants who wished to make a quick buck by hoarding goods.

While the country was going through these economic hardships, Amin's poor international diplomacy began to catch up with him, and exacerbate the problem. The Uganda of the 1970s was virtually a mono-product economy, deriving more than three quarters of its foreign exchange from coffee. Then as now, commodity prices, especially agricultural commodities like coffee could experience large swings, brought about by natural disasters such as frost in the Brazilian crop. Uganda's traditional creditors like the United Kingdom had turned their backs on the country, forcing Uganda to purchase its import requirements on a cash basis. With the multilateral financial institutions such as the IMF, and World Bank, also falling under the sphere of influence of western countries, no new loans were being extended to Uganda, further limiting the availability of foreign exchange.

As the general population complained about shortages, the Central Bank authorities would desperately try to explain the technical issues related to foreign exchange and balance of payments to the cabal of illiterate soldiers ruling the country, who, at one point thought, that foreign exchange was a mysterious person deliberately sabotaging the economy. Amin's vice-president, General Mustafa Adrisi, a one-time driver and cook, who would later confess to a Commission of Inquiry hearing, that he didn't know what "konsitusoni was" nor did he know the country had one, threatened ,

"Foreign exchange anafikili ye ni nyama gani? Kama anayongeza maneno, tunaweza kupiga yeye lisasi kabisa", implying that this animal had better tread carefully, or else they would shoot and kill it.

Fourteen

THE COUNTRY WAS already teetering towards chaos at the end of 1972, when an attempted invasion at Mutukula on the Uganda-Tanzanian border, was orchestrated by exiles based in Tanzania. Many UPC supporters had been hounded by the Amin regime, forcing them to follow their deposed leader, now offered asylum in Tanzania. However, Obote's group was not the only one opposed to the military regime in Kampala. A group of firebrands, mostly trained at Dar-es-Salaam University, had embraced their mentor, Nyerere's pan-Africanism. They were led by a charismatic young man called Yoweri Museveni, the current president of Uganda. Museveni and his cohorts had cut their revolutionary teeth fighting the Portuguese alongside Samora Machel's FRELIMO in Mozambique. In the first few weeks following the coup in Uganda, Museveni could be heard preaching anti-Amin propaganda on Radio Tanzania, Dar-es-Salaam.

Among the most formidable foes Amin was worried about, were Major-General David Oyite Ojok, who was ex-president Obote's right-hand man, and Yoweri Museveni, militaristic by nature, but intellectual at the same time. Museveni had briefly worked in the Obote government as a low-ranking civilian after completing his studies at the University of Dar-es-Salaam. Obote had recruited a cohort of students, including Dr. Ruhakana-Rugunda, Omwony-Ojok, Eriya Kategaya, and many others, who formed the bulk of his UPC Youth-wingers. These young, mostly male brigades, had the ear of the president, and in line with the post-independence rhetoric, could be relied upon to advocate the socialist policies that had been hatched and bred at Dar-es-Salaam University.

The 1972 invasion was a hodge-podge of intellectuals, and diehard UPC stalwarts who wanted to see their constitutionally elected president re-instated. However, while the different groups shared a common foe in Amin, their objectives for removing him did not necessarily converge. It turned out that the younger group were nursing ambitions of their own, thereby rendering the goal of defeating their common enemy, rather futile. Even with backing from President Julius Nyerere, organizational problems emanating from disagreements in the chain of command, set in, leading to near catastrophe during the implementation of the operation.

Amin's intelligence services got wind of the impending invasion as the plan was still being hatched, and feigned ignorance of the goings-on, as Amin himself mobilized his counter-insurgency troops to repel the enemy. He armed the Masaka battalion, which he had nicknamed "suicide", to the teeth, and put it under fearless commanders like Maliyamungu. He then waited for the invaders to fall into the trap. As part of their strategy, the exiles had sent a few saboteurs and scouts across the border, with the aim of causing some commotion, which would cause some riots in the general population, to which the invaders would rally behind militarily. When this failed to materialize, the invaders who had already crossed into Ugandan territory, found themselves having to fight a more hardened force, which was both numerically and militarily superior. The invasion expedition was quickly abandoned as the perpetrators scampered for cover, some blending into the general population, while others were slaughtered mercilessly by Amin's soldiers. The Mutukula invasion marked the beginning of Amin's viciousness. Prominent people, especially those associated with UPC and its leader, Obote, began to disappear mysteriously. It was a few weeks after this invasion, that my brothers and I nearly met our maker at a road block mounted by soldiers near the entrance to the Simba Battalion in Mbarara. Although we were neither political, nor followers of Obote, the invasion had revealed to Amin, that most people from the western region of the country did not like him. Within the invading force itself, the group led by Yoweri Museveni was predominantly from Western Uganda, composed of mainly Banyankore, and Bakiga ethnicity. At the roadblock, therefore, we became guilty by virtue of falling within these ethnic groups.

Following the invasion, Amin's rule became increasingly erratic and brutal. By early 1973, the President's erstwhile supporters, including the British and Israelis, had all but abandoned him due to gross violations of human rights. Amin in turn, did a diplomatic about-turn, relying more and more on his Islamic brethren, mainly from the middle-east. As the Arabs continued beating war drums against their arch enemy Israel, they embarked on a diplomatic offensive around the world, urging any Moslem leaders, and their sympathizers, to savor relations with the Jewish state. No one championed this cause more than the mercurial Colonel Muammar Qaddafi, who had seized power in Libya by overthrowing King Idris in 1969. Awash with petro-dollars, Qaddafi filled the void left by the withdrawal of western aid, after most of the western countries closed their embassies in Uganda.

The chill in relations between Uganda and the United Kingdom was epitomized by the Dennis Cecil Hills incident. Mr. Hills, an aging Englishman who lectured in the English Department at the National Teachers College at Kyambogo, had lived in Uganda for many years. He had recently published a book, in which he had compared Amin's rule to that of a village tyrant. For that, Amin had ordered his arrest and subsequent trial, and was threatening to try him by court martial, which at that time, was headed by semi-illiterate soldiers. With no embassy to handle the case within the country, Britain's Foreign Secretary, Lord Callaghan at the time, ended up jetting into Uganda, on Amin's insistence, to negotiate with him, in order to spare Mr. Hills' life. The rendez-vous for the two titans, was itself a kind of humiliation for the British top diplomat, as he had to endure crawling through a low entrance to a grass-thatched hut that Amin had put up for the purpose at his countryside home in Koboko, West Nile district. However, Amin, a showman by nature, also knew the limits to his brinkmanship. Lord Callaghan flew back to London with his fellow Briton, leaving Big Daddy to prepare for yet more stunts.

With very few friends to turn to, Amin tried every means to exploit his Islamic faith by getting as close as possible to lead-ers in the middle-east. Col. Qaddafi, whose maiden state visit to Uganda was in November 1973, in my freshman year at Makerere University, soon became a regular guest in Amin's State House. Other prominent guests of the era included King Abdallah-Aziz of Saudi Arabia, Yasser Arafat, Emperor Bokassa of Central African Republic, and Omar Bongo of Gabon. My memory of Bokassa, is that of a heavy-set man, with a chest bedecked with so many military medals, that they pulled down on his upper body, making him walk with a stoop. President Omar Bongo, on the other hand, was a vertically challenged man, whose five-foot frame, made him look like Big Daddy's son on the podium. His attempt to compen-sate for a stout frame gave Kampala the "Bongo style" of dressing in high-heeled shoes and bell-bottom pants. Amin's unpredict-ability also began to unfold as world focus turned on the country's human rights record. In a desperate attempt to polish his image, he continuously sought out people with integrity, whom he incor-porated into his cabinet to bolster and fend off both internal and external criticism of his government's record. For instance, late in 1973, while addressing Makerere University students on the cam-pus, in the presence of Col. Qaddafi, Amin turned in the direction of his then foreign Minister, Lt-Col Obitre-Gama, and told him he was relieving him of his job. In the same breath, he appointed Princess Elizabeth Bagaya of Toro, a Cambridge-educated lawyer, and one time model to replace him.

But, as always, Amin had other ulterior motives for these appointments, as Princess Bagaya would soon learn, much to her chagrin. The president, whose "Dada" nickname, (Swahili for sister) had been acquired when he was caught red-handed by his superiors hiding a young woman in his dorm against regulations during his army training days, had miscalculated on Bagaya, thinking that she would be easy prey for him. However, when his advances failed to yield the desired results, Amin witch-hunted the poor woman, first, by murdering her boy-friend, and later, implicating her in a concocted sex scandal purportedly having occurred at the Charles De Gaulle Airport, using amateurish photography to attach her face to a hooker's naked body. After this humiliation, the princess narrowly slipped his grip and went into exile in London, and would later be appointed by the Museveni regime as Uganda's Ambassador to the United States in 1987.

After the closure of the Israeli embassy in Kampala, and following the Yom-Kippur War of October 1973, Amin's rhetoric against the Jewish state became increasingly belligerent, often sending verbal missiles at then Israeli Prime Minister Golda Meir, sometimes with statements including unmentionable body parts. But Amin's undiplomatic language was not limited to Israel. He also targeted Israel's ardent supporters such as the US and Britain, whom he continually referred to as the Imperialist-Zionist coalition. In a 1974 telegram to then US Secretary of State Dr. Henry Kissinger, he wished President Richard Nixon a quick recovery from Watergate, a reference to the illegal break-in into the Democratic Headquarters at the Watergate Hotel in Washington DC in 1972. To further provoke the British, Amin had added the title "Conqueror of the British Empire" (CBE) to his already overflowing list that included, Field Marshall, VC, MC, DSO, most of them meaningless and self-imposed.

In 1975, Amin stunned the Makerere university community, the sole university in the country then, when, as Chancellor by virtue of his position as president of the country, he demanded that he be awarded an honorary doctorate. After a few protestations and resignations from the nation's foremost academic institution, the president got his wish, marking what would be a steady decline in Makerere's prestige for a long time. That same year, Amin hosted a summit for the heads of state of the Organization of African Unity, at the end of which he was elected chairman, after a motion moved by none other than Egyptian President Anwar Sadat.

For the catholic faithful, 1975 ushered in that period which comes every quarter century, during which, St Peter's Basilica in the eternal city of Rome, opens its doors for the laity to make a pilgrimage to pray and walk the grounds of Catholicism's holiest site. My father, although fairly well-traveled inside Uganda, had never left the country. Through his relationship with Mzee Paul Ngorogoza of Kabale who had made an earlier pilgrimage in 1950, my dad used to express his wish to visit Rome. The Catholic Church in Uganda, to which approximately forty-five percent of the population belongs, expected to send a large contingent on this once-in-a-lifetime experience. My brother Matia, whose wife Jane was scheduled to go, suggested that we sponsor the old man for the trip. Our cousin, Francis Kasura, too decided to sponsor his dad, so that Mzee would be in good company. By the time the full list was drawn, a number of prominent men and women from the Rukungiri area, including pre-eminent transporter Kalori Bakesigaki, had jumped on board. The group then joined others from various dioceses around the country for the two-week trip that would change their lives for good.

This trip illustrated Mzee, among other traits, as a man who thought on his feet. As he narrated the story to us upon his return, one afternoon, while on one of those guided tours, he strayed away from his Ugandan group to visit the bathroom. By the time he got back, however, they were long gone. Unable to speak either English or Italian, he did the next best thing he could think of.

He approached one of the Italian carabinieri, and using a combination of pantomimes and his Runyankore, told the security man,

"Nyowe ninduga Uganda, kwonka abantu bangye bansigaho", meaning, "I come from Uganda, but my people have just left without me". The man must have heard the key word, "Uganda", because he immediately led the oldman on a search, that soon re-united him with his group.

Mzee's unique character also has to be seen from some of the deeds he performed over his fairly long life. With the Mbarara family, refugees from Rwanda, whom he received and fed daily at their darkest hour of need, when the rest of the community kept a safe distance, he demonstrated how the best concept of what Archbishop Desmond Tutu of South Africa called "ubuntu", meaning humanness, or that unique quality that separates humans from other creatures, manifests itself during a crisis. In another one of those brave acts, a Langi man by the name of John Emuna, a friend of my brother Matia, earmarked for death during Amin's pogroms of Acholi and Langi ethnic groups, was hidden at Mzee's home for several months until that danger period subsided. Both Mbarara and Emuna, to this day, revere Mzee, referring to him with the highest respect any child could ever give a father.

I had given some money to my sister-in-law, Jane, to buy me a nice Italian suit, as my graduation was soon approaching. She brought back a nice checkered gray-colored woolen suit, which I tried on and then put away. By that time, I had moved out of Mitchell Hall, which had been my primary residence for the first two years of my stay at Makerere University. My teaching diploma had enabled me to secure a teaching position at Kitante Hill Secondary School, paying me a salary that kept me above the average lifestyle of a typical student at that time. The extra income had allowed me to purchase a Suzuki motor bike, a rarity among students in those days. Although I shared a rented house with two other university students near the Law Development Center canteen, it was my presence or absence that was most conspicuous due to the sound of my bike.

One day, I had to teach a class in the morning before my scheduled statistical methods lecture. I was barely gone for one-and-half hours before I returned to find my room completely ransacked, and everything gone, including a stereo system that I had purchased in Nairobi the previous year. However, there was one puzzle to the act. None of my roommates' stuff had been touched, despite having a communicating door between my room and theirs. Although I reported the case to the Old Kampala Police Station, just across the valley, within the hour the sloppy detectives they sent to investigate the robbery seemed bent more on getting their "chai" than going after the culprits. In the end, I just wrote the whole thing off as a loss, and moved on, donning my old blue suit for graduation.

A year later, when I had moved out of that residence to a house on Mawanda Road, another robbery took place there. My former roommates, who were still living in the house, surprised me by showing up with a detective while I was teaching a class, and asked me to go show them around my house. I complied with their request, even going so far as inviting them to feel free to go search my brothers' residences in Kampala, and satisfy themselves that I had nothing to do with their loss. It was at that time, that I confirmed what many of my friends had told me regarding the initial incident. My roommates had probably connived with some characters to relieve me of my property while I stayed with them. Years later, on one of my visits to Kampala, I run into one of those former roommates, who seemed to have fallen on hard times. Although I was going for lunch in one of Kampala's good hotels at the time, and could have given him a meal, the grotesque act he and his friend had committed against me, militated against my embracing him. Apart from exchanging a few words, I decided to part company and move on.

With the chairmanship of the OAU under his belt, Amin had attained the ultimate jewel in the crown, and for a little while, the world seemed to have accepted him despite his flaws. But this honeymoon would not last long, given his unpredictability. Since closing the Israeli embassy in 1973, Amin had courted many Arab leaders, among them, Palestinian leader Yasser Arafat. He had, in fact, embraced the Palestinian cause with the zeal of the outsider who weeps more than the bereaved. The Palestinian mission in Kampala had been elevated to ambassadorial level at a time when a lot of nations, including some Arab countries mostly paid it lip-service. Arafat himself was a fairly common sight in Kampala, sometimes seen on Kampala streets, being driven in a military jeep, seated next to Amin.

Fifteen

THIS COZY RELATIONSHIP with Yasser Arafat was soon put to a test, when on June 27, 1976, an Air France Airbus A300B4-203 jet, Flt # AF139 , with 248 passengers and 12 crew members, en route from Ben Gurion Airport near Tel Aviv, to Charles de Gaulle in Paris, was hijacked by Palestinian freedom fighters, after a refueling stopover at Ellinikon International Airport, Athens, Greece. Shortly after its 12.30 pm takeoff from Athens, the plane was commandeered by two men belonging to the Popular Front for the Liberation of Palestine (PFLP), in conjunction with a man, Wilfried Bose, and a woman, Brigitte Kuhlmann, both from the Revolutionary Cells, or Revolutionare Zellen, a German leftist militant group formed in the early 1970's. The flight was first diverted to Benghazi in Libya, where it spent seven hours, and, one female passenger, faking a miscarriage, was let off.

Once airborne, the hijackers demanded to be flown to Entebbe International Airport in Uganda, where they were joined by another group of four Palestinian freedom fighters, with a nod and wink from Ugandan Military strongman, Idi Amin. Right from the moment Big Daddy allowed the plane to land, until the Israel Defense Forces mounted their daring 2500-mile rescue mission, dubbed "Operation Thunderbolt", Amin's actions looked and smelled suspiciously like collaboration, rather than an act of mercy on the mainly Jewish passengers, which he claimed was the main reason he had allowed the flight to land at Entebbe. The hijackers demanded immediate release of 40 Palestinian prisoners held mainly in Israel, but also in a wide range of countries, including Switzerland, France, West Germany, and Kenya, failure of which they threatened to start killing the hostages by July1, 1976.

The hostages, who were being held at Entebbe's old airport terminal building, had by then been isolated by nationality, and grouped into Jewish and gentiles. This unfortunate demarcation, reminiscent of Hitler's death camps, prompted one holocaust survivor, to display his inmate number, embossed on his forearm, to Bose, one of their captors, prompting him to protest, that he was not a Nazi, but an "idealist", whatever that meant. Upon the hijackers' insistence, that the non-Jewish passengers and crew board another Air France plane, Captain Michel Bacos of the ill-fated flight refused to budge, reminding the hijackers, that all the passengers, Jewish or not, were his responsibility, and that he would not depart without them. His crew backed his decision, and they all stayed with the rest of the hostages, despite the enormous risk. All in all, a total of 105 hostages, composed of 85 Israeli-passport holders, and another twenty, including the entire crew, remained behind.

Israel, which ordinarily adopts a policy of not negotiating with terrorists, was in a bit of a quagmire. It had only been four years since its Olympic athletics team was nearly wiped out by another terrorist group during the 1972 Olympic Games in Munich. And, complicating this particular event, was the fact that it was located half a world away, out of its usual operating distance range in the middle-east. However, in spite of these hurdles, the Jewish state was not about to abscond from its obligation of securing its distressed citizens, no matter where they were, and what it cost them to do so.

Idi Amin had trained in Israel before becoming commander of the Uganda Army in the 1960's. Although he had severed relations and closed the Israeli Embassy in Uganda, there remained, among the IDF, men like Col Bar-Lev, his one-time trainer, whom he still considered friends. The Mossad knew this fact, and they were prepared to exploit it along with any military options they could come up with. Further knowledge could be obtained from companies which had commercial interests in the country. For starters, an Israeli construction company, Solel Boneh, had constructed the new terminal building at Entebbe, just about a quarter of a mile from the old one, where the hostages were being held. The airport itself is located on the shores of Lake Victoria, away from the heavily-populated civilian centers. Moreover, the infrastructure was rather scanty, making it possible to isolate each building easily.

Amin's involvement in the political cauldron of the middle-east had not been welcomed by the majority of Ugandans. His orienting the country towards Islamic causes had caused a rift within the country, whose majority population was, and remains Christian. To most Ugandans, already grappling with the plight of their own suffering under the dictator, the Palestinian cause sounded distant and peripheral. It was therefore, no surprise that, giving the Palestinian freedom fighters sanctuary to hold hostages on Ugandan territory was not wholesomely entertained, except by a minority, mostly Muslims who shared Amin's faith. The Israelis knew these sentiments held among the Ugandan population. However, as a dictator, Amin held sway over who controlled the destiny of the country. To salvage the situation, they would either negotiate with him directly, or fight against his military establishment. None of the options was considered smooth-sailing.

Amin had been commander of the Uganda Army before overthrowing Milton Obote, and therefore had a good sense of military maneuvers. Although the Israeli Defense Forces (IDF), counts among the best combat-ready armies on the globe, its operations in a rescue mission of this nature would stretch it to the limit. The second option of negotiating with the President was already rendered futile by his expulsion of Israeli citizens, followed by the closing of their embassy in Kampala. Any negotiations, therefore, would be approached from an individual, rather than a national approach.

Although the Ugandan Army was considered no match, against an elite unit of the IDF, regionally, it was viewed as strong, and with a home advantage, could inflict a lot of damage to a superior fighting force with no reliable backup to call upon in case of trouble. The Israeli cabinet had designated a retired IDF Col Baruch "Burka" Bar-Lev, a longtime confidante of Amin, to be their point man. The Ugandan president had been chairman of the Organization of African Unity (OAU) for a year since hosting the African heads of state in Uganda in 1975. This position was on a rotational basis, being bestowed on each host of the summit. Amin had urged the Israelis to postpone their negotiations over the hostages until the OAU summit, which that year, was to be held in Port Louis, Mauritius, ended. President Amin would have to attend the summit, and hand over the chairmanship to the host, Sir Seewoosagur Ramgoolum of Mauritius.

Col Bar-Lev made many calls to "his friend", during the hostage crisis, assuring Big Daddy of Israel's good intentions. However, little did Amin realize that Israel was using the Colonel as a deflection from their real intentions of rescuing the hostages. The four-day extension for the negotiations allowed the Israelis to prepare and refine their plans for the rescue. The cabinet approved the dare devil rescue mission on July 3, 1976. The IDF had selected the crème-de-la-crème of their military brass for this unique operation, nothing of which had ever been attempted by the Jewish state.

The overall commander of the operation was Major General Yekutiel "Kuti" Adam, with Major General Matan Vilnai as his deputy, while Brigadier General Dan Shomron was appointed to be in charge of operations on the ground. Israel's Mossad, through extensive interviews with the non-Jewish passengers who had been released from the hijacked plane, was able to reconstruct a partial replica of the terminal building at Entebbe. Among the released hostages, was a Frenchman of Jewish descent, with a military background, and supposedly, a photographic memory, who helped the IDF assess the number of personnel involved inside the airport, along with the kind of weaponry they carried. These efforts were further aided by Israeli civilian contractors who had built the actual terminal structure. The contractors were detained as guests of the IDF until the end of the raid, in order to maximize secrecy about the impending operation, and prevent any possible leakages from spilling out.

After rehearsing and going through the routine many times over, four Hercules C-130 transporters took to the skies under the cover of darkness, flying over Sharm-al-Sheik, then south over the Red Sea, at altitudes of about 100 feet, to avoid radar detection by Egyptian and Saudi Arabian radar. The planes then went on a zig-zag route that took them over Djibouti, Somalia, the Kenyan rift valley, and finally, over Lake Victoria, to land at Entebbe at 23.00 hrs. Meanwhile, two Boeing707 followed the four cargo planes. One of the Boeing aircrafts carried medical equipment, and landed at a secluded area of Jomo Kenyatta International Airport in Nairobi. During this stopover, the lights at the airport conveniently went out. The second plane, with Major-General Yekutiel Adams on board, continued to Entebbe, and circled the airspace while the operation was taking place on the ground.

The operation on the ground, constituting about 100 troops, had been divided into various task forces, ranging from assault and rescue, to protecting the hostages as they boarded, and the destruction of Amin's squadron of Russian Mig fighters, to prevent a possible interception by the Ugandan Air force. Lt-Col Yoni Netanyahu, elder brother of current Israeli Prime Minister Benjamin Netanyahu, was put in charge of the assault task force.

As the cargo planes landed, the cargo-bay doors opened to unload a black Mercedes-Benz, similar to Amin's limo, accompanied by military jeeps with fake Ugandan tags, to give the impression that the President was returning from his OAU trip to Port Louis. Unknown to the Israelis, two sentries, aware that Amin had recently traded in his black Mercedes for a white one, became suspicious, and tried to stop the convoy of Israeli commandos from proceeding. Fearing that this may abort the mission, by creating some commotion around the airport, one of the IDF commandos drew his pistol, fitted with a silencer, and stuffed the unfortunate sentries with a few sluggers. But they did not die right away. Another commando, in the vehicle following the first one, noticed the wounded soldiers crawling away from the scene, drew his Uzi machine gun, and finished them off.

However, this brought some unwanted attention to the operation, due to the pop-corn sound from the rapid fire. The rescue team therefore had to redouble their efforts in order to successfully conduct the mission.

Lt-Col Netanyahu's men burst into the main lounge of the old terminal building, in which the hostages were spread, some seated on airport chairs, the elderly lying down on mattresses which had been provided by Amin. The IDF commandos shouted in Hebrew and ordered everyone to lie down, emphasizing that anyone who remained standing would be deemed to be part of the hostage-takers, and shot on the spot. One 19-year Frenchman, who had earlier, identified himself as an Israeli Jew, despite carrying a French passport, mistakenly stood up, and was quickly shot. A few other hostages were caught in crossfire as the commandos exchanged fire with the hijackers. Within a short period, all the seven hijackers lay dead. Once the IDF had killed and accounted for all the hijackers, Netanyahu gave the green light for the rescue to begin.

Sensing an invasion was in progress, but unsure as to who was behind it, the Ugandan Army guarding the airport made a tactical withdrawal to assess and regroup. So, as the Israeli began the evacuation of the hostages, they were suddenly met with a barrage of hostile fire, and had to fight for dear life to extricate themselves from the quandary. In the ensuing process, Lt-Col Netanyahu was mortally wounded, as he oversaw the last stages of the rescue. A few of the commandos had to fight a bloody battle, to retrieve his lifeless body and take it with them for the flight back. He became the only casualty of the IDF rescue force, although a number of soldiers were seriously wounded in the process. The final tally included all the seven hijackers, three hostages killed, and about ten wounded, and about forty five Ugandan soldiers killed in action.

One elderly hostage, Mrs. Dora Bloch, who had been taken to Mulago Hospital in Kampala, after choking on a fish bone, was later abducted and killed on Amin's orders, apparently in retaliation for what the Israelis had done. Various stories abound as to whether her remains were ever found and later flown back to Israel as claimed, or simply fed to the ever-hungry crocodiles prowling the River Nile near Karuma Falls.

The entire episode did not only humiliate Amin, whose army's mystical strength was revealed as hollow, but it also left a bitter taste in the mouth for those Ugandans, who, on the one hand sympathized with the plight of the hostages, while on the other, were puzzled by Israeli's penchant for collective punishment, inflicted on all Ugandans by way of destroying all the airport's facilities, including the terminal building, runway, and many aircrafts. It took nearly twenty years of painstaking work to rehabilitate Entebbe Airport back to normal. Prime Minister Netyanahu's overtures to build a monument for his slain brother at Entebbe, was therefore seen by many in Uganda, as a slap in the face, that opened up old wounds on a subject most would rather forget.

Sixteen

FOLLOWING THE JULY 4, 1976 humiliation by the successful Israeli hostage rescue, Amin turned increasingly more brutal. First, he laid the blame squarely on the carelessness of the military personnel who guarded the airport facilities, although they had suffered quite a number of casualties in an attempt to fend off the enemy. All the senior officers in charge of airport facilities, were relieved of their duties, some actually court-martialed, and in all likelihood, joining their compatriots in the dungeons of his terror machinery.

In spite of his brutality, however, some media houses, and reporters, especially western journalists took liberty in spreading some innuendos and exaggerations about the regime. A case in point is an article which appeared in the Sunday Monitor of October 10, 2012, with the heading "Was Amin's terror exaggerated?", citing what Professor Ali Mazrui had called "the Makerere Incident". In an article published for Third World Quarterly, Vol 2, No 1, (1980), titled, "Between Development and Decay: Anarchy, Tyranny under Idi Amin, the renowned professor writes how, through British journalist David Martin of the London Observer Newspapaer, he learned about a supposedly massacre that had taken place in Freedom Square right in front of the main Administration Building at Makerere University in early August 1976. According to David Martin's story, upwards of 100 students were brutally slaughtered by Amin's soldiers, while hundreds more were maimed, including the raping of female students, and cutting off their breasts.

According to the Sunday Monitor article, the good Professor was puzzled by the story narrated to him by the journalist in Dar-es-Salaam, at the exile home of the late President Milton Obote of Uganda. For Prof. Mazrui, the facts of the story could not add up, given the open location of the site mentioned, and the mere fact that no other reporter could collaborate the gruesomeness of such an act at what was then, the only university in the country, and located on a prominent hill, about two kilometers from downtown Kampala.

Not one to take any story at face value, Professor Mazrui did his due diligence, over several months, interviewing tens of people of different nationalities who claimed to have been on the campus on that day. None of them could recall having seen a single dead body, although, all agreed that the soldiers had, indeed been there, and roughed up the riotous students. In the end, according to the article, Professor Mazrui concluded that the massacre never happened, and considering that David Martin was filing his reports from Lusaka, Zambia, and Dar-es-Salaam, Tanzania, the Observer journalist was, to say the least, spreading what's known in Swahili, as "wolokoso", or simply "hot air.

Although I am, by no means, an apologist for Amin's heinous crimes, reading through this article, made me wonder how much we heard or read in the papers about him was fact, and how much was fiction. The incident referred to by Professor Mazrui is one that has imbedded itself in my memory because I witnessed the event first hand from beginning to finish as it happened, albeit from the shelter of the University Administration Building.

In March of 1976, I had graduated from Makerere's Institute of Statistics and Applied Economics, and had joined the civil service, taking a job as a statistician with the Ministry of Education's Planning and Statistical unit. Makerere University, as a public institution, drew its funding almost entirely from the central government budget.

In early August, top officials from both the Ministry of Education, and the university, were slated to meet and discuss the university budget for the forthcoming academic year. Students on the "Hill", as Makerere was referred to, were getting increasingly edgy over harassment incidents by the unruly military, sometimes over petty issues related to rivalry over female students. But as the economy continued to deteriorate as a result of sanctions imposed on the country over its human rights record, the university became less of a priority for Amin's regime. Conditions at the once so-called Ivory Tower, plummeted to a point, where students had to get by on cornmeal known as "posho", and beans infested with weevils. I had opted out of Mitchell Hall of Residence, in my second year, in order to control my own diet. About a month following the Israeli rescue of their hostages at Entebbe Airport, students at the university rioted over the poor food and inadequate rations. That week, I had been asked by the Higher Education officer, Mr. Eyoku, to accompany the Ministry team to Makerere, and serve as their statistician on the university Grants committee.

The high-powered committee, that included the Vice Chancellor, Professor J.S. Lutwama, deans of faculties, heads of departments, and senior government officers from the Ministry of Education, held their meetings in a boardroom adjacent to the Vice Chancellor's office in the Administration building. I was given space in Mr. David Musoke's office, who was, at the time, the university's Public Relations Officer. Both of these facilities have a commanding view of the main thoroughfare to the university, and a quadrangle known as Freedom Square in front of the Administration building. So, on the day the riots happened, we could easily discern what was happening outside from the windows facing the square. The students began by boycotting lectures, and forming small groups in front of the administration building. Soon, these groups grew into crowds of shouting students. Nobody knows who called the soldiers, but soon, we were stunned to watch as the armed soldiers descended on the helpless students and almost immediately, began to brutalize them with just about anything they could lay their hands on. As the students scampered for cover, the soldiers gave chase, capturing some who couldn't run fast enough, and tossing them in military vehicles, and driving off with them.

Meanwhile in the committee meeting, many people urged the Vice Chancellor to go outside and talk to the marauding soldiers, or even place a call to the President to order his soldiers to stop. But all I remember hearing Prof. Lutwama say, was, "Mwagala bankube?", meaning, "Do you want me to be beaten up as well?". Among the students was my late young brother Simon, who was at the time, a resident of Livingstone Hall. Later that evening, we searched everywhere for him, to no avail, until he showed up a day later, with serious bruises on his back, apparently the result of beatings with a gun butt. After the riots were contained, the soldiers sealed off the gates of the sprawling university campus, allowing neither entry nor exit by students. From our vantage point on the second floor of the Administration building, we saw the soldiers in action, manhandling the students. Amin's son, Taban joined the soldiers, and he clearly was among the people shouting out commands. Nevertheless, for all the harassment that took place on that day, I do not recall seeing bodies of students lying on the ground. In fact, all the students who had been hulled into army vehicles and taken to the infamous Makindye barracks, including my brother Simon, were later released after giving them a thorough beating, sometimes, using gun butts.

As I still carried my university student ID, I expressed my fears to Mr. Eyoku, who in turn told the Minister of Education, Brig. Barnabas Kili, of our predicament. The minister was gracious enough to authorize his driver to drop me, and Ms. Kawesa, the secretary to the committee, at our respective residences.

My last encounter with Amin's soldiers happened when our UNESCO experts and I went out on an upcountry tour of western Uganda, to meet and brief education officials and heads of schools about a national education census we were preparing. After spending a night at the White Horse Inn in Kabale, we had an early breakfast, and soon after, our driver, Jamada Mawanda, was racing the Toyota Land cruiser at breakneck speed through the gorges of Muko, on our way towards Fort Portal, via the floor of the western rift valley. The Ishasha route runs almost parallel to the Congo (DRC) border. In happier times, this area would have been a tourist mecca. It includes the world famous mountain gorillas in nearby Bwindi impenetrable forest, a lineup of volcanoes and crater lakes, on the borders of Uganda, Rwanda, and DRC, the famed Queen Elizabeth National Park with its tree-climbing lions and a multitude of bird species, and finally, the indomitable Rwenzori Mountains, known since Ptolemy referred to it as the Mountains of the Moon.

The distance between Kabale and Fort Portal is about two hundred miles, give or take a few miles. Ordinarily, this journey would take no more than four hours, with the kind of vehicle we had. However, the nature of the terrain, and hazardous roads, make this a whole day's operation. The whole journey had been smooth, until we came to the junction, where the Ishasha Road branches off towards Rwenshama, on Lake Edward. A military detachment had been deployed there, and had placed an obscure stop sign that was illegible to a speeding motorist. I was seated in the front passenger seat, next to Jamada, the driver, while my colleagues, Messrs Anand Srivastava, and Padhmanbhai, both UNESCO experts in education statistics, occupied the back seat.

Not anticipating any vehicles in such a remote station, Jamada had driven a few meters past the sign, when from the side window, I saw two soldiers waving us to stop. I immediately urged Jamada to stop, as the soldiers approached us. With their machine guns cocked at the ready, the duo ordered all of us out of the car, demanded to see our "bitambulisho", or ID's, then ordered us to seat on the ground. As we sat down, the two soldiers continued bombarding us with the same questions, over and over again, despite Jamada and I, having thoroughly briefed them on the nature of our mission. Within a few minutes, they were joined by maybe, six of their colleagues, who had been taking refuge from the afternoon sun, under a tree, just a hundred feet or so, from the junction. Meanwhile, the two Indian experts were really quaking in their pants, cognizant of the fate that had befallen the Indian community earlier in the decade. Jamada and I could overhear the thugs debating in Swahili amongst themselves, whether or not to shoot us all.

Finally, after about three hours of painstaking negotiations with the soldiers, a little sense prevailed, after being convinced that we were, after all, harmless civil servants. They only asked us for money to buy cigarettes, for which we were more than happy to oblige.

Arriving at the Mountains of the Moon hotel about two hours later, a little shaken, we took up our rooms, freshened up a bit, and, after a little rest, proceeded to Bundibujo to visit the hot springs. The road to Bundibujo traverses a section of the Rwenzori Mountains that is prone to landslides. While we were at the hot springs, some downpours washed away a section of the only earth road that links it with Fort Portal. It took a lot of expert maneuvering by Jamada, to navigate through part of the debris, to steer the Land cruiser back on solid ground. By the time we got back to the hotel, the police had been mobilized for a search-and-rescue mission, which happily, never had to be implemented.

President Amin became increasingly belligerent after his humiliation by the Israeli rescue. He began to distrust everyone around him, including those in his inner circle. Since he could not reach the Israeli perpetrators, his anger turned inward against those he suspected of collaborating with the enemy, whose definition was hard to nail down. The country was already engulfed in a general malaise, with the social and moral fabric slowly, but surely, getting eroded. Kampala became a ghost city by night, as fear of the unknown manifested itself in any resident who dared to walk the streets. As in Dracula's world, the vampire could appear and strike from anywhere. It didn't matter that you kept a low profile, if you had a nice house, or a beautiful wife, or a car that some soldier coveted, any of these could get you in trouble.

As the shortages of goods and services got more acute, people got compromised for survival's sake. In one macabre incident, a female student from Africa Hall at Makerere University, who had been bugging her soldier boy-friend, for expensive watches and jewelry, was invited for a ride to go and get what she had been asking for. Her boy-friend picked her up, and they headed east on Jinja Road, on what the poor girl thought would be a leisurely afternoon drive. About fifteen kilometers outside Kampala, the man got off the main road, and headed for the depth of Namanve forest. A short distance later, he stopped the car and ordered her out, beckoning her to follow him behind some overgrowth. Upon reaching the site, the girl encountered a freshly killed body of a beautiful young woman like herself, completely bedecked with glittering earrings, and an expensive watch still on her arm. The boy-friend turned to the now shocked girl, and said,

"Here is all that you've been asking from me, take all you want, because this one here won't need them anymore".

Between sobs and protests, the girl asked the boy-friend to take her back to her hall of residence. Needless to say, her taste for the glamorous life changed for good.

Night-time shooting (or popcorn as it was called), became de rigueur, as some drunk and unruly soldiers exploded their guns in amusement, in total disregard of the general population. Other times, this occurred while they were arresting someone in the dead of the night. I heard these shootings quite often, from my duplex on Mawanda Road. My immediate neighbors to the west were an army captain, his wife, and kids. Other military families lived in a storied building to my right. My saving grace was the simple fact that I worked at the headquarters of the Ministry of Education.

"Oyo musomesa", (that's a teacher), I once overheard the captain's Musoga wife describing what her neighbor (me) did, to her guests as they sat in her sprawling compound sipping Uganda waragi and other drinks, and smoking heavily. Nobody considered a mere teacher to pause any threat.

A day or two, or even a week, might pass without a major incident. Then all of a sudden, you see everybody in a hurry, moving in one direction, say, towards Old Kampala. You would be a fool not to join the herd and take refuge in numbers. And, since we had long abandoned the idea of trusting the word of the "military spokesman", whom everybody knew was Amin himself, we would crowd in someone's living room, wherever we ended, and tune on foreign radio stations such as BBC, Voice of America, Radio Tanzania, etc, for them to elaborate on the nature of the local incident that had caused a stampede in the city center the previous day.

One sunny morning on February 17, 1977, I arrived in my office on the 9th Floor of the short tower of the Crested Towers Building. This edifice is one of Kampala's landmark buildings, constructed in the late 1960s. At the time, it housed three government ministries, including education. Most of the education functions, including the offices of the Minister and permanent secretary, were located in the short tower, while the inspectorate division was located in the 22-story tall tower. The building overlooked the grounds of the Nile Hotel and International Conference Center. The complex was built in 1974 by Energo Projekt, a Yugoslav construction firm, in preparation for hosting the Organization of African Unity summit for African heads of state, who congregated in Kampala in 1975. It has since been sold to HRH, The Aga Khan, renovated, and renamed Serena Hotel and Conference Center.

That morning, there was a lot of activity on the sprawling

grounds of Nile Hotel. President Amin had summoned all heads of government ministries, from the rank of permanent secretary and up, religious leaders of all denominations, and other dignitaries, including ambassadors, for a special announcement. In true Amin fashion, the real topic would remain a mystery, until announced by Amin himself. My office which was located on the western side of the building had a commanding view of the grounds. And, since the place had also been fitted with sound systems for the occasion, it was easy for me to discern the words being uttered, especially if I kept my wide window open.

By about nine, the invited guests began to take their seats, the purple colors of the clergy, clearly distinguishing them out from the rest of the crowd. A short time later, Mr. Colin Sentongo, my boss, and head of the Planning and Statistics unit came to my office, and we both stood there, watching the unfolding events from my window. Amin had never disguised his disdain for the Acholi and Langi people of northern Uganda, from whom he had wrested power during his coup against Milton Obote. Unknown to us, that day, there were two prominent sons of Acholiland whose fate would be determined during that meeting at Nile Gardens. The first was Archbishop Janaan Luwum, the head of the Anglican Church of Uganda. The other was Mr. Y. Y. Okot, the Chief Inspector of Schools in the Ministry of Education. Both men commanded a lot of respect, not only among their fellow Acholi, but also throughout the entire country. Amin had lately put them under the radar screen, accusing them of being disloyal, and carrying on acts of sabotage against his regime. As Colin and I stood by my window, digesting the events, Mr. Okot emerged from the Crested Towers complex, walking alone, climbing the stairs near the Kasisira Restaurant, to cross the road at the roundabout and head straight to the Nile Gardens. Colin turned to me, and mumbled these words,

"This man is crazy. He shouldn't be going to face Amin at that gathering". We both followed him almost step-by-step, until he arrived at his destination and got swallowed up in the crowd. As it turned out, Colin and I might have been the last people from the Ministry to have set our eyes on him. Meanwhile, at Nile Gardens, we could hear President Amin, booming his baritone voice in the microphone, asking about two other men, whose lives would end that same day.

"Wapi Oboth Ofumbi, wapi Erenayo Oryema?" we heard Amin's voice inquiring. Mr. Oboth Ofumbi was Amin's Minister of Internal Affairs (Interior Secretary), while Mr. Erenayo Oryema was the Inspector General of Police. They were, also apparently under suspicion of being disloyal to the regime.

As Colin went back to his office, I closed my window to block the deafening noise that came from Nile Gardens, and I went about doing my job, occasionally glancing at the colorful crowd. By early afternoon, we broke off for lunch while the gathering was still there. When I returned in the afternoon, the grounds were clear, and by all accounts, things appeared to be normal. But in Amin's world, appearances could be deceiving as we were to learn the following day. That evening on Radio Uganda, a military spokesman announced the arrest of Archbishop Luwum, Y. Y. Okot, Oboth Ofumbi, and Erenayo Oryema, on charges of sabotage detrimental to the functioning of the Military Government of Uganda.

Early on Wednesday, the following day, Kampala, and, the world at large, woke up only to be shocked by pictures of mangled bodies of Archbishop Luwum, Oboth Ofumbi, and Oryema, in the daily newspaper, the Uganda Times, against a background of an equally quixotic auto accident, amateurishly-staged in a Toyota Celica saloon car. The bizarre explanation regarding their death was that they tried to overpower the driver as they were being driven to the notorious Makindye Barracks Prison. All conventional wisdom however, pointed at the three men having been badly tortured, riddled with bullets, and finally dumped in a car that was deliberately run over by a heavy truck to create a make-believe car accident, Hollywood style. Mr. Okot's fate was less clear, although no less tragic. He disappeared without a trace, and his body, like a number of Amin's other victims, was fed to the ever-hungry Nile crocs. The world protested these gruesome murders by further isolating Idi Amin's regime. New economic sanctions were slapped on the regime, while earlier ones were tightened. Nevertheless, despite the protests, Amin held on to power for another two years, indirectly aided by mostly Islamic regimes in the middle-east. After all, despotic regimes were considered the norm in Africa.

By 1977, it was apparently clear, that the loose economic union, known as the East African Community, that bound Uganda, Kenya and Tanzania together, could no longer survive under the animosity and verbosity, flying like missiles, especially between President Amin, and his Tanzanian counterpart, Mwalimu Julius Nyerere. The ten-year institution that was once hailed as a model for developing nations, came tumbling down, leading to a great loss of employment opportunities for many people across the region. Each of the partner countries retained the portion of the common assets that were located in its territory at the time of the breakup. Nairobi, which housed the headquarters of both East African Railways and East African Airways, inherited the most valuable assets. Arusha, the once lively headquarters of the East African Community went into doldrums for more than two decades, until the concept of the community was revived again in the late 1990s. Uganda retained the headquarters of the East African Development Bank (EADB), the only one of the original community institutions that was never dissolved, and still functions.

Seventeen

DR. ASH HARTWELL, a US citizen from the Aloha state of Hawaii, who headed the UNESCO office in Uganda, had been searching for a suitable institution to send my colleague Peter Okongo, and I, for further training in educational statistics. By June of 1977, he had secured both of us scholarships, albeit, from different places. Peter was to proceed to the International Education Institute in Paris, France, while I would travel to the United States of America, to spend about a year at the International Statistical Programs Center of the US Bureau of the Census, located in Suitland, in the state of Maryland. Both of us had been recruited to the Ministry of Education's Planning and Statistical unit as local counterparts to UNESCO experts, with a view of replacing them sometime in the near future.

Peter and I were excited to have secured the scholarships, which would give us a little breathing room, away from Amin's killing fields. We both planned to be back in the country as soon as our courses came to an end. In late July, we both went on one last upcountry tour, and returned to Kampala to make preparations for our journeys. About one week before leaving, my mother, who had been undergoing treatment in Kampala for minor ailments, insisted that I invite my dad to be present when I left the country. Until then, only my brother, Matia, had ever traveled outside the country for a prolonged period. Although I tried to argue that I would not be gone for long, my mother would have none of it. In the end, she won, and we sent for Mzee to come in time for my departure. It was just as well that her prophetic sense prevailed, for it would take me another seven years before I could set my eyes on them again.

My travel arrangements developed a glitch due to the prevailing circumstances. I could not obtain a US visa, because the US had closed its embassy in the country. The only way to get a visa was to travel to Nairobi, Kenya, but even then, there was no guarantee that I could get one there. Fortunately, my handlers found a solution through the UNESCO office in Paris. I was to proceed to the French capital with temporary travel documents, whereupon arrival, US travel papers would be processed for me. My ticket had been booked on Air France, which was one of a handful of airlines that still maintained flights into Entebbe International Airport, albeit, at reduced frequency. However, on Monday, August 22, 1977, the very day I was supposed to travel, we were told that Air France would not be making its scheduled weekly flight. No plausible explanation was offered for the cancellation, although conventional wisdom pointed at the prevailing trend of western businesses closing in protest against Amin's regime.

The news of the cancellation sent Dr. Srivastava, the UNESCO expatriate into a panic, as we rushed to Kimathi Avenue, home to the airline offices, and moved from one office to another, desperately trying to find an alternative. But as luck would have it, an Aeroflot flight from Johannesburg was making a stopover that day, on its way to Odessa en route to Moscow, via Cairo. A little behind the scenes negotiation conducted by one Uganda Airlines agent yielded us a seat on the Russian carrier, and by mid-afternoon, I was airborne, in a mixture of anticipation, and apprehension at the same time. Anybody who got a chance to get away from the chaos and agony, that were the hallmark of the Idi Amin regime, counted himself among the lucky. At the same time, one could not help feel a sense of apprehension, which comes with the knowledge that while you managed to save your own skin, you left behind all your loved ones, still exposed to the same calamities you run away from.

As we left Ugandan airspace, my eyes focused on the snake-like figurine of the River Nile, the only natural link Uganda has with Sudan and Egypt, the two Giant Arab countries separating us from the Mediterranean Sea. We made a brief stop in the sweltering heat of Khartoum Airport, without disembarking, and after another two hours of flight, I began to see silhouettes of the massive edifices from my window seat which announced to everyone, that we were floating above the land of the pharaohs.

A few passengers, including myself, left the Odessa-bound flight in Cairo, only to find some commotion in the main terminal lounge, as hundreds of stranded passengers scrambled to find booking on alternative flights. There was a trans-Atlantic pilot strike which was affecting virtually all flights going to Europe and the Americas. Although I was able to get booked on an Air France flight to Paris, I, and the other passengers on the same flight were told to wait for further announcements regarding the departure. To give us a little more comfort from the summer heat, we were booked in an airport hotel within walking distance of the terminal building, from where we could watch the activities, and even listen to some announcements. Unfortunately, the hotel was only equipped with window cooling units which were inadequate for dealing with the excessive desert heat of Cairo airport. Used to Uganda's fairly mild temperatures, and this being my first time to experience the intensity of the northern summer heat, I found myself wondering if I would survive these weather extremes.

About twelve hours later, things eased a little, and we got on our flight to Charles de Gaulle, where I was met by an official from UNESCO. He drove me to a small hotel called Tourisme Hotel, located at 66 Avenue de la Motte-Picquet, within easy access of Paris landmarks such as the Eiffel Tower, the Champs-de-Mars, and easily connected by metro, to main places of interest, such as Champs-Elysees, the grand cathedral of Notre Dame, etc. He showed me where to go for inexpensive cafeteria-style meals, and afterwards, left me to walk around by myself to get a better feel of my new environment. I spent the next week absorbing the goings-on of la ville de lumiere in the summer, when love birds promenade the streets, hand-in-hand, searching the numerous cafes for the latest in Parisien cuisine. One Ugandan family leaving in Paris, hosted me one evening for a delicious meal, after which they took me on a ride to see Paris by night, ending the evening at a theater near the Arc de Triomphe, where we watched John Wayne's last movie, "The Shootist".

On August 31, 1977, after spending a week in Paris, I boarded TWA 867 at Charles de Gaulle, headed for Washington DC. The little time I had spent in Paris had further raised my expectations about life in America, since the general belief, whether real, or contrived, was that the American way of life was above everyone else's. My sponsors had given me about US$400 of spending money for the trip, but that was before the unanticipated delay in Paris. To someone who was earning perhaps no more than $150 a month during Amin's inflationary spiral, this had appeared like a windfall. At Entebbe Airport, my brothers and a few other relatives and friends who had come to see me off, had helped themselves to some of my nicest shirts and shoes, which I used to purchase in Nairobi, arguing that carrying them with me, was equivalent to "taking sand to the Sahara". I had acquiesced, only to learn, to my chagrin, when I got to Paris, that my so-called generous allowance would not stretch that far on Ave Victor Hugo. By the time I got to Dulles International Airport in the northern Virginia suburb of Washington D.C, I probably was left with a princely sum of around $200. Luckily for me, the UNESCO people in Paris had arranged for my pickup from the airport, so I still held tight onto my little treasure by the time I checked into the Presidential Hotel on Eye Street in Washington D.C.

My friend, Frederick Kalema-Musoke, who was slated to

attend the same program with me, had arrived a few days earlier, and had also been accommodated in the same hotel. The hotel itself was a non-decrepit, run-of-the-mill rooming building, used by US government agencies to accommodate students, and other non-diplomatic visitors to Washington officialdom. We were to stay there for a little while, as we settled down and searched for an apartment. The Washington D.C I arrived in at the time was quite a disappointment from my hyped concept of America. Most of the buildings were run down, some left over from the riots of the late 1960's that followed the assassination of Dr. Martin Luther King Jr. I had walked on Nairobi streets such as Government Road and Kenyatta Avenue, and lately, the glittering boulevards of Paris, and was expecting more from the US capital city. Yet, there they were, dilapidated buildings on 14th, Euclid, and U streets, and even some along Pennsylvania Avenue, just a stone throw from the White House, that citadel of American presidents.

That evening, after settling down in my room, I decided to take an exploratory walk around the city. I stopped at Du Pont circle, a sprawling open place in the heart of the city, where travelers and residents rub shoulders. My first shock was how many people were aggressively accosting strangers for "spare change". In Uganda, the beggars sat in strategic locations such as near places of worship, or near the entrance of a major market, and simply extended their hand for the generous ones to drop something. As I stood there, watching crowds move in beehive fashion, something unusual caught my eye. A few feet away, a scuffle broke out between two young men, one white, and the other black. I couldn't tell what it was all about, except that, within a split second, the black man had thrown his adversary to the ground, and was punching him really hard. The crowd stood there watching, but making no real attempt to separate them. It took the intervention of two policemen, to pull them apart, and drive away with them in their patrol vehicle. I had watched a few movies about violence in America, but this was Hollywood in real time. The incident sent some shock waves through my spine, as it bust the whole myth about the tranquil life in America.

Later, as I got settled in the system, I would witness more of such incidents in different environments. However, by then, I had rationalized that no system, however advanced, is immune to the usual fracas that come with every genre of humanity competing for dominance in their space. Over the years, I came to realize, that pockets of violence, especially in neglected inner-city neighborhoods notwithstanding, America, is, by and large, a safe place to live, compared to a lot of countries worldwide. If one is law-abiding, he or she will get by, and adjust to the occasional nuances of life, which happen from time to time. That sort of freedom is by no means always guaranteed in many places around the world.

Fred and I took up an apartment in Marlo Heights, a Maryland suburb of Washington D.C, where we stayed for four months, to be close to the International Statistical Program Center, and the US Bureau of the Census, which is located in Suitland, Maryland. The original course was meant to last one academic year. However, through a special arrangement struck with The George Washington University, more graduate courses were to be taken at the university, extending the program to eighteen months, for a Masters degree. At ISPC, we had a wonderful time, as the program was a mini United Nations of a sort, drawing students from as far afield as Indonesia, India and Bangladesh in the orient, to Venezuela, Nicaragua, Antigua, and Barbados in the Americas, not forgetting various African and the middle-eastern countries. Since everyone on the program was sponsored, either by their government, or one UN agency or another, flexibility was built in, allowing the students to travel to various cities in the US for pre-arranged seminars or conferences.

This new arrangement with The George Washington University brought with it, an unwanted problem. My UNESCO sponsors had only agreed to finance me for a stipulated period of one academic year, typically, September to May. But now, I was extending it by an additional six months which was not funded. My inner voice kept telling me to take the risk, so I did, much to the displeasure of my sponsors, but even more so, to my bosses in Kampala, who had expected I'd be back within a year. I have a nephew, Xavier Mugisha, who was, at the time, pursuing his Ph D at the University of Manitoba. We grew up together, went to the same high school at Butobere, and I always respected his wise counsel. So as my UNESCO sponsorship was coming to a close, I flew to Winnipeg for a tete-a-tete with him. We both concurred that it was best that I stay and complete my Masters degree. With a new resolve, I returned to Washington D.C, and followed up on my determination, occasionally having a run-in with a guy called Harvey Schneider in the Students accounts office, for falling behind on my payments.

Then, in December 1978, just as my course was drawing to an end, news broke out, that President Amin, in his quest for expansion, and self-aggrandizement, had sent a contingent of his military to the Uganda-Tanzanian border, who invaded and occupied a strip of land known as the Kagera Salient. This is where the River Kagera, one of the major tributaries that flow into Lake Victoria, forms a natural geographical border between the two countries. For Tanzania, this was the straw that broke the camel's back. Mwalimu Julius Nyerere of Tanzania, who had no love lost for the mercurial Ugandan despot, seized the opportunity to make a swift decision to smoke out the "snake in the grass". Within a matter of days, the Tanzanian leader mobilized the national army, the Tanzanian People's Defense Forces (TPDF), and put them on the offensive to flush out the invaders, and regain their territory. At the same time, this availed the Ugandan exiles, mainly based in Tanzania, to join their brethren in liberating the country from the claws of a megalomaniac dictator.

So, we held our breath and watched day in, and day out, as the war drums were sounded on both sides of the border. News still traveled the old-fashioned way, via newswire clips from the world-wide established agencies like Reuters, Associated Press, and AFP. There was no CNN, internet, or You-Tube to transmit the news instantaneously. The U.S television networks in existence at the time, ABC, CBS and NBC, hardly covered any news items about Africa, unless there was some catastrophe somewhere. One could follow up on news stories in a library, but oftentimes, these would be a few days old.

My adrenaline rose with everyday that the war continued unabated. With funds running precariously low, my immigration status heading into the gray zone at the end of the course, my options were fast running out. I went to Indiana Ave in downtown Washington DC, where the Immigration and Naturalization office was located, and filed for a work permit. Things weren't as heady as they are today, in the post September 11th environment. Back then, if you had a genuine reason like I had, especially, running away from dictatorships, the officials gave you a sympathetic hearing. I easily secured a work permit, and thrust myself into the Washington metro's job market.

I got my first job at a company called Applied Management Sciences, one of those referred to as "Beltway bandits", a multitude of firms dotted around the Washington D.C metro ring-road, taking advantage of the abundant federal funds from Capitol Hill. The company was located on Georgia Avenue in the heart of Silver Spring, Maryland. Among other things, the firm specialized in analyzing data on healthcare issues. So, one of my tasks at the time, was to spend a couple of hours at the National Institute of Health (N.I.H), in Bethesda, Maryland, researching and compiling data about Health Maintenance Organizations (HMOs). In the pre-internet days, this was growling work, requiring a lot of patience and agility, peering through volumes of files in order to extract any meaningful and consistent data.

The same week I started on my job in April 1979, things began to tighten around Amin in Kampala. The Tanzanian army, the

TPDF, in a joint collaboration with Ugandan exiles, had mounted a whirlwind putsch that put Idi Amin on the run. Around the world, Ugandans in the diaspora, were expressing their solidarity with their compatriots at home, by taking over diplomatic missions abroad. Washington was no exception, in fact, it was in the lead. There was, at the time, a small, but symbolically important Ugandan community. The few families that resided here were associated with such powerful organizations as the World Bank, IMF, and Intelsat. Men like Zerubaberi Bigirwenkya, (R.I.P), Frank Mwine, George Alibaruho, Pascal Mukasa, (R.I.P), James Ogoola, Dr. Ruhakana Rugunda, Ezra Suruma, and Joseph Kakooza, were part of the Washington scene.

A number of us lived in the Alexandria/Annandale area of Virginia, a suburb of Washington D.C. At the time, I shared an apartment off, Duke Street, with Nassani Tandekwire, a young brother of Dr. Frank Mwine. As bachelors, our apartment was a popular gathering place, where connoisseurs could sit and relax over a Budweiser beer, or a bottle of wine, while pouring their hearts out on a range of issues. And, because the Ugandan community was still so small, the place gave us an excuse to throw parties at very short notice.

On the day Amin was chased out of Kampala, Dr. Rugunda, led the Ugandans in the Washington area to the Embassy building, a rather non-decrepit two-story structure, located on 16th Street, in upper northwest Washington DC, near the famed Walter Reed Military Hospital. There, in front of flushing cameras, and D.C police, who were there to protect embassy property and personnel, Rugunda and his group, demanded that, Mr. Musa, a semi-illiterate man of Amin's Kakwa ethinic group, who had been the acting Charge d'Affairs, hand over the keys of the facility "back to the people". The day ended with the Chancery building being locked up for some time as the country sailed through the political murky waters while fishing for a new leader.

No sooner had Amin fallen than the political shenanigans

started their games again. There was a brief lull, from April, when Amin was chased away, till the beginning of 1980, before the vultures were at each other's throats once again. In the Tanzanian town of Arusha, best known as the headquarters of the East African Community, competing factions under the umbrella of the Uganda National Liberation Assembly (UNLA), went through a tumultuous conference aimed at resolving the leadership conundrum facing Uganda. Every faction leader, military or civilian, wanted to play the leadership role. Mwalimu Nyerere's preference was for his friend, exiled former President Obote, to be re-instated, something that didn't sit well with all groups. After a few nights of haggling, and behind-the-scenes deal-making, a compromise was reached. The man chosen was Yusuf Lule, an academic, and previously, the Vice Chancellor of Makerere University, who had been in self-imposed exile in London. Nevertheless, this choice neither diminished the hunger for power among the protagonists, nor did it eliminate the behind-the-scenes maneuvering to undermine the newly anointed authorities.

Milton Obote, as the last duly elected president of Uganda, felt strongly that he had a legitimate reason to reclaim his throne. However, with nearly nine years of exile under his belt, some new kids on the block, particularly the Fronasa group, led by Yoweri Museveni, considered this claim as rather outdated. To these young Turks, Obote's long absence had changed the political dynamics in the country so much, that the leadership was up for grabs. Moreover, opposition to Amin's military dictatorship had created some quasi-military factions, with a mindset that believed, only the military can uproot the military. Unfortunately, this attitude has taken on a rather permanent discourse that has dogged the country up to today, making it difficult for a non-military leader to emerge and assume effective leadership. This would manifest itself in the coups and counter-coups which followed Amin's overthrow.

Eighteen

PRESIDENT LULE'S TRANSITIONAL government was a very brief one, lasting a mere sixty-six days, from April 13, to June 20, 1979. Many reasons are given for his downfall, the most prominent of which was his lack of deference to his military king-makers, such as Major-General Oyite Ojok. But his fate was sealed by Lule himself. As a conservative Muganda, who seemed to harbor sentiments of the primacy of Buganda over other regions of the country, he started on the wrong note, when he gave his inaugural address, primarily in Luganda, including the use of the expression "Kyetwasubizanga embazzi, kibuyaga assudde", literally translated as, "what we expected to earn through protracted struggle, we've achieved for free". Many Baganda royalists saw his ascendance to power as Buganda's opportunity to avenge itself on its detractors, mainly Obote and his followers, whose regime had desecrated the Buganda kingdom, the once shining city on the hill, humiliating the Kabaka, who later died in abject poverty in London.

Lule's failure to recognize that by focusing on the narrow aspirations of Buganda, rather than the wider problems of a desperate nation that was in search of a "Moses", to deliver it out of the jaws of a dictator, did not ingratiate him to the general population beyond Buganda. From this perspective, therefore, many non-Baganda did not shed a tear, nor did they participate in the "No

Lule no work" campaigns that were staged by Baganda, following his removal, shortly after assuming office.

Professor Lule was replaced by a fellow Muganda, Godfrey Lukongwa Binaisa, in what could be seen as an attempt towards appeasing Buganda. Mr. Binaisa, a London-trained barrister, was once President Obote's Attorney General following Uganda's independence in 1962. However, his reputation among the Baganda, had been tarnished by the role he had played in authoring the so-called pigeon-hole constitution of 1967, which abolished monarchies in Uganda, including that of Buganda, the most powerful and influential. His appointment, therefore, was suspiciously viewed by some monarchists at Mengo, as "warming the seat" for his erstwhile boss, Obote, whom they had come to hate with a passion. Mr. Binaisa, a man with a sharp mind, and an effervescent character, did all he could to calm the waters in a tempestuous storm, using a combination of humor and wit, as when he told an audience soon after taking office, to "Be-nicer" to him, a phonetic version of his name.

Mr. Binaisa tapped two people in the Washington community to serve in his government. Dr. Ruhakana-Rugunda, who was undertaking his residency as a pediatrician at Washington D.C General Hospital, went to serve as a personal physician to the new president, while Mr. Gideon Nkojo, left his World Bank economist position to serve as the Governor of Bank of Uganda. But Uganda had gone through such tremendous shock and awe under Amin, that it would take more than doctors and economists to fix it. The headstrong militaristic characters such as Major-Gen Oyite Ojok, and Yoweri Museveni, who pursued competing, but divergent agendas, could not be accommodated under one roof without blowing it off. Sensing the potential for undermining him, President Binaisa tried to take preventive measures, first by moving Mr. Museveni from his position of deputy Defense Minister to Minister of Regional Cooperation, while Oyite Ojok was appointed as Uganda's Ambassador to Egypt.

The two protagonists felt that the president, who had fled to New York after Obote's ouster, and had devoted very little time to freedom fighting, was giving them a raw deal by his actions. They both refused to budge, and, using their influence in the military, they engineered an internal coup which resulted in the removal of Binaisa from the seat he had once described as "Entebbe ewooma", or literally, the chair is tantalizingly tempting. His administration had lasted a mere eleven months.

I, like a host of other Ugandans who had been scattered outside the country during the Amin regime began to develop some cold feet about returning, after watching two successive regimes fall within less than two years. Reports coming out of the country told of a chaotic situation, where people disappeared under unexplained circumstances, and properties were destroyed, sometimes, in what appeared to be acts of vengeance. It was no place for someone to plunge himself again, especially, if one had already had a chance to escape it. It was time to look for a more permanent job that paid a living wage. I undertook a serious search, until I got a chance to interview for positions in the Research Department at the World Bank, where I secured a job in November 1980.

By that time, Uganda was being ruled by a military commission headed by Paul Muwanga, who made no secret of the fact that he was warming the seat for Milton Obote. During his tenure, one of the most contentious elections in the history of the young nation was organized. There were four contending parties, namely, Uganda Peoples' Congress (UPC), headed by exiled former president Obote, the Democratic Party (DP), led by Paul Ssemogerere, the Uganda Patriotic Movement (UPM), of Yoweri Museveni, and the Conservative Party (CP), under the stewardship of Joash Mayanja-Nkangi. Both DP and UPC were the nation's oldest and well established parties. However, UPC had lost credibility in Buganda, following the skirmishes of 1966 which resulted in the exile of Kabaka Sir Edward Muteesa II, and subsequent abolition of the kingdoms. By effectively being locked out of Buganda, which was the nation's largest voting block, UPC's chances of winning in a fair and competitive race were slim.

But Paul Muwanga had his own idea of a level playing field. By the time the Commonwealth Observer Team left Kampala, it was apparent to everybody, that DP had won the polls. And that's when Muwanga, then Chairman of the military commission, swung into action, and hijacked the entire process, telling the nation that, he and only he alone, would announce the results of the election. By the time the results were presented to an anxious nation about two days later, all the figures had been tampered with in favor of UPC, and Muwanga stunned the nation by inviting his former boss, Milton Obote, to come back from exile in Tanzania, and take the helm of the affairs of state.

From the outset, there was serious objection to Obote taking back power under those cloudy circumstances. DP, the presumed loser, and most aggrieved, took to the courts, with no clear resolution. The most vocal of all parties, turned out to be the latest one on the block, UPM, under firebrand Yoweri Museveni, who vowed to stop Obote from taking office, militarily, if need be. By January 1981, Museveni, along with a small group of twenty six like-minded hotheads, launched a guerrilla movement in the Luwero Triangle of Buganda, which would turn out to be an expensive protracted war lasting five years, and costing the nation hundreds of thousands of mostly innocent lives and property. With the war in full gear, I could not even contemplate going back home until it was over. I started on my job in the research department of the World Bank on November 3, 1980, immersing myself in economic and data issues that the bank is famous for.

Once the guerilla war started in the Luwero triangle, Kampala became extremely dangerous, as any facility in town became a prime target of sabotage. Bombs could be hulled at innocent crowds of people, buildings, or taxis at a moment's notice. The government of the day first gave the impression that it was fully in control, but the more they claimed that, the more determined the other side was to discredit them. During the Amin regime, whenever someone was abducted and murdered, there was one side to lay blame on. But with the raging war, people started disappearing the same way as before, except this time, no one was ready to take responsibility, instead, the two antagonists took turns blaming each other, leaving the general public thoroughly confused as to who was behind this saga.

Meantime, those of us that were caught outside couldn't go in. In the summer of 1982, a number of us at the World Bank and IMF flocked to Nairobi for home leave. These institutions had devised a means to accommodate those members of staff who, for one reason or another, could not directly go home to their countries of birth, to go to the nearest country, where they could be visited by family members. There were plenty of countries that fitted that category then. Some, like Uganda, Nicaragua, and Afghanistan, had raging wars going on, while others like Poland and other Soviet Satelites, though not under war, were under the strict grip of totalitarian regimes that denied their citizens free entry and exit. I clearly remember the day, while on that vacation in Nairobi, when I called my family, gathered at my brother Matia's home in Kampala. I had been away from the country for five years, and I was getting homesick. I took turns to talk to each one individually, exchanging some warm greetings and wishes. When the phone was finally handed to Mzee, after extending his good wishes, he told me in a firm voice, not to attempt "coming home", and to stay where I was for as long as the situation was volatile. It was a hard situation to swallow, but so grave was the situation in the country, that it would have been suicidal to go against my father's counsel.

Later that afternoon still embroiled in the thought of being so close to home, yet unable to actually go there, I urged Lawrence, a nephew of mine who lived in Nairobi, and worked for Kenya Airways, to take a drive with me. We drove around for a while, till we found ourselves on Gilgil Road, the same road that goes to Kampala. Upon reaching Gilgil town, we stopped for a soda, and then headed back to Nairobi after about an hour. Those days, one met a lot of Ugandans in Nairobi. Some had been living there since running away from the Amin regime, and others were more recent arrivals. Dr. Rugunda, who worked at Kenyatta General Hospital at the time, played host to numerous people, who would later constitute the leadership of the National Resistance Movement in Uganda. At least, all these groups appeared to agree on one thing, getting rid of the Obote regime in Kampala. Beyond that, each group seemed to have its own agenda. I returned to Washington, and resumed my job. I would not make another attempt at entering Uganda for another two years.

In 1983, something happened, which made the Obote regime's demise, all but certain. Major-Gen David Oyite Ojok, who was President Milton Obote's dyed-in-the-wool loyalist and chief military strategist, was killed in December when the army helicopter he had traveled in to the war front in Luwero, exploded in mid-air immediately after takeoff. The circumstances of this accident have remained a matter of speculation, although sabotage could not be ruled out. Never considered a good and strategic commander-in-chief, Obote scrambled to replace his fallen protégé, and, against some expert advice, he by-passed, more experienced Acholi officers such as Lt-Gen Bazilio Olara Okello, to appoint a relatively young officer, a fellow ethnic Langi called Brigadier Smith Opon-Acak as Chief of staff of the army. The ethnic in-fighting that followed Brigadier Acak's appointment tore away at the internal cohesion of the UNLA, and laid the grounds for the Acholi-led coup in July 1985, that dethroned Milton Obote from the presidency for the second and last time.

Since nothing had changed in Uganda, as far as security was concerned, I had planned to go back to Nairobi, only this time I had planned to bring my parents to see me there. I took a flight to Paris and checked into a hotel, expecting to board a

Nairobi-bound flight the following day. Then as I relaxed in the hotel, watching the news on TV, the first headline said that there had been an attempted coup against President Daniel Arap Moi of Kenya, and that all flights into Jomo Kenyatta International Airport had been suspended indefinitely. I was determined to take my vacation outside Washington DC, but where could I go at such a short notice? My nephew, Xavier Mugisha, had been teaching at the University of Botswana for about a year since leaving Winnipeg, Manitoba, where we had last met a few years earlier. Among my advantages at the time was that I carried a Laissez-Passer, the quintessential United Nations passport issued to the staff of the UN and its affiliated agencies. I knew that I could easily get an entry visa in Botswana with the document. I contacted Xavier from my hotel, and he seemed happy to have my company, especially that he was alone, since his wife was still completing her course in Canada. The following morning, I went to the Swissair office in Paris and changed my destination to Gaborone, via Johannesburg, instead of Nairobi.

Botswana, a country of less than one million citizens at the time, has remained steadfast in its approach towards development. It remains one of the few countries in Africa, if not the world, that has not been tainted by rampant corruption. The discovery of ample deposits of diamonds which catapulted the semi-arid Southern African country to the top position of producers of this precious metal had not been accompanied by the usual myth of a resource curse which has afflicted many other countries in similar situations. While countries like Nigeria, Angola, Gabon, and Sierra Leone, for instance, wasted the revenues received from exporting oil and diamonds through the porous hands of the leadership at the top, through Debtswana, the mining conglomerate set up jointly by De Beers of South Africa, and the government of Botswana, the country used its receipts to develop good infrastructure, and human resources, both a pre-requisite for attracting foreign investors into the country. As a result, the country scores near the top of development Indices, be it the UN's Human Development Index (HDI), or the more recent Mo Ibrahim Index, specific to African countries. The only major setback has been the high prevalence of HIV in the country. But even that has been handled very well, due to the country's ability to afford medical facilities such as anti-retroviral drugs that prolong the lives of those already inflicted with the virus.

Nineteen

IN DECEMBER 1984, I resolved to visit Uganda after an absence of seven years. I had not seen anybody from my family for all those years, except for an occasional phone call. These too, were infrequent due to the breakdown caused partly by poor maintenance, but also by military sabotage from the guerillas. Although the situation on the ground was not getting any better, it was clear that the pendulum was beginning to swing in the direction of the rebel movement. The protracted war had taken its toll on the whole country, limiting the movement of people and goods to just a few hours of daylight. In the Luwero triangle, the center of axis for the war effort, civilian life had been disrupted so much, that most residents had been reduced to a life-style akin to a mouse that only scavenges for food at night, and hides in its hole during daytime.

Hoards of military men from UNLA, the national army, regularly visited and combed villages in search of insurgents, committing many atrocities along the way. Families suspected of giving sanctuary to any member of the NRA, were singled out, the head of the family tortured and sometimes killed on the spot, simply to instill fear among the off-springs, and discourage them from following in their father's footsteps. But this act of retribution was not limited to the national army. The NRA itself exacted severe punishment on those villagers who for one reason or another, cooperated with the enemy. Lately, stories have surfaced that seem to implicate the NRA in some of the most gruesome disappearances and killings in the area, where NRA soldiers donned uniforms stripped from fallen UNLA fighters, and went ahead to terrorize citizens with the sole purpose of tarnishing the name, and discrediting the government of the day. Although the NRM government continues to deny this, the fact that the leaders seem to be scared of a commission of inquiry into the 5-year guerilla war, as recently suggested by Mr. Olara Otunnu, one of the presidential aspirants, suggests that there are a few skeletons in their closets which they would like to keep undisturbed.

I had arrived in the country without fanfare, quite aware of the risks that were present under the prevailing circumstances. Kampala itself appeared calm, but then again, that's the nature of guerilla warfare. Sometimes things will appear normal for a relatively long time while the insurgents are scouting for an opportunity. When that chance finally comes along, things can quickly take a dramatic turn for the worse. I had slipped into the country via Nairobi, because there were no major airlines flying into Entebbe International Airport at the time. I proceeded immediately to my home town of Rukungiri, where a party was organized at my parents' home in my honor. At the time, no parent in his or her right mind could admit that their child had joined the rebels. My cousin, Francis Kasura, a member of Parliament representing Rujumbura County, used my presence to explain the disappearance of his son Daudi, who had joined the rebel movement. Sitting in a bar in Rukungiri town one day, he introduced me to Mr. Kezekia Biryabarema, one of the staunch supporters of the ruling UPC government in the area, as "the man who looks after his son in America". Later, I was to learn, that Alfonse Kikoro, my nephew, who had also disappeared mysteriously in the early 1980's, had been among the NRM's early recruits. His nom de guerre of Lt Nyakagyeme, referred to our sub-county bearing the same name.

During the party at my parents' home, I encountered what I believe was my first case of an AIDS-inflicted victim. While moving among the crowds outside, I heard what I thought was a familiar voice of someone calling me. I turned around to face what at first looked like a skeleton moving on stilts. First, I hesitated, unsure whether this figure was a real man or a ghost. Then, Manuel extended his bonny hand, and called my name again. The face was unmistakable. We had attended primary school together, but he had branched off early after the eighth grade, to go to Ibanda Teachers College, where he qualified as a primary school teacher. He had been posted at a school near Rubindi, in Kashari County, where he met and married a woman that turned out not to be very compatible. In the ensuing fights between the two, one of them had a one-night stand with an infected person. The wife died first, leaving a sickly Manuel to care for three young children without much help or money. Manuel himself passed away in 1985, a year after I saw him.

I spent about three days in the village, reconnecting with my parents and other relatives who couldn't seem to get enough of me. Then, on the day we were to return to the city, we filled the trunk of Matia's Toyota Corolla with bunches of matoke (green bananas, chickens, etc), and then, six of us packed ourselves in the compact sedan, and headed for Kampala with my brother Marcel on the wheel. Those days, almost all motorists traveled during the day in order to avoid any possible deadly encounters with soldiers or their imposters at roadblocks. We whizzed through Mbarara and Masaka towns quickly, except for brief stops at gas stations for fuel. Ordinarily, these two major towns along the way would have been rest stops for a relaxed lunch or cold drink before proceeding to Kampala.

Matia was particularly adamant about our driving to the city almost non-stop. This contrasted sharply with Marcel's approach of easy-going style. Around one-thirty in the afternoon, as we approached Nsimbe agricultural estate, Matia's son Steven, then about ten years old, fidgeted about in his seat, indicating that he wanted to answer nature's call. Marcel pulled on the side and stopped the vehicle, much against Matia's protests. We all jumped out of the car and took advantage of the opportunity. But, as we were returning to the car, we heard what was probably the sound of a breaking twig, and we all stared in that direction, only to reveal a group of about five soldiers heading in our direction. With lightening speed, we dived into the car, and took off with a screech of the tires. This particular area with its dense vegetation, had gained the notoriety of being a "no-stop" zone. About half an hour later, we were back in Kampala, our hearts in our mouths, but glad to be safely home all the same.

I had planned to remain in Kampala for another week, but things took a dramatic twist that Sunday night we got back into Kampala. The Obote regime, in a move to boost morale within the military, and also re-assure the nation that they were still fully in charge, used a helicopter to drop some propaganda leaflets all over the city, announcing that the guerillas had been totally vanquished, and were on the run. Many people did not believe the government's version, and true to form, by Monday morning, it was reported that the Insurgents had invaded the military base at Kabamba, taking with them a large cache of ammunition and other military materiel. People panicked, fearing that the city would be engulfed in gunfire, reminiscent of the Amin overthrow period of five years earlier. Fearing that I might be caught in crossfire, and fail to get an outward flight, I rushed to Airlines House on Kimathi Ave, and managed to convince the British Airways agent to change my travel date to that evening. I made whatever hasty arrangements I could, and in the afternoon, I got on Kenya Airways at Entebbe, to connect with my BA flight in Nairobi to return to Washington, via London.

At the World Bank, I began getting restless after five years. The environment there was very competitive, often favoring people who had emerged from Ivy League institutions such as Harvard, M.I.T, Stanford, or London School of Economics. A young African man with training from commoners' colleges like

George Washington University, or Makerere, was unlikely to advance very far. But I was clearly caught between a rock and a hard place in as far as alternatives were concerned. Leaving the Bank would thrust me in a precarious immigration status that would demand that I return to my native country, where war was raging. None of these options were acceptable to me. Instead, I toiled with the idea of going back to school for an MBA. That option too, proved untenable at the time. I would have had to either obtain funding from the Bank, or resign my position altogether.

In June of that year, I had married my wife Christine, and we were already expecting a baby towards the end of the year. At the time of the wedding, Uganda, and in particular, Kampala, was a total war zone. Although I had formally informed, and even invited my parents and brothers to the wedding, I knew none would come, given those circumstances. In the end, I got Mr. John Kamuhanda and his wife Joyce (R.I.P), to stand in for my parents. The Ugandan Ambassador to the US at the time, H.E John Wycliff Lwamafa and his wife Rosemary (both since deceased), also graced the occasion, as did all my colleagues in the Country Analysis Division of the World Bank.

However, I had only been five years on the job, and now, with a wife, a mortgage to pay, and a baby on the way, I couldn't afford to walk off the job. I approached my Division Chief, Jed Shilling regarding the prospects for Bank sponsorship. Although he was receptive about further training, he was non-committal about the sponsorship. He suggested I talk to the Director, Mr. Jean Baneth, whose attitude proved even colder. The situation became a replay of my earlier school days, when I was stuck in a teaching course that I didn't like. Late in November, my wife gave birth to our son, Tobias. We named him Tobias Ngazoire, after Mzee. Although this gave me a lot of gratification, as my brother-in-law Dan instilled it in me at Fairfax Hospital soon after the birth, I needed to always wear my seat belt, since I no longer was responsible for my life alone, but also that of the toddler I had just brought to this cruel world.

Then, one morning in December, I received a call from Pascal Mukasa. Pascal was Francis Kasura, my cousin's brother-in-law, and culturally, my in-law too. He and his wife Marcela, lived in the Bethesda suburb of Washington DC.

"Francis is dead", he announced, "He was gunned down at Pope Paul VI Center by unknown assailants" he told me as I rubbed some remnants of sleep from my eyes.

The news was devastating to me, Francis had been like a favorite uncle and a big brother rolled in one. At the time I was born, he used to remind me, he was staying at our home commuting the short distance to Kahoko Primary School, where his father, Uncle Francis Xavier Kitarara taught as a vernacular teacher. As kids, my brothers and I used to be amused as we watched the old man make repairs on the tires of his Raleigh bicycle, whose inner tubes had undergone so many patches, that you could hardly trace the original tube. As a result, the tires rolled in a rather irregular fashion, akin to the movement of an earth mover chain. It was my cousin Francis who had wanted me to attend Saint Mary's College Kisubi, his Almer Mater, instead of Butobere. Later, as an employee of Shell Oil Company, stationed in Port Harcourt, Nigeria, he dissuaded me from going to Ife University (now Chief Awolowo University), on an inter-university exchange scheme, instead advising me to go to Makerere University, which he had attended. It was the same Francis, who, a year earlier, had used me as a decoy, to deflect questions from those curious to know where his son Daudi had disappeared to, and telling them he stayed with me in America. I was particularly fond of him, and I felt a tremendous sense of personal loss from his demise. Daudi Kasura is currently a Lieutenant-Colonel in the UPDF, serving as the Director of the Leadership Institute at Kyankwanzi.

By July 1985, President Milton Obote had been overthrown for the second time in his presidency, in a military coup d'etat, staged by senior Acholi officers, led by Brigadier Bazilio Okello. These officers had installed, a semi-illiterate septuagenarian fellow Acholi General, named Okello Lutwa as president. But the NRM guerillas under Yoweri Museveni, who were beginning to smell success, refused to silence their guns, and instead turned them against the new fledgling regime. That December, it became clear that this regime, too, would fall, unless they invited the NRM to join them into some kind of power-sharing coalition. Through the auspices of President Daniel Arap Moi of Kenya, the two antagonists were invited to Nairobi for Peace Talks (later dubbed Peace Jokes by some pundits). An agreement for a power-sharing arrangement was reached, signed and handshakes were made. But while all this was going on, the guerillas were inching closer and closer to Kampala. No sooner had the negotiators returned from Nairobi than the final assault on Kampala began, literally sending the peace agreement up in smoke. Within a month, following the daily barrage of gunfire, Kampala fell to the guerillas. On January 26, 1986, Yoweri Museveni, at 43, wearing his military fatigues, was sworn in as the nation's president at Parliament Buildings.

In his maiden speech, he promised the nation that his regime was no mere change of guards, but rather, one which would usher in a real fundamental change. Among the criticisms he made about African leaders, was their reluctance to leave office when their mandates are long worn out. He also castigated them for indulging themselves and their cronies in luxuries such as private jets and limousines, while their fellow citizens make do with bare feet infested with jiggers, and their children walk around naked, with distended stomachs and jaundice, sure signs of kwashiorkor. For a while, the nation was captivated by this teetotaler, who carried a chalk board wherever he went, and lectured his fellow citizens on the basics of political organization and economic development. He even initially promised to throw away the imported beds and cups in State House, and replace them with the Banco beds and aluminum cups manufactured by the local company Tumpeco.

Twenty

IN 1986, WITH the war practically over, most of us were scrambling to go home, if only to check for ourselves, what was left of that once beautiful country of ours. My wife and I, together with our then one-year old son, got on a British Airways flight that would take us to Nairobi, via London. There were no direct BA flights to Entebbe then. One had to go through Nairobi, and endure the layovers, which sometimes lasted eight hours or longer. The airport had also recently acquired a reputation for relieving transit passengers of their valuables, mostly snatched during the process of transferring luggage between planes. We checked into the Intercontinental Hotel for one night, and coincidentally, Mr. Oliver Tambo, then President of the African National Congress (ANC) happened to be staying in the same hotel. We learned about this first hand when we encountered a swarm of journalists in the hotel lobby, angling to snap a shot of him as he emerged from the hotel. His graceful but slow and deliberate walk was unmistakable.

Although I was taking my wife and son home for the first time, the youthful adventurer in me was still fresh, and I was about to embark on yet one more. Before leaving Washington, I had called my nephew Xavier, who was, at the time, teaching at the University of Umtata in the Province of the Eastern Cape, South Africa, home of the indomitable Nelson Mandela. I said I would stop by, and then we would drive together to Uganda. The political and economic chaos of the early-1980's in Uganda had created such a vacuum for goods and services in the country that anybody with an opportunity to go out, usually returned with a few extra items in their suitcase to sell on the open market. Some enterprising souls were going as far south as Johannesburg, Maseru (Lesotho) or Gaborone (Botswana), purchasing vehicles, and driving them to Kampala, and disposing them for a handsome profit.

Xavier and I had planned on joining this pack. We would purchase our vehicles in Maseru, and then join a few other friends to drive up north in a convoy. However, when I got to Umtata, neither Xavier, nor his friends were ready. Yet my vacation time was limited and ticking away. I decided to embark on the project "solo", turning it into a real once-in-a-lifetime adventure. Instead, Xavier and I, in the company of Dr. Iraka, another Ugandan domiciled in the so-called Bantustans at the time, drove to the Lesotho capital of Maseru, where I would leave them to proceed on my sojourn. Lesotho is a tiny southern African mountainous kingdom, with the unique characteristic that it is completely surrounded by its giant neighbor, the Republic of South Africa. During the hey days of apartheid, many black South African freedom fighters crisscrossed the borders of the tiny nation for sanctuary, although the vicious regime often violated the international border with impunity in hot pursuit of its victims. Basotho is one of the distinct ethnic groups within South Africa.

Lesotho's high and cool mountains with altitudes averaging above 6,000 feet above sea level, and cresting at around 11,000 ft in the majestic Maluti Mountains, are endowed with the one vital resource South Africa lacks most, fresh water. The two major Rivers in South Africa, the Orange and the Thukela, trace their origins in these mountain ranges. At the time I was there, the country, with the help of the World Bank, was developing a giant water project based in the mountains north-east of Maseru, which it would pipe to thirsty South Africa. I visited a few car dealers in Maseru before settling on a small blue Toyota station wagon which I knew would get me home trouble-free. Xavier and Dr. Iraka stayed in Maseru for two days, and headed back to resume their tasks in Umtata. I stayed behind two more days to finish the paperwork on the car, and in the afternoon of the fourth day, I crossed into South Africa at Maseru Bridge. We had meticulously mapped out a route I would follow, including hotels and lodges to use as rest stops, something I came to appreciate even more as I sped through winding roads of unknown territory for miles, sometimes late at night, on roads that did not carry clearly marked signs. Heading north-west, I drove through the well-laid out city of Bloemfontein, a conservative bastion of apartheid, stopping once to fill my gas tank. At the gas station, I asked the owner, a white man, for directions, and he was surprisingly courteous, in a country that was at the time, considered a pariah for its rigid racial laws. It was getting dark, so I took to the road again, following a smooth, but fairly lonely road that meandered through well-tended farms, whose size I could hardly figure out from the flickering lights on the seemingly palatial homes beyond.

By two o'clock, I had reached the small town of Mafikeng in what was called Bophutaswana , a country no-one else recognized, except South Africa, another one of those social-engineering projects of apartheid South Africa. I checked into one of the lodges on my list, only to stretch out my bones from the long drive, before checking out again at 6.00 am, to head for the border post at Lobatse, which marks the border between South Africa and Botswana.

In Botswana, I stopped for about two hours at the Presidential Hotel in downtown Gaborone, just to recharge my internal batteries before moving north towards Francistown, the country's second largest town, located 420 kilometers NE of Gaborone. Luckily, the road was smooth, although, seemingly lonely. The countryside itself was sparsely populated as this arid country of

224,000 square miles is home to only 1.6 million people today (2012), and was occupied by less than a million souls at the time I drove through. I arrived at the Beautiful Nata Lodge, located in an oasis in the Mokolwane palms, which form part of the extensive Makgadikgadi Salt pans of the Great Okovango Delta. After registration at the main reception, I was given keys to a cozy charlet with a thatched roof, but with all the creature comforts an exhausted traveler could ask for. After soaking myself in the shower to wash off the dust, I headed for the dining room in the main house, where I settled for a sumptuous meal of juicy, mouth-watering Botswana beef. The country was, at the time, and remains one of the few African countries that export beef to the European Union.

A deep sleep followed the exhaustion of the long drive, but by morning, I was very refreshed, and eager to take to the wheel again. After a quick breakfast of tasty sausages and freshly-squeezed juices, I headed for Kazungula border, marking the international border between Botswana and Zambia. At the time, there was no bridge crossing the Zambezi at this point. Instead, an old ferry plowed the river, shuttling passengers and their wares between the two shores. However, a serious accident in 2007, in which an overloaded truck from Zambia caused the pontoon ferry to capsize mid-river, was attributed to the absence of a bridge. Zambia and Botswana have since collaborated in the construction of a bridge across this 400- metre stretch of the Zambezi. In Livingstone, Zambia's second largest city, and named for the famed English explorer, Dr. David Livingstone, I drove through the streets searching for a restaurant to have a decent meal before continuing north on my sojourn. The Zambia of the 1980's, like many other sub-Saharan countries, was a wasteland, devoid of such basics as sugar, flour and soap. I stopped by several shops in town, open, but with hardly any merchandise on display on the shelves. Most did not even stock a soda, referring you to another shop, a few blocks down, only to get there and be referred back to the place you just left. With all the arable land available in the vast country, there were food riots at the time, following a government increase in the price of the national staple of corn meal. The price increase was in reaction to the IMF-World Bank structural adjustment policies that recommended doing away with government subsidies, in return for their lender-of-last-resort loans to countries that were strapped for cash, with no other option. The copper mines in the nation's copper-belt of Kitwe-Ndola, were standing nearly idle, as copper prices for the country's major export, had all but collapsed, throwing thousands of Zambians out of work. A lot of Zambians took to the bottle purportedly to ease their pain, prompting the humanist President Kaunda, known for sporting white handkerchiefs, to shed many tears in public fora.

In Livingstone, I offered two middle-aged women a ride to Lusaka, the capital, after they explained to me that they had been stranded at the bus station for two days, hoping a bus would eventually show up, akin to "waiting for Gordot". The women, although barely fluent in English, nevertheless, painted the dire circumstances the country was facing at the time. Some of the stories sounded grimmer than what I was used to hearing and digesting from my desk in Washington D.C. Some hordes of young people surrounded your car as soon as you parked it, and literally began washing it even before asking you whether or not you wanted it cleaned. Upon asking them how much their labor was worth, they simply said "anything". However, behind this façade, there was a little trap, that an unsuspecting new visitor in town was unlikely to extricate himself out of. Once you left the washing bay, a few of them followed you, in case you parked at another spot nearby, where they would automatically wash the vehicle again, asking you to pay "anything". And that anything had better be paid, or else, at the next parking, the vehicle might be stripped and abandoned, or disappear altogether.

Driving past Mulungushi, a small town in central Zambia made famous by former President Kenneth Kaunda's socialist policies announced there in 1968, I was getting hungry, when all of a sudden, my attention was captured by an old billboard by the roadside, welcoming drivers to a luxury hotel a few miles ahead, where they could wash off the dust, relax in comfort as they dined on the best cuisine the country could offer. I followed the sign to the letter, and parked my little car in the ample parking lot, which, except for a handful of old vehicles, perhaps belonging to managerial staff, appeared empty. Approaching the reception desk, the manager on duty was polite and courteous, inquiring whether I needed a room to stay for a night. I told him I only wished to have lunch and continue on my trip. He asked me what I wanted to eat, but, upon checking with the kitchen staff, as it turned out, none of the items displayed on the menu were available. Finally, the frustrated, and apparently embarrassed manager, called in one of the boys that worked in the restaurant, and instructed him to go outside and check if the lady that sold eggs outside the hotel still had any eggs left. The young man hurried outside, and soon returned with a half-tray of eggs, from which the manager ordered him to prepare me an omelette.

The Socialist ideology was very much in vogue in many countries on the continent during the 1970's and 1980's, a period dubbed the "lost decades", on account of the retrogression of the continent's economic performance. Among the main proponents of this doctrine, was Mwalimu Julius Nyerere of Tanzania, who emphasized self-reliance through village communes known as ujamaa. Following the Arusha Declarations of 1967, the Tanzanian economy was to be run on a policy proscribed as Ujamaa. Under this experiment of an African development model, people were forcefully herded to far-flung empty villages, and given basic agricultural tools such as machetes, hoes and seeds to start cooperative farming, whose yield was expected to be shared among the residents of the ujamaa village. Lack of agricultural extension workers, coupled with natural resistance to an unpopular policy, drastically reduced food production in the country, year in, and year out, turning Tanzania from a self-sufficient food producer in the 1960's to a perpetually food deficit nation throughout the 70's and 80's. By the time Mwalimu Nyerere handed over the reigns of power to Ali Hassan Mwinyi in 1985, it was abundantly clear that the ujamaa policy had been nothing but a disaster for the nation.

In spite of the poor economic performance, however, Nyerere's patriotic legacy still rings in hundreds of Tanzanian villages which he strung together to form the United Republic of Tanzania, one of a handful of countries in sub-Saharan Africa that have so far avoided internecine squabbles that have plagued other African countries.

Tanzania and Zambia's socialist policies garnered them a helping hand from the Chinese, who linked the two neighbors with the Tazara Railway. But this project seems to have been conceived and implemented in a hurry by the Chinese, with very little input from the intended beneficiaries. As a result, the system has more often been out of service, as a result of poor maintenance, and insufficient rolling stock. With China's re-emergence on the continent, and its emphasis on infrastructure, there is hope that projects such as the Tazara Railway will get a new lease on life.

Leaving Zambia, I entered Tanzania through the border post at Tunduma. The road had been rough from around Kapiri Mposhi, all the way to the border, and at one time in my haste, I run the speeding car into a giant pothole, that relieved the car of the muffler. Unsure of where I was, I stopped long enough to pick up the exhaust pipe and throw it in the extended trunk, which I had enlarged by folding the back seat in the station wagon. Unlike border crossings further south, I had been warned that customs agents would pester me for "kittu kidogo", payment of which, or failure to do so, could mean spending a few hours or an extra day of waiting for the "right official". A bearded gentleman by the name of Rutaremwa took my passport, saw my name, and immediately broke into the Kihaya dialect of north-western Tanzania, which is similar to my mother tongue of Runyankore.

There was some indirect relief on my part, although I knew that this common heritage alone was not enough to exonerate me from greasing his palm. Within about two hours, my documents, including the vehicle, had been processed, and I parted with $20, mainly as an appreciation gesture to Mr. Rutaremwa.

Heading towards the south-western regional town of Iringa, the hilly terrain, covered with banana trees and coffee plantations, resembled that of my home district of Rukungiri. As I did not carry any Tanzanian shillings, I knew it would be hard conducting even the most basic of transactions, including buying fuel. Once I reached the town, I approached one gentleman on the street, and asked him where the nearest bank was. "Hapo karibu", meaning it's nearby, although typically omitting the actual distance. I had found Tanzanians in general, to be, by most measures, an affable and approachable bunch of people, judging from the interactions I had with fellow classmates like Mwakabaja and Umfundizi at Makerere University, although they (especially Umfundizi), had a tendency to linger on the bottle much longer than the average student, turning him into a chatterbox on steroids.

One former Tanzanian student I met in the late 70's in Winnipeg, Manitoba, while narrating to us some stories about his carousing nights in Katanga Valley, and Makerere Kivulo, dubbed Makivu by students, both of them shanty towns near the university campus, was stunned when we solved his mystery of who "Enguli" was. Enguli is a Luganda word that describes a highly intoxicating spirit, akin to 'moonshine", derived from distilled banana juice. It is typically consumed by low income groups who can't afford its more purified cousin known as Uganda Waragi, which some connoisseurs compare with Gordon's Dry Gin. Many local consumers of the illicit liquor die after imbibing too much of the toxic stuff. Some have lost eyesight after drinking a concoction of this, mixed with methyl alcohol. While at the University, this gentleman told us, "Enguli" was his preferred drink of choice, because, above all, it gave him and his light-pocketed colleagues, more bang for the buck. However, everyday, he used to read in the local newspapers, headlines like,

"Man found dead in Bwaise, enguli suspected". Since they always referred to their drink by the generalized name of "waragi", which is a corrupted name of "war gin", they remained oblivious to the fact that the same runaway killer on the loose known as Enguli, was one and the same as the hellfire that gave them perpetual hangovers.

I went straight to the branch of National Bank of Commerce, and asked for the foreign exchange department. The bank teller scanned me from head to toe as if I was from Mars, and said the bank didn't have one. Instead he referred me to the manager, who occupied a small paneled office at the other end of the hall. I went over and knocked at his door, and Mr. Juma Mkitani said, "Karibu Bwana, ingia", meaning, "Please enter". At first he addressed me in the beautifully-flowing coastal Kiswahili that is the lingua franca of Tanzania, but soon, he realized my deficiency in the language, and switched to English. Although most East Africans in urban areas, claim to speak or at least have a semblance of understanding the language, it's the Tanzanians by far, who have perfected the language. Swahili is a language spoken widely in eastern and central Africa, but, with good targeted planning, could unite most of the Bantu-speaking groups extending all the way to southern Africa. It is, by all accounts, a truly international language, having its roots in a cornucopia of Bantu, Arabic, and Portuguese languages.

Those were the days of controlled foreign exchange regimes, so whatever foreign currencies the regional banks collected, they were required to remit the proceeds to the central Bank, which in the case of Tanzania, was in Dar-es-Salaam. As I was only in transit, I figured I would not need a lot of local currency, so I only purchased about forty dollars worth. Tanzania, whose gallant soldiers had helped in ousting and dislodging dictator Idi Amin from power a few years earlier, still loved to reminisce about their national pride in the act. The bank manager kept me talking for nearly two hours until I implored him to let me go.

Driving through the vast wilderness that forms part of the Ruaha National Park, at one point I encountered a swarm of insects which kept smashing into my windshield, making the glass impossible to see through. I attempted cleaning, but soon, the only piece of cloth I was using got overwhelmed, and any further attempt to use it simply added another layer of greasy stuff. But the worst was yet to come. Between 10.00 and 11.00 pm that night, while speeding through the park towards Morogoro, I hit a large pothole which I couldn't see on the dark road. I knew immediately that something went wrong because the car's steering column became extremely hard to control. Being conscious of my surroundings, I was afraid of getting out in the pitch darkness to trouble-shoot the nature of the problem with the car, least I became dinner for lions and hyenas. Instead, I resolved to sit in the car with only a wheel spanner for a weapon, listening to all kinds of strange noises that are associated with the wild. I could not afford to sleep, because that would have made me easy prey, for both man and beast alike.

As my eyes got accustomed to the darkness, I began to discern some human settlements nearby, marked by silhouettes of grass-thatched huts in the background. But still, I didn't dare venturing in the night under circumstances I was not fully in control of. Towards eleven o'clock, I heard voices of people moving closer towards the car, and I braced myself for a possible assault, or worse. As the two men got closer, I started picking some of their conversation in Swahili, and one of them said to the other, that they should go check out the car. My instincts told me to pre-empt their actions by letting them know that I was aware of their presence. I rolled down the window, and called out.

"Wandugu", Swahili for "brothers", and this immediately disarmed them. I told them I was from Uganda, and they appeared to be willing to help me out. As it turned out, one of them told me he used to work as a turn-boy on a truck that hauled merchandise to the Zambian copper-belt in Kitwe. They told me they lived in the neighborhood, and actually pointed out their huts almost within shouting distance. They had just been out drinking Changaa, a local brew made from corn. Even then, I first sized them up before deciding to get out of the car. Once outside, I noticed that the hood was slanted towards the passenger side, a tell-tale sign that the left front tire was flat. Luckily, I had a spare tire, and a wheel spanner, and now, with a turn-boy's skills available to me, my troubles would soon be over. But it was not to be.

My new nocturnal friends helped me replace the flattened tire with the spare, and I gave each one about a dollar in Tanzanian equivalent, and bade them farewell. But, in my haste to fix the problem, I had only glanced at the other tires without physically examining them. I jumped into the driver's seat, started the vehicle and engaged the gear, only to find the steering column feeling like I was carrying a sack of salt on my shoulders. Now, a little more confident about my surrounding, I got out of the car, and examined each tire individually, only to discover that, the hind tire on the passenger side had burst simultaneously with the front one. I was traveling with only one spare tire, so I knew I couldn't leave this place that night. Not feeling entirely safe staying by my self, I took a bold move and followed my new friends to their hut, and narrated my ordeal to them. I convinced them to come back and share the night with me around the car, promising to compensate them for the inconvenience. This being a rural area with few employment opportunities, they were more than eager to oblige. One of them suggested that we make a fire, an idea I found so enticing, as a gathering around a fire brings out the best camaraderie among humanity, besides being a strong repellant to would-be four-legged nocturnal undesirables. We sat around, and I gave each one a can of Coke as we shared a packet of cookies, from my luggage, an action that endeared me to them, and allayed my fears of anyone harboring some ulterior motives of pouncing on me.

Around six o'clock in the morning, just as I was beginning to contemplate on how I would take the busted tires to the nearest gas station for repair, a Norwegian expatriate, by the name of Karl Johansson, working with the Tanzania Federation of Cooperatives, riding in a Land Rover with another Tanzanian official, pulled over to see what had happened. I stood up, indentified myself, including handing them my World Bank business card, and explained all that had happened. Mr. Johansson graciously offered to take me to the gas station, which was close to Morogoro town, almost twenty five miles away. The two gentlemen patiently waited and chatted with me as the tires got repaired, then, drove me back to my car, pro bono, turning down my offer to compensate them for their invaluable services. I thanked them endlessly, and watched as they headed back towards Morogoro, wondering if this self-less act could ever spread beyond the Olduvai Gorge in the Serengeti plains of northern Tanzania, made famous by reputed paleontologist, Dr. Leakey, as the cradle of mankind.

By now, the sun was up, warming the surroundings very quickly. The chirping sounds of tropical birds were everywhere, interspersed with the cooing of doves. An occasional curious monkey popped out its head from nearby bushes, mimicking as if it expected response, then diving for the nearest branch at the sign of someone moving in its direction. These were reminders of the chorus of music I used to hear in the virgin forests of Rwamashunju, near my home as a kid, before the giant trees were chopped down to cater for the ever growing needs of providing firewood to cook the evening meal. With the repaired tires mounted, I paid my night-time companions, bade them farewell, and I too, sped towards Morogoro, driving past green fields of the sisal plant (agave sisilana), locally known as kamba, used to make twine. During the seventies and eighties, Morogoro town was a non-decrepit dusty town, only known for its namesake, the Morogoro Jazz Band. I had a quick lunch of pilaf na kuku (rice and chicken), then as I was getting into the car to leave, one police officer whose wife and daughter were standing nearby waiting for a bus to Arusha, asked me which direction I was going. Remembering the good Samaritans that had just rescued me that morning, I acquiesced, although I was wary of giving rides to total strangers.

The road infrastructure in Tanzania in the 1980's was all but a shambles. The country's vast interior was not well linked to the commercial capital of Dar-es-Salaam on the coast. Regarding the other two major urban centers of Arusha and Moshi, it appeared as if the road system had followed the East African Community's demise, nearly a decade earlier. At the restaurant in Morogoro where I ate lunch, I run into a few people, who were driving the same route to Arusha, so we formed a sort of convoy. It was early afternoon, perhaps 1.30 to 2.00 pm when we got on the Dar-Arusha road. The tarmac had been worn out on many sections of the highway, leaving giant potholes that on many occasions hit the vehicle's differential system on the underbelly. The road was so bad, that, once caught up in one lane, it appeared rather suicidal to try and maneuver out of the lane without the danger of possibly overturning, since the lanes slanted in opposite directions, leaving a ridge in the middle. Driving the long stretch became hazardous, not so much because of the danger of on-coming vehicles, but rather, gauging when you would hit the next big pothole that might put the car out of commission. Sometime close to 10.00 pm, we made one brief rest stop for fuel, and nibbled on chapattis and sodas before resuming the arduous journey to Arusha.

Shortly before five o'clock, I began to see the silhouettes of Mount Meru in the foreground, and the indomitable Mt. Kilimanjaro further on. I knew there and then, that we had arrived in the Arusha-Moshi region. By that time, however, I was so exhausted from driving, that my eyes could hardly focus on the road. After dropping the mother-daughter passengers I had picked from Morogoro, I simply went against my own risk precautions, parked the car on the street, locked the doors, and took a nap. Waking up about two hours later, with my internal energy batteries recharged, I whizzed through the 108 kilometer (67 miles) to Namanga, the official border post between Kenya and Tanzania. Scores of vehicles were lined up before me awaiting clearance, some of which, upon inquiring from their owner/drivers, had been there for several days. Graft on Kenyan roads has always been legendary, but nowhere is the problem more pervasive than on border posts. The first border security personnel I contacted directed me to a parking area that was already teaming with vehicles.

Once inside the customs office, and after the officer looked through my vehicle's official documents that had passed other countries' scrutiny without a hitch, he declared that my papers were "not in order", and that "the stolen car" would not be allowed to enter Kenya!

"But sir, you've seen all the receipts showing proof of purchase and country of origin, how can you say the car is stolen?" I protested. The fellow ignored me and went on to deal with the next person in line. With the Ugandan economy in a shambles at the time, and most imports into the country entering via Kenya, police and immigration authorities in Kenya had perfected the art of squeezing "kittu kidogo" out the desperate Ugandans, clamoring to make a buck at home by importing all manner of merchandise. Frustrated with my efforts to convince the officer, I withdrew from the building and joined a group of drivers sitting outside, some playing backgammon to pass the time. I narrated my ordeal to two gentlemen, who, sensing my naivety about customs and border issues, advised me to approach the station chief instead.

The chief's home was a little secluded, away from the chaos and noise of the border post. One of the drivers offered to accompany me there, and we took a leisurely walk to the one-story bungalow, whose compound already had several cars parked there. There was a gate at the entrance, but it was unlocked, so we entered and I knocked at the metal grill door. A young boy emerged, still holding a piece of ugali (cornmeal) that he was eating for lunch.

"Kijana, baba yako yiko nyumbani?" I inquired if the father was at home. The boy nodded in the affirmative, and hurried back inside. A few minutes passed before a tall man in Kenyan police uniform, with a captain's epaulets emerged and opened the door. He did not invite us inside, but instead stepped out to stand under the shelter of an avocado tree. After a few pleasantries, I pulled my vehicle papers from the khaki envelope where I kept them, and handed them to him. He looked them over for a few minutes, then turned to me,

"You will leave your car here, go to Nairobi, post a bond, and after that I'll arrange for a police escort to allow you cross with your car to the Ugandan border". It was getting too complicated. Namanga border is about 162 kilometers (101 miles) south of Nairobi, and it was already late in the afternoon. And, since I could not drive my own car, I was only left with the option of hopping on the infamous "Matatu taxis" that plow the Kenyan roads. Any attempt to embark on a trip that late, let alone the possibility of finding anyone to conduct business with in Nairobi, was an exercise in futility. The police chief showed me a spot where I could park my car, and soon after, I drove the car to his compound, parked, locked it, and returned to commiserate with my fellow stranded travelers.

The next morning, at about 8.30 am, I joined other passengers, and we boarded an old Peugeot 404 station wagon bound for Nairobi. Those French-made work horses were very popular modes of transportation in the 70's and 80's, before the Japanese introduced the more efficient, gas-sipping minibus, dubbed "kamunye", because it zips through the road like a hawk dives in the sky. Matatu drivers in Kenya have a reputation for trampling traffic laws by overloading their rickety vehicles, leading to preventable road carnage. The incessant driver kept adding more passengers along the way, despite our protestations, until one could hardly move a limb, because every available space was occupied. A few kilometers past the provincial town of Kajiado, passengers in the middle row seat began to get edgy, complaining that their seat was getting too warm. The driver paid them no attention, and instead stepped on the gas to push the ramshackle even faster. A few moments later, before anybody realized what was happening, we saw a ball of fire rising from the seat in the middle. The driver pumped the breaks, but like everything else in this piece of moving junk, they had given way a long time ago.

Those seated near doors pushed them open and jumped out, some crushing on the bare tarmac, and getting injured. The driver, too, kicked his door and made for the exit, leaving those of us seated in the rear, stuck in the burning vehicle. The driverless vehicle veered off the road and began heading down the slope. By that time, only a few of us were still in the vehicle, but like everyone else, struggling to escape the fire, Finally, the car hit an acacia tree, uprooting it, but the tree managed to slow it enough to suck the momentum out of it. Three of the passengers seated with me behind run out in a stampede. I had a shoulder bag with all my documents. As I was clamoring to get out, the strap got hooked in one of the hinges on the edge of the seat. I could hear people shouting,

"Chimbiya! Chimbiya!", which is Swahili for "Run". I pulled strongly enough at the strap till it snapped, sending me and the bag crushing down in a heap. I got up quickly and moved to where the rest of the passengers were standing, some gathering sand with their bare hands, and throwing it at the burning vehicle. Miraculously, they contained the fire, and the car didn't explode. But then, here we were, in the middle of nowhere, unsure of how we could continue to Nairobi. For about two hours we waited, waving at every vehicle to stop, but each one appeared to be filled to capacity. Finally, when we were getting desperate, a seemingly overloaded bus stopped, and we managed to squeeze ourselves into it. It wasn't until late in the afternoon when we pulled into the Nairobi Bus Park, clearly, too late to conduct business for that day. I had been instructed by the police chief at Namanga, where I should go to post the bond. The following morning, as soon as posted the bond, I rushed to the taxi station. Finding no direct one to Namanga, I caught a Matatu to Kajiado, from where I would easily connect in another to Namanga. The chief accepted a small token for "keeping my car safely", and even dropped the requirement of a police escort.

The date was Christmas eve, 1986, and I had expected to spend the festive occasion with my people upcountry in Rukungiri. However, given the physical distance to cover by road, the prospects didn't look very good. Nairobi lies about 504 kilometers (313 miles) SE of the Ugandan capital of Kampala. Add the distance from Namanga, and another 200 miles from Kampala to my home area, and it becomes crystal clear why I'd not be home for Christmas. Having left Namanga fairly late, I attempted to make up for lost time, picking up speed by taking advantage of Kenya's main trunk roads, which were better than Tanzania's, and still remain superior to those of its neighbors in the region. I stopped in Nakuru briefly to have dinner, and fill my fuel tank. Nakuru (dusty place in the Masai language), is Kenya's third largest city, located about 160 kilometers NW of Nairobi, in the great East African Rift Valley. It is a well laid out city that once claimed the title of East Africa's cleanest city, and a favorite hangout for colonial administrators. Lake Nakuru, nearby, one of the crater lakes dotting the rift valley, is famous for its pink flamingos, numbering more than a million. The pink coloration is derived from the consumption of algae growing in the warm alkaline shallow waters of this lake.

Twenty One

THE NEXT SIGNIFICANT town along this route is Eldoret, whose native son, Daniel Arap Moi, ruled Kenya with a firm hand under a philosophy he termed "Nyayo", which adduces for one to "follow in the footsteps", akin to a hyena trailing a lion in order to pick up the leftovers. President Moi, who took the reins of state power following the death of Mzee Jomo Kenyatta in 1978, coined the term to assure an anxious nation that he would not deviate from the capitalistic policies of his predecessor. Kenya remained steadfast, a sort of odd man in a region where countries were falling over their heads pronouncing themselves socialist this, or Marxist that. The payoff continues to manifest itself in Kenya's status as the regional economic powerhouse, the political hiccup in 2008 notwithstanding. During his last years in office, the "Bwana Mkubwa" steered a grandiose project to Eldoret as a personal memento, but also to remind the nation, and his people in particular, that "pork" still follows the chief. An international airport was built near Eldoret, even when all economic evaluations indicated that the project was not viable, given the popularity of Nairobi to the east as a hub, followed by Entebbe Airport, 30 minutes to the west as an alternative. The project has become Kenya's version of "Road to nowhere". But, come on, this wasn't as bad as le grand vieil homme, Houphouet-Boigny s "Vatican" monumental edifice to himself, built in his birth place town of Yamoussoukro at a cost of $300 million, in a country with a minority Christian population.

I arrived at the Uganda/Kenya border post of Malaba on Thursday, Chrismas Day, 1986, only to find a skeletal staff, most people having gone home for the holidays. Excited to finally be home, I thought they would process my paper work and let me proceed to enjoy my Christmas. However, upon presenting the car documents, they told me I needed to fill import forms, which they said they didn't have there, requiring me to go and obtain them from Kampala. Knowing that Boxing Day is usually a holiday, I knew that the earliest I could find any office open was the following Monday. It would have been an exercise in futility to attempt pressing them any further.

The customs officials showed me where to park the car, directly behind the office building, and I walked the short distance to the taxi park, where I boarded a kamunye for Kampala. The country was in celebratory mood, having been rid of the unruly armies of the Obote II and Okello Lutwa regimes earlier that year. The infamous road blocks were nowhere to be seen, except one near Majansi on the Tororo-Jinja section of the highway. Even this, I was told, was specifically to check on smugglers, who used the alternate border post of Busia. For the rest of the way, I took in the green scenery of Kibimba Rice Project, followed moments later by the extensive Kakira sugar plantations of the Madhvani family, Uganda's equivalent of the Rockefeller scions of the Robber Baron era.

Muljibhai Prabhudas Madhvani, the patriarch of the family, immigrated from Aaslyapat in the Indian state of Gujirat at 18, and arrived, penniless in Uganda in 1908, distraught after losing his mother Laduma in his early teens. He first worked as a shop assistant in his uncle's little shop in what was then a rural small town of Kaliro in the Busoga region of eastern Province. His indefatigable attitude towards work, coupled with his acumen to turn a profit, soon impressed his uncle, who by 1912, allowed him to open up his own shop. Determined to succeed in the sugar business, against the advice of Sir William Frederick Gowers, then Colonial Governor of Uganda, Muljibhai acquired 800 hectares of land from the Busoga Kingdom to establish what would later be one of the African continent's largest sugar plantations. The land was at the time, infested with malaria-carrying mosquitoes, snakes, and even Nile crocodiles. By 1930, he had not only succeeded in taming the land, but had established his flagship sugar factory at Kakira, about 6 miles east of Jinja town, where it still stands and operates to this day. The conglomerate has since diversified into many other industrial products, including steel, cooking oil, textiles, etc. Lately, they have also ventured into tourism, running the two best resorts in the country, Mweya Lodge, and Chobe Safari Lodge, mostly frequented by well-heeled clients.

Before the term corporate social responsibility made its way into the management lexicon, the Madhvani Group of companies had been putting the concept into practice for decades, building housing, schools and hospitals for its workers in an integrated network that made Kakira the heart and soul of Jinja town. Like Henry Ford was to the auto industry in Detroit, you either worked in one of the Madhvani factories in town, or for the government, period. But the company's philanthropy extended further than its immediate surroundings of Jinja, for instance, offering scholarships that benefitted many needy students. We all lived in awe of the behemoth that controlled the sugar we drank down to the matches we used to light the fire for making the tea.

Although the empire was seriously disrupted by Idi Amin's mass expulsion of people of Asian descent in 1972, the younger generation such as Nitin who took the reins after the Departed Asian Properties Custodian Board returned their properties, have continued to run the enterprise with the same zeal their grandfather injected into it.

Muljibhai's uncle was among the wave of Indian coolies, brought in by the British to help with the construction of the East

African Railway, from the Indian Ocean port of Mombasa, to the Ugandan interior.

These were the same rail workers who were constantly terrorized by a pair of lions dubbed the "man-eaters of Tsavo", the fearless carnivores that developed such a taste for human flesh, and whose viciousness has been immortalized in movies and folklore alike. Col John Henry Patterson who was supervising construction of a bridge, hunted them down and killed them after they had devoured as many as 135 of his men. His book documenting the events culminated into the original movie, "The Man-Eaters of Tsavo". Their carcasses were eventually shipped to the Field Museum in Chicago, where they remain on display until today. There are, however, current efforts by some Kenyan patriots, who wish to repatriate the "fugitives", and try them posthumorously in their native land. It is deemed that their Jeffrey Dahmer character may be a boon to the nation's tourism industry.

Entering Jinja, Uganda's former industrial heartbeat, one cannot but help observe the dilapidated state into which the town has been plunged. The old smoke-stack industries including the copper smelter at Walakira have been silenced as industries moved closer to Kampala. Jinja, which means stone in the Luganda language, is famously known as the source of the River Nile. The stone or rock for which it was named, is perhaps, the site of Nalubale Dam (formerly known as Owen Falls), where the mighty River Nile separates itself from the waters of Lake Victoria, thereby beginning its 6650 kilometer northward flow, through the land of the Pharaohs, before emptying into the Mediterranean Sea. Uganda currently generates most of its hydropower from two dams located within a few miles of each other near the source of the Nile. A third one, called Bujagali, located downstream, opened in 2012, adding an estimated 250 Megawatts of power to the national grid. This, plus a few more planned projects such as the 700-megawatt Karuma dam, will help alleviate the energy deficit that often paralyzes industrial production, and hamstrings daily domestic chores in peoples' homes.

The nearly 60-year old Owen Falls Dam Bridge, the only one linking most of Uganda's road trade to the rest of the world, is developing structural cracks, endangering not only Uganda's trade, but also that of the satellite countries such as Rwanda, Burundi and eastern Congo, which rely on the same route. There is, currently, talk of a Japanese construction company replacing this narrow bridge with a wider, and more modern and versatile structure. However, like most other planned developments, it could be a while before we see another functioning bridge. Princess Elizabeth commissioned the current one, back in 1952, just a few months before her coronation to the British Throne. It took her a mere fifty-five years to pay another visit to the country, she claimed was "dear to her heart", when she came to open the Commonwealth Heads of Government Summit (CHOGM) in 2007. What a way to shower love over your subjects, whose lakes (Victoria, Edward, George and Albert), are named after members of your own family, and the best national park (Queen Elizabeth) bears your own name. The Windsors' longevity notwithstanding, it would appear, that we'll be waiting for a very long time before another "gloved one" walks on our soil again.

The Kampala of the 1980's was very different from today in many respects. It used to be said, that, like Rome, the city was built on seven hills, mainly Nakasero, Kololo, Mengo, Rubaga, Kibuli, Muyenga and Mbuya. This is no longer true. Today, the city is an urban sprawl that almost defies any compartmentalization. By some estimates, the population of Kampala swells to nearly three million by day, and perhaps shrinks to no more than a million by night. A visit to the bus and taxi park areas, and the surrounding neighborhoods of Owino Market, Kikuubo, Kisekka Market, and Shauri Yako, gives one the impression that the rural populations have almost abandoned their ancestral villages to try their luck in what has become one of the worst managed cities in the world. Here, any academic interested in expanding the theory of chaos, would hit a bonanza. From William Street, down to Ben Kiwanuka Street, people compete for space the same way that ants run into each other over little specks fallen from bread crumbs. Although many of these people are peddling something, no matter how small and insignificant it appears to a casual observer, the vast majority simply appear to be loitering around aimlessly, drifting from place to place, simply to kill time. This perpetual motion extends into the night, as most of these drifters, faced with over-crowding in their usual places of abode, and lacking permanent places to call home, spend more time on the streets than inside structured home environments.

Woe is the day you are caught near these neighborhoods after it rains. Kampala has many places prone to flooding whenever God releases his sweat to quench the thirst on earth. There is a quick transformation from a dusty scene, where specks of dust, rising from the thousands of feet pounding on the streets, settle down on people's nostrils, throats and eye lashes, giving most the appearance of permanent red eyes. Next minute, when it rains, the pedestrian and motorist alike, struggle to avoid piles of debris, some wrapped up in the ubiquitous buvera (plastic bags), that have taken a life of their own in a city that doesn't bother collecting trash. The reasons for the flooding are easy to discern. The Nakivubo channel which is the water catchment area that used to direct the tributaries into Lake Victoria, has all but been blocked, mostly by illegal structures, allowed by uncouth Kampala City Councilmen, whose inspectors look the other way after pocketing "kitu kidogo", allowing shoddy unlicensed structures to pop up. In the extreme, residential areas such as Bwaise, Kifumbira and Ndeeba, experience floods that carry with them floating raw sewage from above-ground latrines, inflicting a lot of havoc to the communities through such water-borne epidemics as cholera and typhoid.

The former Mayor, Hajj Nasser Ntege Sebaggala, known as Seeya, is an ex-felon, who was nabbed by US customs officials and jailed in the US city of Boston a couple of years ago, for money laundering, and carrying illicit checks known as "bicupuli". His hero-like reception upon release thrust him at the helm of City Hall, propelled there mainly by lumpen characters calling themselves "Ekibiina ky'abatasoma", or the association of the uneducated. Before running for the mayor's job, he had a stint at running for the top job in the country back in 2001, only to be disqualified on account of not meeting the basic academic requirements. Determined to push himself to the next level, he enrolled in a UK correspondence school calling itself Oxford College, (to bluff the unsuspecting public with the impression that he attended the more famous Oxford). And while there, he spent the next two years struggling, albeit failing to polish up on his English language skills. He has since given up hope of ever becoming president, and after curtailing his powers further with the central government's control of City Hall, he was lured into joining the incumbent president's campaign, with perhaps, a promise of an insignificant ministerial position, which too, failed to materialize, after parliament refused to ratify his selection to the cabinet. Ugandan politics has degenerated from a meritocracy, where the country was once admired for its efficient civil service, into a patronage system, managed from the center at the whims of State House. The first signs of trouble manifested themselves around 1991, when the National Resistance Council, the highest governing organ asked for a five-year extension to write a new constitution. At his swearing in on January 26, 1986, Mr. Yoweri Museveni, then, a brazen-looking young man in military fatigues had read the NRM's ten-point program to restore the devastated nation to normalcy. Among his proclamations, was the determination to end the impunity of leaders who conned the electorate by initially enlisting their support in elections, only to turn around and overstay their welcome through subsequent sham elections. He had also castigated those "excellencies" who flew to New York, London and Geneva in luxurious presidential jets to attend conferences where champagne and caviar are served in posh hotels like the Waldorf-Astoria, or Grosvenor, while their compatriots at home barely survive on one meal of sima (pap) and bug-infested beans, their feet swelling with jiggers, contracted from a filthy living environment.

"But what kind of constitution takes five years to write?", asked some of the naysayers at the time, among them, my late brother Matia. "This man, Museveni, is a trickster like the rest of them", Matia predicted earlier on. But in the early days of the NRM regime, talk like that earned you lots of scorn, and most people didn't take you seriously, because you were among the stray sheep that couldn't see the correct line.

As it turned out, 1991 also marked a turning point in my family. Career conditions at the World Bank in Washington were very competitive, requiring one to polish up and keep in tune with events. Two years earlier, I had enrolled for another Masters degree at the American University's Tenleytown Campus on Massachusetts Avenue in Upper N.W Washington D.C. The development banking course had been started, courtesy of the ebullient Professor Jose Epstein, a former treasurer of the Organization of American States (OAS), also headquartered in Washington DC, like its big brother, the World Bank. Before embarking on this course, I had entertained ideas of quitting the Bank job to go to business school, and seek fame and fortune elsewhere after that. However, with a young family, and virtually no considerable savings to rely on, my prospects of completing an MBA at a pricy business school like the Wharton School of the University of Pennsylvania were pretty grim. I had settled for the American University option, after an old colleague of mine at the Bank pointed me in that direction, highlighting the relevance of that degree to the job I was already doing.

In Kampala, my young brother Simon, had joined the regime, and was serving in the President's Office. He was in the good books with some of the high profile people, having been a roommate of the flamboyant Jim Muhwezi at Makerere University's Livingstone Hall. In fact, it was Jim, then the Director-General of the Internal Security Organization, who had enticed him to join him. In a city, devoid of decent accommodation, he lived in a tidy fourth-floor apartment in Bugolobi, considered as one of Kampala's up-market neighborhoods. My wife and I had spent several vacations with him there. He was still unmarried, although he shared the apartment with his fiancée Bea, to whom he was engaged at the time.

On the last Saturday of February, my study group was scheduled to meet at the AU campus, for a discussion regarding a joint paper we were preparing together. Early that morning, I received an alarming call from my other young brother Tony. In somewhat of hushed tone, he said Simon was in a comma in his apartment, and that the prognosis didn't look good. Phone calls cost a fortune those days, and connections to remote stations like Kampala were haphazard at best. I tried to get some more details from him, but sometimes got disconnected in the attempt.

"Contact Dr. Alex as soon as possible", I advised Tony, referring to a close family friend of Matia's . But as fate would have it, that same day, both Matia and Alex had gone to the Kyotera area of Masaka, following a tip about a car stolen from Alex, which Matia had imported for him. There was no contact with them all day, since these were the pre-cell phone days. I reluctantly drove to American University, but was distraught all day, and hardly contributed towards the discussion. Later that evening, after my return, I got the dreaded call. Simon had been rushed to Nsambya Hospital, but the doctors could not revive him back to life. The night he slipped into a comma, there was a downpour, typical of the seasonal rains of March-April period. His bedroom window had been found open, and, the bed itself soggy wet. We'll never know whether he opened the window in a desperate attempt to let in some cool air.

On Monday morning, I went to the office, only to make

arrangements for the emergency travel. I secured a seat on Sabena Airlines, flying to Entebbe via Brussels, the Belgian capital. In Brussels, I run into two prominent government officials who knew him, both of whom attempted to console me. As we alighted from the plane at Entebbe, Princess Dorothy Nnasolo, a sister to Kabaka Ronald Mutebi, and her colleague, Mr. Manzi-Tumubweine, then a minister in the NRM government, offered to give me a ride to Kampala in their official car. However, my brothers in Kampala, who had by then left for the funeral upcountry, had made arrangements for my transportation to my parents' home near Rukungiri. Without fanfare, we left immediately for the six-hour trip, arriving in time for the two o'clock event.

Simon's passing profoundly shook my family in many respects. It was the first death of an immediate family member since I was born, and everybody loved him for his simplicity and openness. I had grown accustomed to him picking me up from the airport, cutting through the airport bureaucracy with his intimate familiarity of both the system and its operatives. But on this trip, I realized that all that had come to a sudden end. I would have to re-adjust my life to suit the new circumstances without him, a very painful reminder of how much I had come to depend on him. Two days after the funeral, a time I spent with my grief-stricken parents, I got on the flight back to Washington, with a heavy heart, but determined to pick up the pieces where I had left off. I rejoined my study group, but overall, my performance in that course was lackluster, although, with time, I healed enough to successfully finish my degree.

Later that year, I stopped over at the Ugandan Ambassador's Residence on Loughboro Road in Upper NW Washington DC, close to American University. The ambassador to the United States was then Princess Elizabeth Bagaya of Toro Kingdom. Her disdain for both the Obote regime which had abolished hereditary rule in Uganda, followed by the brutal Amin era, in which her name was dragged through the mud, were equally matched by her enthusiastic and unequivocal support towards the NRM government. My chance visit found me in the company of Dr. Sulaiman Kiggundu, then Governor of Bank of Uganda, and Dr. Crispus Kiyonga, the Finance Minister. The two were visiting Washington on a consultation mission with World Bank and IMF officials. The Museveni regime in its early phases was deemed socialist. As such, any attempt to convince bureaucrats from the two Bretton Woods behemoths, let alone the dyed-in-the-wool capitalists at Foggy Bottom, was initially, an exercise in futility. I had never met the two gentlemen, but as the four of us sat over lunch (including the ambassador), we had a frank and lively discussion over issues of general interest, which unknown to me, seemed to interest them enough to a point of offering me a job.

One morning a few weeks later, I arrived in my office at my usual time of 8.00 am, and shortly thereafter, the phone rang. I picked the receiver and answered casually, thinking it was one of my colleagues at work, but the caller on the other side said,

"Hello Nick, this is Dr. Sula Kiggundu calling from Paris".

"The Governor?" I asked, gently, not knowing what to expect.

"Yes", he said, "and the reason I am calling you is to ask if you would consider coming to work for us at the Central Bank".

I could not commit myself in any way, but just told him what an honor it was to be regarded by him that way. I promised to give his request some consideration and get back to him at a later date in the near future.

Not long after that, the Minister of Finance returned to Washington, and instructed one of the Embassy staff to call me and ask me to meet with the Minister. I returned the call at his hotel, but was told he was out. The following day, the Embassy called again, but when I called the hotel, they told me he was out again. On the third attempt, I called the Embassy, and told them, if the Minister wanted to see me so bad, he knew where to find me. But the game was not over yet. A few months later, the deputy Governor called me about the same issue, and I was more direct with him, telling him that all the calls didn't amount to anything, because nothing concrete had been offered to me in writing.

Nevertheless, on a visit to the country later that year, I decided to test the waters. I knew the top management of the central Bank, some of them going back about twenty years to our high school days. Upon pressing them further on the issue, I realized that the job they were offering me was not worth the tradeoff with my bank job, financially and otherwise. My two children were both under five years old, and any move would have distracted their lives tremendously. Moreover, a discussion with the principal of Kampala Parents School, the one international school of repute at the time, left me in doubt regarding the efficacy of my actions. After that, I summoned enough courage and told the officials at Bank of Uganda, that if they could find a better qualified person, they should have the liberty to fill the position.

But my restlessness was not over. I was yawning for something more than my research job at the Bank was offering. Meantime, tragedy hit my family once again In October 1992, snatching the life of my sister Lucy from us. I began entertaining ideas of setting up a business of my own. In my final research paper at American University, I had laid down the foundations of manufacturing some charcoal briquettes from coffee husks in Uganda, to, among other things, help the poor obtain an alternative source of energy without wantonly cutting down existing forests. I had tried to market the idea to various funding organizations without much success. However, I was not just about to give up.

During the process of sourcing some briquetting equipment for the project, I had written a letter to a Japanese company that sold the suitable equipment, but I never received a reply. Puzzled, I approached a Japanese colleague from the Marubeni Trading Company, who was at the time, researching some Sino-Japanese trade relations topics from my division. He told me that some small Japanese companies like the one I was inquiring from may not have the English-speaking personnel to handle such issues. He offered to interpret my letter into Japanese and send it. Lo and behold, a few weeks later, I got a positive response, not from Japan, but from their affiliate in the Netherlands, which handled sales in Europe, Africa and the Middle East. The seller also recommended a briquetting company based in Amelo, Netherlands, which I did contact.

For the next few years, beginning in1991, I made numerous trips to the country, to study conditions on the ground and evaluate prospects for setting up my project. However, as I would soon discover, much to my chagrin, the country in general, was not yet ready for prime time. The Uganda Investment Authority, the so-called one-stop shop for setting up a company, was in its infancy, and many of its officials at that time were non-committal at best. Getting a license required clearances from various places, including the Ministry of Finance, and that of Trade, all of which were time-consuming and uncoordinated activities. Banks were few, and extremely cautious with their lending policies, most preferring to purchase treasury bills with yields of 15 percent or more at the time, rather than take on risky local ventures for which they charged eye-popping interest rates of 24 percent and above. Lenders from well-established institutions such as the International Finance Corporation, a World Bank affiliate, required that the sponsor of a project show serious commitment by putting down a sizeable portion of the initial capital requirement of the project, perhaps 25%. Another requirement was to have collaboration with local counterparts who brought in the local expertise to make the project a success. Mostly however, the business environment at the time favored large established businesses with track records.

Doing the pro forma analysis was easy to spell out on paper, but in reality, the situation on the ground was an alien matter. For instance, local counterparts didn't want to part with a dime, although they were eager to partner with you. At the end of the day, the proprietor found himself in a position where he or she was expected to contribute most of the equity capital, and, once the project started, cough out the debt service for the loans obtained, mainly from abroad. This position was untenable for most small business entrepreneurs, no matter how deep-pocketed they appeared to be. I wrestled with the problem, committing a lot of my resources into a project, about which I received little or token support on the ground, until I found myself completely drained, and unable to cope. Finally, I realized that the venture would not work under this kind of arrangement, so I decided to throw in the towel, return to my family which had all along stayed in the US. Anyone who has gone through this experience, can identify with that nonchalant feeling about life in general, that is symptomatic of the aftermath. I had quit my Bank job at the end of 1995 on an optimistic high note, and now, here I was, two years later, back in the same environment, dejected, and feeling like the whole world had conspired against me.

Towards the end of July 1997, I took my elder brother Marcel, who had not been well for some time, to Mulago Hospital, and then I left abruptly for a business trip to Mombasa, Kenya. Two days later, I went to the post office in Mombasa, and made a call home to ask about the patient. The words that my niece Grace uttered to me on the other end of the line still ring hollow in my ears to this day.

"Uncle died the same day you left, and we've been struggling to reach you ever since", she said.

Cell phones were still objects of the very wealthy at the time. Although I had scrambled some cash and purchased a GSM Motorola set from London, it had turned into an albatross when it failed to function in Kampala. After the call at the Mombasa Post Office, I did not even have time to sit somewhere and absorb the shock. I just simply abandoned all I was supposed to do in Mombasa, and booked a one-way ticket on an all-night bus trip back to Kampala. The bus was filled to capacity, and those of us who booked late ended up standing for the best part of the journey of 500 miles or so, arriving the following day, exhausted and haggard. The driver's rather reckless over-speeding on the poorly-lit, and potholed roads, while seemingly devoting more attention to chewing amairungi (caffeine-addictive plant called khat), did not give tired and restless passengers like me, any solace.

Although burial had already taken place at my parents' home, I could not wait another minute in Kampala. So, even in my weakened state, I boarded a Kasaba Bus heading for Rukungiri. Kalori, the owner, and long time family friend, who travelled on the same bus, ensured that I got a seat. But as fate would have it, as we approached Masaka town, the bus developed a mechanical problem, and with darkness on the horizon, it did not appear likely to be solvable. Kalori and the driver went about prowling the local auto garages in search of mechanics to diagnose and fix the problem. Meanwhile inside the bus itself, passengers staged a near riot against the conductor, some demanding partial payment, others adamant for a full refund of the bus fare so they could use it on other buses. One by one, people started abandoning the bus. At first I was torn between the loyalty of abandoning a friend at his hour of need, and the reality of getting home to pay tribute to my fallen brother.

I waited and waited, but when Kalori and the driver still didn't show up, I too, picked my bag and headed for the exit. However, instead of waiting for another bus to continue the journey, I opted to return to Kampala, a trip of just a little more than an hour by taxi. I had been warned that night time travel by bus was risky, because gun-totting thugs often ambushed these buses at night, and robbed passengers at will. The following day, a sympathetic friend gave me a car to drive upcountry, where I once again spent two days with the unenviable task of consoling my parents.

By now, almost drained of all energy and resources, I put whatever household merchandise I deemed salable, on the auction block, losing a lot of money in the process, from buyers who took stuff on promise to pay but never did, nevertheless, freeing myself to leave this environment. It took a while and a lot of cajoling by my wife, to wake up to the new realities, and begin to orient my life in a new direction. Meanwhile, the bills were piling up, and I had to look for a job real fast, to prevent my family from being ejected from our home. I had never savored the experience of being without a job. From my student days, I had transitioned smoothly into decent positions that seemed to give one the false illusion of invincibility. But now, here I was, out of a job, and having drained all my liquid resources on an untenable project in Uganda. I knew I couldn't get my job back at the World Bank due to some release clauses I had signed. However, it was still possible to secure temporary consulting assignments there. I decided to give it a try as the first line of defense. My former division chief, Mr. Uri Dadush, was very accommodative towards my situation, and soon, I was back crunching numbers, buying myself some precious time as I continued searching for a more permanent position.

These temporary assignments are stopgap facilities that the Bank and its sister organization, the IMF, use to give a soft landing to its retirees, especially those who choose to remain in the Washington metro area for one reason or another. Competition for these ad hoc positions is cutthroat, as the number of retirees has grown by leaps and bounds over the years. Besides, consultancies to these institutions is coveted by all kinds of professionals from all-over the world. As such, one assignment, in no way guarantees, that it will be followed by another. Fortunately, I was already aware of this fact of life. So, while I was at It, I relentlessly pursued other channels.

Except for a brief one year period after my arrival in which I alternated between Maryland and Washington DC, I have always lived in Fairfax County, in the Commonwealth of Virginia. This county, west of the city of Washington DC, was created out of the northern part of Prince William County in 1742, and named after an English nobleman, Lord Thomas Fairfax, 6th Lord Fairfax of Cameron, the only member of the British nobility ever to reside in the colonies, according to US historical records.

During the time I first set foot in Fairfax County in the late 1970's, to the mid 1990's, the county, best known for its famous residence at Mount Vernon, the stately home of George Washington, America's first president, had changed tremendously. It had transformed itself from a mostly bedroom community of federal and private sector workers who commuted daily to Washington DC, into an economic powerhouse to reckon with, that rivaled other behemoths like Westchester County in New York State, Orange County in California, Cook County in the Chicago area, and Dallas County in the Lone star state of Texas. Many of America's big corporations appearing on the Fortune-500 list have been setting up shop in the county, to have a foothold near the power centers of the nation's capital.

Using the auspices of the formidable Fairfax County Economic Development Authority, and its outspoken president Gerald L. Gordon, the county registered success after success in creating a business-friendly environment, which attracted more firms to locate here, creating an incredible number of well-paying jobs. Companies like Northrop-Grumman, Volkswagen America, Hilton Hotels, SAIC, etc, call Fairfax County Home. In the process, this managed to reverse the trend for the commuting public. Instead, job-seekers started flocking into Fairfax County from neighboring jurisdictions and beyond. Most economic and other surveys conducted in the last twenty years or so, have ranked Fairfax County and the neighboring jurisdictions of Arlington, Loudon and Prince William Counties, which constitute the sprawling Northern Virginia suburb, among the top choice in the nation as a place to locate and do business. Of particular note, has been the attraction of hi-tech firms to the county, giving it a higher concentration of hi-tech workers than Silicon Valley of Apple and HP fame.

With a gross domestic product of around $95 billion, and an annual budget of around $4 billion, for a population of slightly more than one million residents (2010), Fairfax is one of the ten largest counties in the nation, and its economy dwarfs those of at least five US states, including, Rhode Island, Maine, Wyoming, North and South Dakota, not to mention whole countries in many parts of the globe. Around 2008, the county became the first major jurisdiction of its size in the nation, to register a median annual family income above $100,000.

This rush to the top, has, however, not been devoid of some negative consequences, the worst of which has been the clogging of the road network, resulting in long and frustrating periods of commuting. This has happened in spite of continuous attempts to expand and improve the modes of transportation in the northern Virginia area. Part of Fairfax County's attractiveness has always been the reputation of its superb public school system. At over 170,000 students, with a $2 billion budget, the system is the 12th largest, and consistently ranks near the top in the nation. It also boasts of the largest fleet of school buses of any school system in the nation.

The FCPS system as it is generally referred to, traces its origin to the Reconstruction period, beginning in 1870, following the US civil war that pitted the segregationist southern states against the anti-slavery north. Virginia State was part of the confederate southern states. In the years that followed the emancipation of slavery by President Abraham Lincoln, segregation did not disappear, but rather, took on a different form under the stringent Jim Crow laws. In Virginia, as in the other southern states, constitutions mandated setting up separate systems of education based on race, not unlike the system that prevailed in Apartheid South Africa until it officially ended in 1994. FCPS continued busing its black students to neighboring Manassas in Prince William county, even after the Supreme Court had ruled in Brown versus the Board of Education landmark case of 1954, which stipulated that "separate was unequal". The county did not allow black students into white-designated schools until 1960.

But, as the county population has surged beyond one million, the swelling numbers have put a strain on the system, forcing children to hold classes inside trailers, due to a shortage of permanent classroom space. The cost of housing has also skyrocketed over the years, to a point where it has priced out the average salary worker. For instance, during the years between 2004 and 2007, a period engrossed over by what former Federal Reserve Chairman Alan Greenspan called "irrational exuberance", the median price of a single family home nearly touched $600,000. The high prices greatly affected the ability of first time home buyers, such as young families and low income earners, from affording a home in the county. This is reflected in the fact that only about 40% of Fairfax County employees, who include local government workers, police officers, fire-fighters, teachers, etc, live within the county. The rest have been forced to relocate further out in outlying jurisdictions such as Prince William and Fauquier counties, with some commuting as far away as Warrenton and Culpepper, where housing is still relatively affordable.

However, those residents who stayed put, and new arrivals such as executives relocating on transfer, continue to enjoy a high quality of life, envied, and in some cases, emulated by some societies across the globe. For instance, in South Africa, authorities modeled the suburb of Sandton, north of Johannesburg (also known as Africa's richest square mile), on the planned community of Reston, Virginia, which forms the northwestern part of Fairfax County. The county is characterized by a low crime rate, and a well-educated populace who put a priority on such subjects as clean air, water, and other environmental issues.

This huge economic muscle has given the county enormous leverage in the affairs of the commonwealth state of Virginia, where it acts as a bell-weather against which most jurisdictions rightly, or wrongly, judge their performance. Whether it's the economy, or politics, in Virginia, "when Fairfax County talks", as in the old E.F. Hutton commercial, "the rest of Virginia and the nation, listen". Despite this power, complaints are commonplace among the Northern Virginia political establishment, on how Richmond takes more from this region than it ploughs back. The intractable transportation gridlock that has become synonymous with driving in the northern Virginia suburbs is more often attributable to the fact that the state retains, rather than remit back the funds earmarked for improving this sector.

Likewise, within the county itself, some areas such as McLean and Great Falls flex more muscle than say, Mason District or Sully Station, based on account of their contribution to the county's purse. He, who pays the piper, calls the tune. It all fits in well with the natural laws of capitalism.

Before I took on my current job with the county government, I had no intimate knowledge about Fairfax County, and felt a bit alien to my neighborhood for that matter, despite having been a resident there for almost two decades. My work routine was such that I used to leave home at sunrise, and returned at dusk. But, schedule aside, I suppose the foreign mentality syndrome had rubbed on me. That's the mindset prevalent among those associated with international organizations, be it the World Bank, IMF, WHO, or the UN, where the unwritten rule appears to be that "anything foreign is good and exotic". They wear Italian designer suits, speak foreign languages, read foreign newspapers and magazines (Financial Times, Il Tiempo, Economist and Der Spiegel), send their kids to Swiss or English Prep schools, eat foreign foods, drive foreign cars like BMW, Lexus and Jaguar (stick shift, please), book their travels on foreign airlines, and, yes, even in the delicate matters of the heart, they settle for foreign spouses too.

Whenever they take time off, they go on "home leave", most of which is usually spent in some remote part of the world, after fulfilling the requirement of visiting one's homeland. If not vacationing there, then at least the family would rather jet off to some popular tourist sites like Maui, Hawaii, Acapulco or one of the Caribbean resorts, never leaving enough time for exploring neighborhood attractions. Don't expect them to participate in your weekend neighborhood watch, because theirs is most likely that home whose lights are controlled by the auto switch, since the owners never seem to be there.

It didn't take me long to learn the ropes of traversing the streets of Fairfax county. Believe me, if your life depends on it, you will sooner, rather than later, figure out an easy way to get around. Unlike the number crunching job I was accustomed to at the World Bank, a real estate appraiser's job (also called valuer), requires one to spend more time on the road, combing neighborhoods, and talking to home-owners. One has to develop a good and coherent people-friendly skill in order to survive on the job, because oftentimes, it involves being somewhat invasive, such as those times you have to inspect bedrooms and bathrooms in order to ascertain the quality of the dwelling. In the process, however, one learns a lot about the diverse lifestyles enjoyed by communities like Fairfax.

From the stately homes of Mount Vernon and Gunston Hall in the Mount Vernon district in the south, through old farm houses in Clifton and Sully district, to the nouveau riche mansions of Great Falls and McLean in the Dranesville district to the north, Fairfax County offers a variety of home styles like no other place. And the owners tend to their treasures like mother chicken guards its young against impending danger from a hawk in the sky. Some home-owners subject you to a vicious interview regarding the purpose of your visit, even after establishing your credentials as a government employee. Who would blame them for being so protective of what is ultimately the most valuable asset any family can hold? But by and large, most homeowners are courteous, and will give you the data you are looking for, once they ascertain that you are acting on behalf of the government. After all, as that quintessential American hero, Benjamin Franklin put it, death and taxes are the only certainties that a normal human being can't avoid.

Twenty Two

THE UGANDAN EXPERIMENT in multiparty democracy had seemingly been thriving well since being re-introduced in 1996 in the first election following the 1980 debacle that pushed the country into a prolonged guerrilla war. The trouble was, it was the same play with an improvised cast of characters. The 1996 election pitted Mr. Yoweri Museveni, then, as in 2011, at the helm of the National Resistance Movement (NRM), against his long-serving Foreign Minister, Dr. Paul Ssemogerere, who had inherited the reins of the nation's oldest party, the Democratic Party, from its stalwart founder, Benedicto Kiwanuka. Dr. Ssemogerere had been chosen as the compromise candidate to head the Inter-Party Coalition (IPC), which constituted the two oldest parties, DP and UPC, together with an amalgam of smaller parties, all clamoring to wrest power from incumbent Museveni.

Then as now, some people had expressed reservations as to the wisdom of Museveni's transition from a military strongman into a civilian president. The Consultative Council had already extended his rule by another five years, under the pretext that he would preside over the drafting of a new constitution. The Constitutional Commission, chaired by Justice Benjamin Odoki (retiring in June 2013 as Chief Justice), had traversed the globe, gathering ideas and affidavits from Ugandan citizens and well-wishers, which they would later incorporate in the final elaborate document, finished in 1995. The new constitution, cognizant of Uganda's past turbulence, had spelled out clearly what qualities a prospective president should possess, complete with the terms he or she could serve (maximum of 2 five-year terms). Mr. Museveni had already served ten years prior to the promulgation of this constitution, and some thought he should pass the baton to another leader.

It was then that Mr. Museveni and his bush war veterans began to show their true colors of manipulating every situation in order to cling to power. First, through a hierarchical arrangement that ensured that the chairman of the NRM, and by extension, the commander-in-chief of the National Resistance Army, NRA, would be the automatic presidential nominee, this ensured that Mr. Museveni would reign supreme for a long time to come. At the same time, the Museveni juggernaut slowly, but surely, began to weaken and dismantle state institutions that would have allowed any semblance of a challenge to emerge. Although there is no doubt that Mr. Museveni still commanded a sizeable following in 1996, and would have sailed through the election with little difficulty, his popularity began to wane once these machinations began to be apparent.

In 1999, Dr. Kiiza Besigye, a young colonel who had once served as Mr. Museveni's personal physician during the guerrilla war, dropped a bombshell by publishing a letter in the local media, heavily critical of the NRM's modus operandi. In the letter, he castigated the ruling party as intolerant and prone to stifling any change that would encourage internal democracy. In their reaction, the NRM leadership hung the young man high and dry, labeling him as a renegade dissenter who could not toe "the correct line". Mr. Museveni went to the extent of threatening to court-martial him in a military court. When Dr. Besigye stuck to his guns, and refused to apologize, and decided to quit the military, every roadblock was placed in his way to ensure that he remained gagged under the control of the army. However, he remained steadfast on his mission, and by 2001, when the country was preparing for a second round of elections under the multiparty arrangement, Dr. Besigye got the dismissal he sought from the army, and then decided to throw his hat in the ring as a candidate for president under a newly formed party known as the Reform Agenda.

Dr. Besigye's predicament, it seems, had only just began to unfold. Within a few weeks of his declaring himself as a presidential candidate, the NRM leadership began to trail him and his family, on a twenty-four-seven basis. Some in the NRM establishment, like then Defense Minister Amama Mbabazi,(now Prime Minister), uttered the infamous words, that Dr. Besigye "was jumping the queue", implying there were others more worthy of the position, even though the NRM had preached to the country all along, that their system chose its leadership based on individual merit. As the campaign rhetoric heated up, so did the pressure on Besigye. So much was the hounding and harassment, that immediately after the disputed elections, he finally capitulated by escaping from the country into voluntary exile in South Africa, where he would remain for nearly five years.

In one incident during Dr. Besigye's 2001 election campaign, one of his aides, Captain Okwir Rabwoni, a young brother to Brigadier Noble Mayombo, then President Museveni's aide-de-camp, was arrested violently at Entebbe Airport, to prevent him from boarding the same flight with Dr. Besigye bound for a political rally in Arua, West Nile. Although the flight was scrapped for all, due to the commotion that followed the arrest, many people still wonder, whether the forced arrest was meant to save the life of one soul that otherwise might have perished in a doomed flight. I witnessed the remnants of this fracas, as I arrived at Entebbe airport on a short visit, about three hours after the incident happened.

Uganda was by no means the only country experiencing turmoil. The whole world witnessed in shock, as two fully-loaded jets commandeered by Al Qaeda terrorists smashed into New York City's World Trade Center twin towers within a few moments of each other on that day of infamy that has come to be known as Nine-Eleven. The crash was of such magnitude that it obliterated the 110-story edifice from the Big Apple as one of the most recognizable landmarks, snapping with it, the lives of three thousand innocent people, devastating many families, and shaping for good, the way the world looks at terrorism. Moments after the attack on what has by now, come to be known as Ground Zero, another plane slammed into the Pentagon, that symbol of American might that was thought to be impregnable, killing and maiming many soldiers and civilian alike.

Meanwhile, yet a fourth aircraft, United Airlines Flight 93, originating from Boston like the other three, flying over Shanksville, Pennsylvania, en route to San Francisco, was commandeered in coordination with the other three, with possibly the intention of either attacking the White House, or Capitol Hill. Although the flight crushed killing all on board, it was later learned from the information gathered from some of the relatives of the passengers on the ill-fated plane, that the deadly mission was aborted by the gallantry of those aboard, who fought back the hijackers, even if it meant paying the ultimate price.

That morning, my colleagues and I had packed ourselves in Kevin Greenleaf, our director's office, to catch the horror as it unfolded on TV screens in real time. It remains one of those moments the mind can't erase.

President George W. Bush who had assumed the presidency under a cloud on January 20, 2001, following one of the most contentious elections in American history, suddenly found himself riding high on a wave of patriotism, in which all fighting factions coalesced and rallied behind the commander-in-chief in order to swart the new evil.

In Uganda, Dr. Besigye's daring challenge, it appears, sent a bolt of lightning through Mr. Museveni's spine, who had reigned supreme, until that time. At first, the rift between the two had been dismissed as mere rivalry over matters of the heart. You see, about two years earlier, Dr. Besigye had wed a smart and outspoken woman, called Winnie Byanyima, whom many bush war veterans knew to have been Mr. Museveni's girlfriend during the war (his wife having been shipped to Sweden). However, when some other disgruntled war veterans joined Dr. Besigye's party, it soon dawned on many political observers, that this was more than "skirt warfare". The NRM as an umbrella organization had swallowed up and neutralized the effectiveness of the old parties like the Democratic Party (DP), and the Uganda Peoples' Congress (UPC), making the country a de facto one-party state. It was under this unleveled playing field that, Dr. Paul Ssemogerere of the IPC had contested for the presidency against incumbent Museveni, in 1996.

Although the field had not been leveled since the last elections, Dr. Besigye's party, the Forum for Democratic Change (FDC), had emerged as the only viable opposition to the NRM. Still, the more than two-to-one majority advantage the NRM party enjoyed over the opposition, made it act like a one-party legislature in parliament. The president got his way on most issues, by arm-twisting the NRM caucus to vote his way, even when some of the issues were controversial. In 2003, for instance, a quiet scheme to amend the constitution and remove presidential term limits was engineered by a little-known member of Parliament, called James Kakooza, presumably, with tacit approval from the president himself. Most people in the country were opposed to an idea that would entrench a president in the position, no matter how popular he might appear to be at the time. As the idea gathered steam, it became clear that some among the president's staunch supporters, including his childhood friend, Eriya Kategaya, (died in March 2013), were opposed to it. However, not a man to be distracted, Mr. Museveni, whose cabinet had not been changed for many years, decided to reshuffle his team, dropping those who were opposed, and replacing them with known praise-singers. Determined to prevail, the president used this occasion to drop his infamous "five million shilling" envelop in each NRM parliamentarian's in-box, euphemistically called a facilitation fund, but which everyone else knew was an inducement, or a bribe to vote for the removal of presidential term limits.

After that, the president coxed the NRM members of parliament to vote for the amendment, which they did with the numerical advantage they had in the legislature, effectively paving the way for a life president. With this pseudo-mandate, the president once again presented himself for the nomination, and easily sailed through, since no one in the NRM party appeared willing to challenge him.

Meanwhile, on the opposition side, his old nemesis, who had all along been exiled in South Africa, was being sought out to be the flag-bearer for his FDC party. But the president and his courtiers were doggedly determined to ensure that it wouldn't happen. The president had gone so far as issuing a stern warning, that if the good doctor dared to return from exile, he might be arrested and prosecuted for acts that amounted to treason. At first nobody took the president seriously. After all, the only thing Dr. Besigye had done, was attempting to run against his one-time patient and boss. The country was therefore grappled with surprise, when, within two weeks of his arrival, the Colonel was way-laid at Busega, near Nateete, a suburb of Kampala City, arrested on tramped charges of treason and rape, and immediately locked up at Luzira maximum security prison on the shores of Lake Victoria. However, in spite of all the hurdles the government threw in its way, the opposition party was determined to get its founder nominated as the presidential candidate, even if this meant anointing him in absentia.

The attorney-General, Dr Khiddu Makubuya, opined at the time, that nominating a candidate this way would be illegal, but the people would have none of it. Finally, during one of his standing-room-only High Court appearances, when the presiding judge granted the Colonel and his co-accused, bail, the nation was shocked moments later, as a hither-to unknown rag-tag military offshoot, later identified as "Black Mambas", stormed the court premises, seized the prisoners and whisked them off to a military jail. This grotesque incident was reminiscent of the abduction of Chief Justice Benedicto Kiwanuka, during Idi Amin's reign of terror in 1972, in which the veteran politician, who was the nation's first post-colonial Prime Minister, was abducted, and disappeared, never to be seen again. In a poetic reaction to Dr. Besigye's High Court incident, Justice James Ogoola, the Principal Judge at the High Court, described it as the "rape of the Temple of Justice". The stage had been set, it appears, for these incidents would be repeated over many times in future.

By 2005, President Museveni, the same man who had pinned down Africa's most nagging problems as emanating from leaders who overstay their welcome way past their "sell-by-due-date", had himself laid the stage for doing exactly that. Among the veterans of the 1981-85 bush war that brought him to power, were men and women, who had vigorously opposed the idea of amending the 1995 constitution to remove presidential term limits, and effectively create a de facto life presidency. And, true to form, the son of Kaguta didn't disappoint. By the time it was all said and done, most of those, including well-respected figures like Bidandi Ssali, Amanya Mushega, Miria Matembe, and his childhood friend and buddy, Eriya Kategaya, had all been dumped from the cabinet. It was clear from that moment on that, like Napoleon Bonaparte, no man was considered man enough to deny Museveni what Museveni coveted. Uganda's fate was sealed with yet another dictator, joining the unenviable cohort that have dotted the continent since the independence decade, leaving a path of destruction and wasteland in their countries.

For many observers, Museveni, who was once described by the Clinton Administration as representing a new breed of African leaders, with the intellectual and analytical wherewithal to chart a new course for the lagging continent, his about-turn was particularly disappointing, although to those who knew him more closely, his actions were not surprising.

Twenty Three

I HAD LAST been to South Africa in 1986, at the height of the apartheid regime. The country had changed tremendously since 1994, the year Nelson Mandela was installed as the first black democratically elected president of the new republic. In December 2005, my family and I spent the Christmas and New Year's period, visiting some of the country's popular tourist sites, including the well-laid out capital City of Pretoria, with its grand buildings such as the Union Building, the seat of the presidential power. We also took off time to visit the world-famous Kruger National Park, located in the north-eastern part of the country, straddling the borders of Mozambique to the east, and Zimbabwe to the north. To appreciate the extent to which the country had changed, one would have to imagine the scene at Jan Smuts International Airport in the 1980's, against the current situation at the same airport, now renamed Oliver R.Tambo International, after the late ANC stalwart who led the party during its most tumultuous years, culminating into its unbanning in 1990.

Arriving at this sprawling airport, one of the largest, and by all measures, the most sophisticated on the continent, it is easy to forget that you are indeed on the same land mass, that accommodates the likes of Kigali, Bamako and Entebbe airports. Back in the 1980's, when apartheid was at its peak, the airport was characterized by the tense atmosphere you felt even as a transit passenger, stopping here for only a few hours. Equally conspicuously missing, were black faces in the lounges, except for an occasional cleaning man or woman, hurriedly on their way to carry out their chores. I remember waiting six hours for a connecting flight to Nairobi in the mid-1980s. I run into one gentleman, Peter Kasanda, who was the Permanent Secretary in the Ministry of Foreign Affairs in Zambia, and we commiserated together as we both waited for our flights. At the time, one could not help noticing the overwhelming presence of security personnel in the airport area, prompting Peter to remark that there seemed to be more gun-toting security men than actual passengers.

Years later, one returns to find Oliver Tambo International as a thriving world-class busy airport that seems to have more in common with the likes of Schiphol International airport in Amsterdam than Harare in Zimbabwe or Lusaka in Zambia. Besides the extensive facilities and services available at JNB, as its code is known, the atmosphere is much more relaxed, and this time around, black South African faces are everywhere you look, right from the immigration officers who stamp your passport, to the taxi-drivers who accost you, offering to take you to your hotel. The airport is, however, not without its faults. South Africa ranks high among countries considered to be high crime areas, partly the residual effects of the apartheid regime that ignored the welfare of the majority black population. Once the regime was dismantled, the restricted movements of blacks were abolished, and many, who were once confined to townships, such as Soweto, Alexandra, Mamelodi, and Khayelitsha, flocked to mega metropolises such as Johannesburg, Cape Town and Durban in search of job opportunities.

But most of the township dwellers had limited skills, making it extremely difficult to secure meaningful employment. Coupled with the higher cost of living in a city like Johannesburg, has pushed some of these groups to turn to criminal activities such as car-jacking, burglary, assault or shoplifting in order to survive in the hustle and bustle of city life. Mobile telephony has exacerbated some of these petty crimes, as crime syndicates form and use this new communication tool to track and relay the movements of their intended victims. It is, for instance, considered extremely dangerous for a well-dressed passenger, new to JNB, emerging from the arrival lounge with several suit-cases in tow, to hop into one of those taxis prowling the airport after dark. Many passengers have been relieved of their cash and luggage on their way to their hotels by those benevolent taxi-drivers who had earlier welcomed them to Joburg.

The recent tragic Valentine's day incident in which the celebrated double amputee, and Olympic Games hero, Oscar Pistorius shot and killed his equally celebrity girl-friend Reeva Steenkamp in his gated community residence in Pretoria, exudes the fear factor that hangs on every South African as they retire for the night, even in the most impregnable and exclusive neighborhoods.

Three days after Christmas in 2005, my wife, our two children and myself, bundled ourselves in a Toyota Corolla in Pretoria, and headed east on Route N4 towards the Kruger National Park. The drive to the southernmost gate at Malelane took us about four hours, including brief refueling stops in the cities of Witbank and Nelspruit. Major trunk roads such as N1 that traverses the country from Polokwane in Limpopo Province in the northeast to Cape Town in the Western Cape, or N4 that runs east-west from the Botswana border to Komatipoort on the Mozambican border, are first class bitumen toll-roads, akin to European-style thoroughfares.

Kruger National Park, designated as a world heritage site by UNESCO, is truly, a jewel in South Africa's gazetted parks, and a world-class attraction for nature lovers. Sprawling over nearly 2 million hectares of territory, the park stretches for 390 kilometers from north to south, and almost 60 kilometers at its widest. To visit the park, one needs to purchase a ticket through the South African National Park Service. There are strict rules regarding what you may or may not do inside the park, including observing a speed limit of 40km per hour, and not feeding the animals. Travel restrictions also apply within certain hours, due to the risks involving wild animals. Decent lodging is available within the park at organized sites. Some provide restaurant services, while others are available on a self-service basis, allowing families to enjoy the facilities at their own leisure and budget.

Once within the park boundaries, a cornercopia of all manner of animals turned up by the roadside, perhaps as curious to gaze at us as we were to peep at them. Near Skukuza camp, in the heart of Big-Five territory, a 5-ton bull elephant blocked the narrow road for nearly fifteen minutes, forcing motorists on the narrow road to line up for close to a quarter mile, and cower in their vehicles with rolled up windows, until the indomitable pachyderm decided he had showed us who's boss in this neck of the woods. Arriving at Letaba camp close to the cutoff hour of 6 O'clock, we took up residence in two nicely-thatched, self-contained chalets, typical of camps managed by the South African Park service, which we had booked beforehand. Around nine, we checked into the dining room of the main house, where we dined on succulent steaks and chocolate mousse cake as we savored in beautiful tunes from the resident pianist, a nice way to say bye to the old year, and usher in a new one, as the clock ticked towards midnight.

Walking back to our new domicile after dinner, my wife and I kept shining our flashlight on any object that remotely looked suspiciously unfamiliar, just in case one of our four-legged friends had beaten the odds and scaled over the electric fence that surrounds the camp. Although maximum security is ensured, complete with over-night armed guards, there are constant reminders throughout the night as to who your immediate neighbors are, outside the fence. The cuckoo of a dove perched in the thorny bushveld tree yonder, interspersed with the cry of hyenas, perhaps retreating from a potential attack by the king of the jungle protecting his fresh kill, made up the background music that eventually sent us to sleep in the middle of what is admittedly, one of the few remaining spots of unspoiled nature.

The next morning, after a leisurely breakfast, we set off for Mopani Lodge, further north. The lodge is named for the Mopani tree, common in the South African provinces of Mpumalanga and Limpopo, but also extending into the semi-arid regions of Zimbabwe, Mozambique, and Botswana. The tree attracts the Mopani worm, a member of the caterpillar family, which is a delicacy to natives in this part of the world, providing them a protein supplement to their high-fiber carbohydrate diet of pap. Along the way, we made various game-watching stops, joining groups of other park tourists as they pulled off to watch different families of wildlife.

Among the big-five (elephant, buffalo, rhino, lion and leopard), only the first three could easily be sighted. Everyone along the way, it seemed, was anxious to see the ever-elusive big cats, but none were in sight on our outward drive, although, judging from the stampede of some deer and antelopes that we witnessed on a few occasions, one could guess that these predators were lurking in nearby bushes, only strategizing to chase the errant one that strays from the herd, for their mid-day meal. The majestic giraffes, effortlessly foraging from the canopies of dwarf thorny trees, were a common sight, as were the colorful zebra, mixing easily with hordes of myriads of deer, antelopes, and eland, almost oblivious about our intrusion. It is all a breathtaking experience that sucks one into the intricacies of nature, and almost instantly turns you into a preservationist.

At Mopani Lodge, we checked into a three-bedroom family-style chalet, where modern kitchen facilities are provided. We had carried some provisions with us from Pretoria, well aware that we'd prepare some of our own meals. This being a larger lodge than the one at Letaba, there is, besides the main restaurant, a mini-supermarket with basics such as an assortment of meats, bread, tea, coffee, milk and other survival items that you can purchase as ingredients for a delicious family dinner. Near sundown, we ventured out for a drive, to catch a view of some of the nocturnal animals as they came out in search of food. Due to the relatively high summer temperatures, the majority of the animals take lazy naps during the day, coming out to graze after the sun has subsided in the evening. Safety precautions provided by the South African Park Service, warn visitors to stay within their vehicles, unless accompanied by an armed ranger from SAPS, to avoid becoming part of the food chain. At one time, we stopped to watch sunset over the ubiquitous baobab trees that dot this landscape, soon after, driving back to gather around the kitchen, as each of us pitched in to cook a lovely evening meal.

Early morning the following day, we set off on our way back to Pretoria. We were still hopeful that we could see the remaining two of the big five, namely, the lion and the leopard. One of the official residents at Mopani had told us that the chances of sighting a lion were better than encountering a leopard, easily one of the most elusive of the predators. He had told us that, to improve our chances, we needed to drive further north, towards Punda Maria, close to the Zimbabwean border. But we had neither budgeted for the time nor the money for another day in the park. We stopped briefly at Skukuza camp for a quick lunch, and browsed around in the tourist shop before hitting the road again. The sun was getting hot, and we were planning on getting back to Pretoria by around five O'clock. About half-way between Skukuza and Berg-en-dal, a car occupied by an Indian family, and headed in the direction we were coming from, slowed down, and a young boy aged about twenty, leaned out and asked us jovially,

"Want to see any lions?" He quickly added, "Give me twenty bucks". We didn't take him seriously, so we pressed on. However, about a mile ahead, we noticed other drivers slowing down, turning right on a narrow gravel road and parking. We decided to check for ourselves, and did the same. I rolled down my window and asked the driver of a car that was pulling out, what it was people were curious about.

"A pride of lions", he said. "See those bushes over there under the tree?" he asked while pointing towards a cluster of thick bushes. "There are at least four or five lions basking in there".

We all sat there in anticipation, nobody daring to get out of the car. After about fifteen minutes of seeing nothing, a young Afrikaans boy seated with his family two cars ahead of us, slowly pushed his door open, grabbed two pieces of rock and cast them towards the bushes. The desired effect came instantly, as a pair of male lions rose up to full height to investigate the source of noise. The whole crowd shouted kudos at the young man who threw the rocks, as some of us fumbled with our cameras to snap photos of the giant carnivores before they retreated back to their shade to continue their afternoon siesta.

We rejoined the main trunk road toward Malelane, exited the Kruger National Park, and drove past vast irrigated fields of sugarcane plantations that reminded me of the Madhvani plantations near Jinja in Uganda, and the Mumias in Kenya. It was past 6.00PM when we got back into beautiful Pretoria, also christened Jacaranda City due to its extensive coverage with the jacaranda species of trees, initially imported from Brazil. The purple flowers add some spice in late spring, to the well-laid out city that, until Nelson Mandela was installed as the first democratically-elected chief executive in 1994, epitomized the symbols of apartheid, with the Union Building, and Voortrekker Monument, both now embraced as national symbols.

Twenty Four

NOWHERE HAS THE continent been as devastated with the HIV/ AIDS virus as the wider southern African region, particularly South Africa, Botswana, and Swaziland. Although the region was a little behind the curve compared to their eastern African counterparts, once they caught on, their infection rates quickly surpassed those of other regions of the world, in some extremes, communities in Swaziland registering infections of one in four.

Large migrant populations associated with the giant mining sector in South Africa, confined male populations in dorm-like conditions away from their families, often forcing men to go "offline" with infected communal partners. During the Thabo Mbeki Administration, South Africa lost a lot of ground in introducing measures to combat HIV, by engaging in an unwinnable debate on whether or not HIV causes Aids. In the latter part of his second term, however, under tremendous pressure at home, and international criticism abroad, the administration, using the country's higher resource base, accelerated its efforts towards containing the spread of the pandemic, whose prevalence is among the highest in the world.

Despite the Bush Administration's gun-boat diplomacy which climaxed with the unprovoked invasion of Iraq in 2003, right on the heels of the 2001 Afghan war that ousted the Talibans, it's credited with forming the Presidential Emergency Plan for Aids Relief

(PEPFAR) initiative which has saved thousands, if not millions of lives. Under this project, the Bush Administration committed $15 billion over a five-year period between 2003 and 2008, to cover such areas as anti-retroviral drugs, research etc.

Uganda, long, hailed as a global model in the fight against the Aids pandemic, with its ABC slogan (Abstain-Be faithful-or use Condoms), took on the lion's share of these resources. Uganda's Daily Monitor of July 16, 2011, quoted Dr. Wuhib Tadesse, the Director of the Atlanta-based Centers for Disease Control project in Uganda, as saying that, between 2004 and 2010, the country garnered a whopping $1.2 billion, or nearly ten percent of the committed funds from PEPFAR. But, although drastic progress had been achieved in the first two decades since the virus was identified, dramatically reducing the infection rate from near 30%, down to around 7%, this level has since stagnated, with new surveys showing increasing rates of infection. This can partly be attributed to complacency that came with wider use of anti-retroviral drugs that have reduced the perception of HIV from an automatic death sentence, to a manageable disease. Uganda's utilization of ARV's has risen from a mere 10,000 patients a decade ago, to over 200,000 today.

Still, with an estimated 110,000 additional infections every year, over a looming possibility of fund reductions, the CDC and other agencies involved fear that the country's once-stellar performance could be reversed, especially in a country with a galloping population growth rate, estimated at about 3.2 percent per annum. As of this writing in July 2011, a recent clinical test conducted in both Uganda and Kenya over discordant couples, showed that persistent use of ARVs by the infected partner reduced the chance of infecting the other party by as much as 73%. Provided that funds can be obtained to further avail ARVs to such couples, the results point at a possibility of containing, or even reducing infection rates from their current levels. There is fear of complacency setting in with success of such programs. People will resort to their old promiscuous lifestyles without the looming fear of death hanging over their necks like a millstone. More troubling, however, is the new trend of increasingly younger female adolescents turning to the oldest profession, due to lack of alternatives in the economy. Some of these are children orphaned as a result of parents dying of Aids. Burdened with adult tasks of looking after their young siblings without any help, they are very vulnerable, and soon fall prey to the tantalizing benevolence of "sugar-daddies", who dangle a few coins before them. Hunger and desperation militate against these young victims, who sooner, rather than later, follow in their parents' footsteps, contracting the very disease that thrust them under dire straits in the first place.

Many recruiting syndicates are now present in the shanty suburbs of Africa's burgeoning cities, creating a new lucrative industry of "sex tourism", a la Bangkok. These pimps go to impoverished villages in the countryside, and lure the kids to the cities, promising them well-paying jobs in the service industries such as hotels and restaurants. Upon arriving in the city, however, the kids find themselves gullible, and beholden to ruthless benefactors, whose only goal is to exploit their bodies for profit. Unable to extricate themselves out of such pathetic conditions, some are resigned to fate, until some NGO manages to get in contact and rescue them. Most countries have some law or statute barring child prostitution and trafficking, but few have the resources, or the will to bring the full force of the law to bear on the perpetrators of such crimes. As a result, instead of the problem of child trafficking being in retreat, it appears to be spinning out of control worldwide, with its array of attending social consequences.

Populist programs like Universal Primary Education (UPE) in Uganda, introduced hurriedly by the NRM government prior to the 1996 general election, without prior research, more than doubled enrolment in primary schools overnight, without increasing facilities proportionally. As a result, diminishing returns set in, to the extent that today's student, if he or she ever makes it to the seventh grade, does so less equipped with the three R's of Reading, writing , and arithmetic. But the mere process of being at school raises their expectations beyond the peasant surroundings. It is this same group that soon flocks to the cities soon after dropping out of school, in the hope of finding something better to do, than live the rest of their lives condemned to tilling the unforgiving soil like their forebears before them.

Nobody is advocating doing away with such a vital service that took a lot of burden off poor people's backs. However, the system has been in place now long enough for authorities to have learned from their mistakes and make an effort to correct them. For instance, it does not take a rocket scientist to know that poorly paid teachers are less motivated to teach and excite their students. The high truancy rates registered in UPE schools is partly a manifestation of failure on the policy makers to realize this shortcoming. The liberalization of the education sector in Uganda, that has allowed a quantum leap in enrolment at all levels, without the accompanying quality checks, has so diluted the standards to the point where today's university graduates are half-baked. That's quite an indictment for a country that was once synonymous with high quality education on the continent.

During the structural adjustment wave that swept through these countries in the eighties and nineties, the twin Bretton Woods institutions (the World Bank & IMF), had insisted on privatizing semi-government run operations, arguing that the private sector would inject not only some new capital, but much needed efficiencies. But, with no operation manual to go by, every country went about this task in its own way, displacing thousands of experienced employees, and replacing them with more inefficient family members. What were once government monopolies quickly turned into family-run franchises that staggered on for a little while, before collapsing and throwing more people out of work.

In Uganda, a well respected company, the Uganda Development Corporation (UDC), which had been set up in the

60's as an incubator for industrial production, folded due to mismanagement. The Uganda Transport Corporation, once a thriving enterprise with a fleet of buses that traversed the whole country on a daily basis, disintegrated only to be replaced by the present day chaos of kamunyes and boda bodas. The Cooperative Bank, which stabilized farmers' incomes by maintaining buffer stocks was let go without any substitute, leaving individual farmers at the mercy of unscrupulous crop traders. The absence of these key institutions together with others like a reliable railway transport network, have created a vacuum in the system that looks insurmountable. For a land-locked country, this adds to the cost of doing business, thus making the country less competitive.

President Museveni, adept at heaping blame on others, except himself, has had a field day, blaming all the laxity in his ruling NRM party's performance on the opposition. However, lately, the opposition appears to have found his Achilles heel, and started to effectively turn tables on him. The walk-to-work campaign, for instance, which started in April 2011, paralyzed Kampala, and the rest of the country for more than a month, as battle-hardened police and the military, fought daily pitched battles on the streets. The initial objective of the walk was to protest the escalating prices of food and fuel, which had greatly impacted the welfare of the average citizen. But, a jittery president, freshly returned into power with what many internal and external observers alike, viewed as a fraudulent and manipulated election, construed this as a direct challenge to his legitimacy.

His reaction was predictably swift and heavy-handed, especially in targeting his arch-rival, Dr. Kiiza Besigye, the leader of the main opposition party, known as the Forum for Democratic Change (FDC). With tacit connivance of the police, the country held its breath as they witnessed hither-to, unknown shadowy security groups set upon unarmed civilian opposition participants, brutalizing them in a style reminiscent of the deplorable Amin-era. Dr. Besigye was particularly singled out when a young man called

Gilbert Arineitwe Bwana of the Rapid Response Unit, smashed the windshield of the former's car with a gun butt, and nearly emptied a can of pepper spray into his face, including directly into the opposition leader's eyes. This action, which temporarily blinded the retired Army Colonel, was captured on camera by some journalists, and later shown to shocked world-wide audiences. The brutality was such that it took the intervention of diplomats from the US and other countries, to push the government into allowing the victim to travel to Nairobi, Kenya for treatment.

All this happened as the president scoffed at citizens' cries for the government to take drastic measures in addressing the country's economic woes. For his part, the president first called the inflationary trend "good for farmers", whom he said, would now reap higher prices from their agricultural products. Put to task to explain how this would happen, since farmers faced higher transportation costs with rising fuel prices, the president told the nation that gas price increases were "a global phenomenon", about which he could do nothing. In any case, the government needed to maintain the revenue stream from gasoline taxes, and therefore his regime was not just about to commit the cardinal sin of starving itself of the discretionary income it needed to purchase the military arsenal to control those recalcitrant opposition leaders.

However, mindful of the Bouazizi effect, which ushered in the Arab Spring awakening in Tunisia, Egypt, Libya, Syria, Yemen and Bahrain, Africa's strongmen no longer take their positions for granted. African people, long among the most oppressed, have started displaying a kind of boldness they never showed before, unyielding to the ever-present intimidation ploys that their entrenched leaders have always employed to quell potential riots, and keep the populace in tow. From Kenya's December 2007 riots, after a flawed electoral process that legitimized the perceived loser of the elections as the president, to Comrade Bob's unleashing of terror over his opponent, Morgan Svangarai in Zimbabwe, and more recently, Museveni's systematic targeting of his erstwhile comrade-in-arms, and personal physician, it's now apparent that these iron-fisted leaders will take no prisoners.

The riots that started in London's Tottenham borough during the weekend of August 5th to 7th , 2011, following the shooting dead by the police, of a black young man named Mark Duggan, and quickly engulfed other poor neighborhoods of London, Birmingham and Liverpool, had an eerily familiar tone. Would British Prime Minister David Cameron, after spitting fire in a hastily called parliamentary session, in which he promised to hunt down and punish the perpetrators of these criminal acts, wag the same finger at the Musevenis, Mugabes, or Bashar Assads, whose regimes were battling the same elements in their impoverished societies? The world has been transformed so much with the advent of social media like the internet, Face Book, You Tube and Twitter. This new weapon is fast being embraced by both the affluent and down-trodden alike in a way no present leader can mobilize society in order to address their grievances.

Suffice it to say that, the common theme that the London riots appear to share with those in Cairo, Lilongwe and Santiago Chile, is that, while capitalism at its best, rewards enterprising individuals beyond their wildest dreams, it at the same time leaves the less fortunate masses, in a more precarious vulnerable position. London, home to Scotland Yard, renowned for its efficient police work, is now turning to Los Angeles Police Chief, to learn how the city transformed itself in the wake of the riots that followed the LAPD's brutal mishandling of a black man named Rodney King, nearly twenty years ago in 1992. Rodney King's "Can't we get along?" quote in an interview then, appears as relevant today as ever.

Twenty Five

THE ELECTION OF Barack Obama to the presidency of the United States in November 2008 was as electrifying as it was polarizing in some sections of American society. When the Junior Senator from Illinois climbed on the steps of the state capital in Springfield, the same background used by Abraham Lincoln one hundred and fifty years earlier, nobody gave the lanky young man with "a funny name", one chance in a million, of cruising his way to 1600 Pennsylvania Avenue on January 20, 2009. The American presidential campaigns, easily the longest in the world, are as excruciating as they are costly. But soon, the American people, as well as the rest of the world who follow these events hour by hour, began to notice that this new kid on the block was attracting audiences larger than other traditional mainstream candidates.

Was America finally shading its past, and embracing a black man in line with Thomas Jefferson's penmanship of "Every human being is endowed by the creator, with inalienable rights of life, liberty and the pursuit of happiness", enshrined in the US constitution, or would this come to pass, as it had before, when non-traditional candidates such the Rev. Jesse L Jackson stood in the 1980's or Congresswoman Barbara Jordan had done in the 1970's, only to remain as erasable dots in the American political landscape. From the moment he splashed on the scene with a rousing speech at the 2004 Democratic Convention in Boston that nominated John Kerry as the flag bearer, the skinny, big-eared state senator from Illinois had left an indelible mark on many political watchers. It would be just a matter of time before some promoter would push him to the frontline of American politics.

Black Americans gave him a cool reception at first, feeling a sense of déjà vu, with candidates who said all the right things, but with no chance to win the ultimate prize, in a country where the majority white citizens would be calling the shots for a long time to come. For candidate Obama, with a foreign-sounding name, there were other sentiments that militated against supporting him. With a white mother and a Kenyan father who never planted his roots in the country, some viewed him as an "imposter", unschooled in the traditions of a black candidate with scars from the acrimony of the civil rights movement. Obama's experience had been shaped by his stint as a community organizer in Chicago's poor housing projects after leaving Columbia University in the 1980's. This was long after the riots and street battles with the police, which followed the assassination of revered civil rights legend Dr. Martin Luther King Jr.

To many African Americans therefore, it was inconceivable, that a young man, born and raised in a middle-class white household in far-flung Honolulu, Hawaii, would inherit the mantle once held by Dr. King, from those who were clobbered by police with him in the streets of Selma, Alabama, fire-bombed in churches in Mississippi, jailed in Atlanta, and humiliated in every aspect of their lives elsewhere. True, Dr. King had paid the ultimate sacrifice, fighting for inclusion based on character rather than skin color, which was the theme he preached about in his famous "I have a dream speech", delivered during the March on Washington, at the Lincoln Memorial on August 28, 1963. But still, many people from all walks of life, were unconvinced that Obama had paid enough dues to deserve the prize of the most powerful position on earth, ahead of the stalwarts of the civil rights movement.

"Why waste your vote over a candidate that will never win?"

was a typical question heard over radio waves, barber shops and black churches everywhere, during the early stages of Obama's campaign. Media personalities like Juan Williams and Tavis Smiley, both strong Dr. King adherents, never attempted to hide their disdain for him, during his quest for the highest office, and even after he attained it. In their most recent zeal, Mr. Smiley was joined by famed academician Dr. Cornell West of Princeton University, on what they dubbed as an "anti-poverty" bus tour around the country, to raise awareness, especially among African Americans, emphasizing how Obama's economic policies have maligned them. Luckily for the president, not everyone is sold on the duo's motives. Prominent among them, have been firebrand types like Reverend Al Sharpton, who questioned why the duo did not mount similar campaigns against white occupants of 1600 Pennsylvania Avenue, like Reagan and the Bushes, whose policies were even less-friendly to the poor in general.

It took the endorsement of Talk Show Queen Oprah Winfrey, on her show, to turn the tide, and convince rather skeptical black voters, that this was the "real McCoy", whose vote would deliver the proverbial forbidden fruit. Until that time, Hillary Rodham Clinton, then a junior Senator from the Empire state of New York, and wife to former President Bill Clinton, had been anointed as the front-runner for the presidential nomination of the Democratic Party. Sentiments were very high among the supporters of the former president, who had been nick-named "the first black president", due to his closeness with high profile black leaders such as Vernon Jordan, Congressman Charles Rangel, and civil rights icon John Lewis of Georgia. Indeed, for many black voters, it came down to a choice between "the devil you know", and an "estranged brother".

While campaigning for his wife in Charleston, South Carolina close to the Super Tuesday primaries in February 2008, Bill Clinton sealed his wife's fate, when he made a comment about the civil rights bill of 1964, which seemed to elevate the role of

President Lyndon Johnson over that of Dr. King. Many black voters interpreted this as the usual condescending attitude of the white establishment towards black people no matter how qualified they may be for a position. The result was an overnight switch of loyalties from the Clinton campaign to Obama's. In a classic case, Congressman John Lewis, whose constituents gave him an ultimatum to vote for Mrs. Clinton and risk a recall from his seat, made the famous quote that "he didn't want to be caught on the wrong side of history".

With that turn of events, what had been considered a fait accompli for Hillary, began to look like a long shot, since in American politics, no other group even comes close in loyalty to a political party, like African Americans consistently deliver to the Democrats. Super Tuesday's vote showed overwhelming support for Obama, an endorsement that had eluded him up to that point. Having secured their vote, candidate Obama worked even harder to earn their trust and ingratiate himself to them, a bond he seems to have maintained ever since, despite the harsh economic times that have characterized his administration, much to the detriment of the very group that forms his solid base. But hard as he tries, the President's job was doomed from the beginning by the conditions he inherited from his predecessor. The Iraq and Afghan wars, both of which have sucked more than a trillion dollars from the US Treasury, were the first major wars to be entirely financed through borrowing, without raising revenue devoted to the purpose, as had happened with previous war efforts.

President George Walker Bush, whose first term had been under a cloud, due to the disputed 2000 election against Vice President Al Gore, had been forced by the un-anticipated circumstances of September 11, 2001, to declare war on the Taliban perpetrators of the US invasion. The Iraqi war, which followed two years later, based on dubious intelligence about Saddam Hussein's possession of weapons of mass destruction, (WMD), ensured that the US would be fully engaged in the war theater for the next decade, no matter which party, Democrats or Republicans, won elections.

Nevertheless, when Obama entered the presidential race in 2007, he campaigned strongly as an anti-war candidate, promising to "bring our troops home", spiced with a resonant message of "change you can believe in". A war-fatigued American audience listened, and, in the heat of the moment, with the prospects of a history-making event of electing the first Black man ever to hold this office, euphoria turned into a frenzy, culminating into the swearing in of President Obama on January 20, 2009. During President Bush's second term the US economy had steadily deteriorated every year, until in his last year, the bottom appeared to fall off completely. The credit crunch that seized the entire global financial system had not been seen since the economic depression of the 1930's when Calvin Coolidge was president. American icons such as Lehman Brothers, a 150-year Wall Street fixture, got caught on the wrong side of the balance sheet, and were forced to cease their operations. Even Fannie –Mae and Freddie-Mac, once thought of as impregnable due to their heavy backing from Uncle Sam, were thrust on the receiving line of the stimulus package.

Thus, right from the beginning, Obama's challenge was to replicate Franklin Delano Roosevelt's heroic measures of rescuing America's sinking ship, and restore the country back to glory, while sailing against recalcitrant Republicans violently opposed to raising taxes. He would soon find out, that Washington, particularly Capitol Hill, abhors change, the same way nature abhors a vacuum. It was easier to give speeches and get away with campaign rhetoric than getting populist policies through a bickering Congress. Most presidents usually get a grace period soon after election, during which both the press and the public treat them with deference in an unwritten code of conduct. But Obama hardly got any. The Republican rightwing ideologues, initially led by radio personality Rush Limbaugh and Fox News hosts like Bill O'Reilley and Sean Hannity, launched their vitriol almost from day one. Then there was the formation of the Tea Party, mostly composed of Sarah Palin disciples. Sarah Palin had been a completely unknown entity until Senator John McCain, Obama's Republican challenger in the 2008 presidential race, picked her as a vice-presidential running mate. At the time, she was Governor of the wayward state of Alaska. Ms. Palin, a flashy personality, turned out to be "mostly hat and no cattle", as Texans would say. And soon, after gaining fame and fortune from her best-selling book, entitled "Going Rogue", the public quickly discovered that there were more looks to her than substance. Her popularity quickly waned, and has been going south ever since.

Still, Obama's problems would have persisted, with or without the rightwing.

"It's the economy, stupid", as James Carville, former President Bill Clinton's campaign manager often says. Compounding the problem, is an economy that has been in the doldrums longer than any other since the Depression. The massive US$700 billion stimulus package that he managed to rush through Congress in his first year, promising that it would put Americans back to work, has yet to deliver the goodies. The national unemployment rate in the early part of 2012 hovered around 9.1 percent, and in states like Michigan and Nevada, closer to a whopping twelve percent and worsening (National unemployment rate now down to around 7.5%). Within the African-American community, his safest base, unemployment rate topped fifteen percent for adults and perhaps double that among young black males. These are the kind of statistics that give any occupant of 1600 Pennsylvania Avenue, some extra grey hairs and a wrinkled face, both of which have been visibly apparent on the president lately.

Nevertheless, those on the extreme right, who professed that Obama would be a one-term president, should remember that Bill Clinton was equally cornered, when in 1994, former Speaker Newt Gingrich led a campaign he dubbed " A Contract with America". In what was a mid-term landslide victory for the Republican Party, young Turks captured many seats previously held by Democrats, almost making it impossible for President Clinton to get any of his proposed bills passed in Congress. The president methodically fought back, relentlessly focusing "as a laser beam", on issues that affected peoples' pocket books, eventually winning himself both friend and foe, so that by 1996, he trounced Senator Bob Dole, to win a second term with a very comfortable margin.

Americans cannot be fooled by the Tea Party rhetoric, sometimes tinged with racist subliminal messages. While the president was struggling to get Americans the jobs they lost, most rational people realized that none of the individuals among the coterie of GOP candidates would offer any better solutions for the nation, let alone the whole world yearning to recover. In that case it boiled down to a case of "better the devil you know". The president, whose persona is devoid of the sort of scandals that bedeviled his immediate predecessors, retained individual appeal, which, combined with his effective communication skills, became his saving grace. It is apparently clear, that the majority of Americans have transcended the issues of petty racism, to a point where, like the Chinese say, "they don't care about the color of the cat, as long as it catches the mice".

In mid-January 2009, I hurried back from vacation, to return to Washington, just in time for the inauguration of President Obama. I wanted to witness the historic event of seeing the first black man ever to assume the world's most influential position. Winters around Washington DC can sometimes turn bitterly cold, but I was used to that. If you have to be away from the house for a prolonged period, the trick is to leave the heat on, and set the thermometer at about 65 degrees, just warm enough to prevent water pipes from freezing. But all rooms in a house cannot adjust to the same temperature, as some are more exposed to the outside than others, while those nearest to the garage may be poorly insulated. During frigid temperatures, the heat in the house sometimes becomes inadequate to keep the less-insulated spaces from freezing.

As the KLM flight from Amsterdam touched the tarmac at Dulles International Airport, I turned my phone on to call my sister so that she could pick me from the airport. But, just before calling, I tried to check my voicemail for messages. There were two messages, one from my sister, and the second one from my son in Chicago. They all said the same thing.

"Please do not go directly to your home, as the water and power have been turned off by the Fire Marshall". They also provided a telephone number of the police officer who had accompanied the fire men to the scene. Had my home caught fire in my absence? My heart was racing to my mouth as I dialed my sister to find out what exactly had happened.

"A water pipe burst from upstairs, and flooded the house", Monica told me. "But how did the cops get involved in all this?" I asked.

"It appears one of your neighbors noticed the water gushing out of the house, and knowing that you were away, simply decided to call the authorities", she said. Thank you neighbor, whoever you are, I said to myself, for my house would have turned into a mini lake, a frozen one at that. I still wanted to see and assess the situation for myself, so when Monica arrived at the airport, we drove straight to my home. It was after 7.30 pm, and with the short days of winter, there was no light, except for the lone street light that illuminates the area around the mailbox.

My first puzzle was how to get into the house, since the garage door operates on an electronic device, that couldn't work since the power was off. Then it dawned on me that the police must have forced one of the windows open to enter the home. I called the police captain again, and he confirmed my suspicion. I went back to the car trunk, and fished out a flashlight to allow me to see the damage inside. What I encountered was not a pretty sight. The frigid water was more than ankle-deep, stretching all the way from the garage to the living room and kitchen. Only two years earlier, I had sunk a lot of money in a major renovation that had gotten rid of the 70's look in my house. Now all this would have to be redone, provided my homeowner's insurance would pay for it.

I proceeded to my sister's home in Alexandria, but in spite of the exhaustion from a long flight, I couldn't catch any sleep at all. Before going to bed, I placed a call to my Insurance Company to let them know about the emergency. It was about mid-night, and nobody was in the office, so I left them an urgent message for someone to call me as soon as possible. The following day, January 20, 2009, was Inaugural day, and it was a national holiday. The temperatures were a bone-chilling 13 degrees Fahrenheit (-10.5 C), stretching most home heaters to a break-down point. As soon as I woke up, I rushed to my home to get a better view under natural light. Upon arrival, the situation appeared even worse than I had seen it under the dim light of the flashlight. For the next two hours or more, I called the Insurance Company back and forth, hoping that they could send someone to assess the damage. And for the umpteenth time, the underwriter on the other end told me that the earliest they could get someone to come in was Wednesday or Thursday that week. It was Monday.

Finally, frustrated and numb from the frigid temperatures inside the house, I left the house and headed for my sister's home to continue searching for a solution, at least from a warmer place. By that time, I had abandoned any plans of joining the multitudes that thronged the streets of the nation's capital of Washington DC for the inauguration. Instead, I turned the TV on, along with a VCR, to capture as much of the historic event as I could, while spending more time on the phone in search of a plumber to repair the busted pipes. By mid-day, my insurance agent had arranged for Service Master, a company they frequently engaged in such emergencies, to bring some heavy-duty driers to my house and start drying out the place. This operation would turn out to last more than a week, during which time I found out that a lot of my stuff, especially those that had direct contact with the ground, had sustained more damage than could be repaired.

The flood in my house had turned my life topsy-turvy, and the holiday had not helped the cause. Most plumbers I called promised to come in a week's time, citing backlogs created by the inclement weather conditions. For the next month or so, I commuted from Alexandria to my work at Government Center, stopping by my house every morning, to open for the repair crew, and set the program for the day. Finally, when the insurance adjustor came by, after about a week following the incident, it became a test of wills, arguing over what the insurance would or wouldn't cover. When they finally gave me the list of what their liability was, I took it grudgingly, and followed it with a complaint both to the Better Business Bureau, and the State Insurance Regulatory Commission in Richmond. It would not be until mid-March, that the home was ready to occupy again. But, as the saying goes, every dark cloud has a silver lining. The flood gave me an opportunity to do most of the delayed maintenance I had put off for years. Now, I look back with a little trepidation, at the prospect of going through the same experience each time old man winter rears his head.

Meanwhile, President Obama's job remains a tossup as the US economy remains stuck in neutral. America almost always, votes their pocket, not ideological gobbledygook. Although the current lineup of GOP candidates is far from inspiring, if the national unemployment rate does not drop below the eye-popping 9.1 percent in the next few months preceding the first presidential primaries in January, the American voters will most likely hire someone else to sit in the Oval Office. However, the American economy cannot grow in isolation, considering the Euro zone's insurmountable problems which continue hitting the US with a debilitating blow.

Earlier this first week of October, Sarah Palin, looked in the mirror, took a deep breath, and declared herself "not fit for duty", ending the speculation surrounding her intentions to jump into the

2012 presidential race. Her exit might benefit the GOP top-tier candidates like former Governor of Massachusetts, Mitt Romney, or his closest Republican competitor, Texas Governor, Rick Perry, but not the president himself, since all polls conducted so far suggest that, pitied against her, he would win easily. But the GOP also has this habit of parading some "also-run" black candidates against Obama, in the hope that their blackness will somehow stop, or even neutralize his advance. They planted Allan Keys in his Illinois Senate race, and when that didn't work, they later promoted Michael Steel, former Lieutenant Governor of Maryland as the spokesman of the GOP in the hope of attracting more African Americans and other minorities to the party. But Mr. Steel's appointment only produced disastrous results, probably maligning the party from them even more due to this kind of tokenism. Now they are at it again, parading former Godfather Pizza czar Herman Cain, who is affiliated with the Tea Party, as the anointed one to lead them to the Promised Land. He talks of race being inconsequential, while at the same time promises to siphon black voters from the president. If race indeed doesn't matter in America anymore, why not concentrate on all these other groups that would garner him a majority vote?

Of late, beginning in late October 2011, scandal's natural process of selection had began taking a punch at Mr. Cain's campaign, as one blonde after another came forward to accuse the pizza man of having made some unsolicited advances towards them during his reign at the American Restaurant Association. These allegations were naturally followed by vehement denials, and the usual "conspiracy theories" about "modern day high-tech lynching". This line of defense was first used by a combative, later-to-be, Justice Clarence Thomas, while defending himself against accusations of sexual harassment from one time subordinate Anita Hill. Both men referred to a deliberate attempt by some section of the American public, to bring down some "uppity blacks". While this may have some grain of truth, the bulk of the problem is self-inflicted. Many political heavy-weights have succumbed under the weight of illicit dalliances. Former Senator Gary Hart of Colorado missed the democratic nomination in 1988 due to "Monkey business", while more recently, Governor Elliot Spitzer of New York, was forced to tender in his resignation after admitting some payoff to a young escort. Mr. Cain's dropping out of the race will place him in very good company.

As an American citizen of African descent, I would naturally, like to see President Obama do something special for the continent of his fore-bearers, along the lines of President George Bush's PEPFAR, or Bill Clinton's AGOA initiatives. But I would also quickly point out that this is a rather selfish approach. A more pragmatic view however, is that, given the prevailing domestic circumstances, and the fact that he has been a trailblazer in a role once considered out of reach, I'd rather see him succeed here first and prove all the naysayers wrong, that the roof will not cave in on the most powerful country, simply because a black man occupies the best seat on the table.

But, as many of us know, a president can at best, do little more than set the moral campus of the nation. The current imbroglio surrounding the shooting to death of an unarmed black teenager named Trayvon Martin, by a Latino man on neighborhood watch in Florida on February 26, 2012, shows how impotent presidential influence can be in such matters. Under a Florida statute referred to as "Stand your ground", in which a person can be justified in using maximum force if he or she perceives an adversary as threatening, the trigger man, named George Zimmerman, with a white father, and a Peruvian mother, is still walking free. This is happening, despite daily calls from a cross-section of the American public, with President Obama, proclaiming during a Rose Garden ceremony, that "If I had a son, he'd look like Trayvon", and calling for justice to prevail. Some in the black community have likened the case to the 1955 lynching of another black teenager named Emmett Till, although the circumstances are vastly different.

When Emmett Till, a fourteen-year old black boy from Chicago took a train to visit his folks in Money, Mississippi in the summer of 1955, he was dreaming of receiving the southern hospitality that his mother so often talked about. Little did he know that the American south was still engrossed in Jim Crow laws, which punished a black man for as frivolous a reason as staring, let alone talking to, or making a pass at a white woman. The Chicago and Detroit areas had become magnets for southern black Americans, fleeing Jim Crow's stringent segregationist laws of the Deep South, which relegated them only to a life of a sharecropper, and picking cotton and tobacco on the white man's plantation.

Passing by a store, one August afternoon, after boasting, and showing his friends in Mississippi, a picture of a white girl from Chicago, whom he purportedly said was his girlfriend, they dared him to go in and talk to the daughter of the white owner. Naïve about the unwritten codes of the sweltering delta, he entered the store, bought some candy, and, on the way out, said "bye baby" to Carolyn Bryant, who happened to be the wife of Roy Bryant, the owner, and a prominent member of the Ku Klux Klan.

A few days passed without incident, and it appeared as if the brazen boy from yonder north had made good on his promise. But, later that week, two white men, Mr. Roy Bryant, with his brother-in-law JW Milam, showed up at Emmett's uncle, Mose Wright's cabin in the middle of the night, and demanded to see the boy. They drove away with him in their pickup truck, and three days later, his mutilated body was discovered on the banks of the Tallahatchie River. One eye had been poked out, and the unrecognizable face had been bashed in, probably with a sledgehammer.

At first, all decent citizens of Mississippi showed disdain towards such a heinous crime, and the authorities vowed to visit some justice on the perpetrators. However, when Mamie Bradley, Emmett's mom, involved the NAACP, turning the incident into a national tragedy, and insisted that the body be shipped back to

Chicago, and be viewed in an open casket, "so the world can see what they've done to my son", the southern whites resented the way the northerners portrayed Dixieland, and threw their support behind the murderers. For the trial, which began on September 19, 1955, at the courthouse in Sumner, Mississippi, the prosecution initially couldn't find any white person willing to sit on the jury. They equally had a difficult time finding any witnesses, especially, black ones, willing to testify against white men, never mind that these were murderers. Things just simply weren't done like that in the Mississippi of the 1950's.

Finally, with a lot of prodding, Mr. Wright, Emmett's uncle, relented, and the prosecution managed to convince him to testify in the case. Asked if he could identify the perpetrators, he looked in their direction, and said "Dar he", "There he is". He was, however, rushed out of state soon after, for fear that he too, would be lynched. The all-white jury deliberated for a little over one hour, before returning a "Not guilty" verdict on September 23, 1955, the 166th anniversary following the signing of the Bill of Rights.

Jury duty is one of those sacrosanct tasks that every adult individual in a free society should aspire to do at least once in their lifetime. Apart from casting my vote to choose the president of the United States, this was the only other aspect which I felt would anoint me into a fully-fledged citizen of this great Republic. I had envied my wife when, a couple of years earlier, a summons had arrived in the mail, ordering her to appear at the Fairfax Circuit Court as a potential juror. Oftentimes, many people are called, but very few ever get selected to actually perform this very basic, yet extremely important role of participatory democracy.

My turn came while my wife and I were on vacation in Uganda, during which we had to take care of my ailing mother. Our daughter had stayed in the house, picking the mail as it came, and accumulating it until we returned. Having developed a disdain for junk mail over the years, I tend to go through the pile rather quickly, visually sorting out what I consider relevant, and putting it on one side, while tearing to pieces, the rest which I deem to be useless. A white non-decrepit envelope with a blue insert stared at me, and I was about to do to it what I had done to other pieces, until I read the address on the top-left hand corner, "From: The Clerk of the Circuit Court of Fairfax County". This immediately grabbed my attention, and I slit the envelop open, only to reveal a summons for me to appear on Monday at 8.15 am to be among the pool of people from which to select jurors. This was Saturday afternoon.

Emerging from the multi-story parking garage B on Monday morning, I joined the seemingly endless lines of those waiting to be cleared by security at the entrance to the five-story edifice. Our cell phones, and any electronic gadget deemed capable of taking photos were relieved from us. Realizing I had not communicated with my workplace about my possible absence for the day, I approached one of the security officers at the check-in, and told him I needed my phone to make a quick call.

"See that yellow phone over there?", he said as he pointed towards the reception desk beyond the screening booths, "Go use that one". With the stern look on his face, I did not wish to appear too cheeky, so I proceeded towards the phone, where two or three other people were already waiting to do the same. After the call, I took an elevator to the third floor, where a sea of people were verifying their parking tickets at the counter, before gathering in a large room to await further instructions after watching a brief video exhorting the virtues of participating in jury duty. After a little while, several uniformed bailiffs showed up clutching clipboards, and each one read the names assigned to each individual group. I listened very attentively, until my name was read out, directing us to gather in Court Room 5H on the fifth floor.

There, Judge Jane Marum Rouch, of the 19th Judicial Circuit Court was already seated at her elevated desk, while the County prosecuting attorney and the defense attorney stood up and watched us as we filed into the chamber. After brief instructions from the Judge, jury selection started in earnest. First the bailiff called the names she had retained on her original list after consultations with the two legal counsels. Those of us whose names were read were told to move to the "jury box", after which further screening took place with each individual answering a battery of questions. Those who couldn't answer the questions satisfactorily were eliminated, until only twelve of us were left. At this point, the bailiff ordered us to stand up and raise our right hands for the swearing in as jurors. Our colleagues, who for one reason or another had not been inducted into this select group, were excused from the chamber, and told they could go home. The Judge once again briefed us about the nature of the case (criminal), and told us, that barring any unusual circumstances, we could expect to spend the full day on the case, and depending on the evidence we had to sift through, two days or more were the norm. There was, we were told by the Judge, to be no discussion of the case, either in the corridors, bathrooms, or cafeteria, except in the jury room, located just behind the court room. Next thing we knew, the prosecutor was presenting his evidence, some of it extremely graphic in nature. We had been given some note books in which we were allowed to jot some notes for the express purpose of discussing the case. Anybody needing a break, including visiting the bathroom, had to be escorted by the bailiff, so we were told.

The lengthy presentation by the prosecution dragged us into the late afternoon hours, forcing the Judge to sound an early warning that we could not deliberate on the case until the following day. Before dismissing us for the day, the Judge repeated her warning to us, not to share anything about the case with our families. The following morning, I had to make another call to my office that I was still needed for jury duty. Once again, I endured another round of searches at the entrance to the Circuit court building, as I rushed to join my colleagues, before being ushered in the court room by the bailiff.

After brief remarks by the Judge, the prosecutor invited the police officer who had arrested and interrogated the crime suspect, to give testimony, which he did with relative precision. In an ironic twist, the defense attorney, a bulky bearded man, reminiscent of Raymond Burr of Perry Mason fame, put on what most of us in the jury box, admitted was mediocre performance. He occasionally put in an objection here and there, most of which were overruled by the Judge. Even when he finally put his client on the stand, his cross-examination technique appeared to give more ammunition to the prosecution than saving his client. The last witness was the subject's aging father, a reverend, whose testimony also did very little to help his son's case.

After both the prosecution and defense made their closing remarks, the Judge released us to go and deliberate over the case in the jury room. The strong video evidence presented by the prosecution had been incriminating enough, leaving no doubt in any juror's mind which way the vote would go. The two hour debate we had in the room was therefore, more about the nature of punishment to fit this crime. Some leaned towards a light jail sentence, arguing that certain crimes exacerbated by the internet had become so prevalent in society, that to give this poor man a stiff sentence would only make him a sacrificial lamb. In the end, however, we settled over a mid-way position that levied both jail time and some punitive monetary reparation, if only to remind him that he had inflicted some damage to his young son, with whom he shared the lurid material.

Having arrived at a unanimous decision, we selected a captain among ourselves, who would deliver it to the Judge. As we marched in single file back to the court room, I took a glance at the poor man on whose future we had just put a permanent scar. My conscious was clear that I'd just done the right thing. As the Judge dismissed us after the verdict, my mind went back to the jury selection video we'd watched in the assembly room the previous day. At the end of it, the presenter said, "I may not have changed the world, but I certainly did my part".

Twenty Six

EARLIER TRAVELS IN South Africa had left me with an unfulfilled curiosity since my first visit there in the early 1980's. However, that was during the apartheid era when I could not have traveled through the country freely. Nevertheless, the little exposure I had gained driving solo on a long stretch, from Maseru in the tiny kingdom of Lesotho to Lobatse on the Botswana border, had showed me a different side that one rarely picks up in a newspaper or magazine article. Now I had a chance to satisfy that void. My wife and I agreed on absorbing the scenery by taking a road trip from Pretoria to Cape Town. That was towards the end of December 2007. Both of our kids were on Christmas vacation, and it would therefore, be a great time to coalesce as a family and enjoy an outing together.

I am used to adjusting quickly from driving on the right in the US, to driving on "the wrong side" or left as they do in Britain and most of its former colonies. For the uninitiated, however, the sudden switch can be intimidating, and even incredibly dangerous. One wrong move can result in a head-on collision, especially on the narrow two-lane roads common in countries like Uganda. Luckily, the South African highway system is as close to a European one as one can get, more than any other country on the continent. The system offers a smooth, well-planned dual-carriage network, with maps and toll booths which ensure that revenues are available for regular maintenance. Some major trunk roads like N1, N2, N3 and N4, run for long stretches of this vast country. N1, for instance, stretches from Polokwane in Limpopo Province to the north-east, down to Cape Town, a distance in excess of one thousand miles.

If one has a reliable car like we did, a drive through the countryside can offer tantalizingly beautiful vistas of the landscape. I had sampled some of this awesome scenery from a previous trip, during which we drove to Durban. This beach city, located on the Indian Ocean in Kwa-Zulu-Natal, or KZN, is, to South Africa, what Miami is to the US, vacation land. It is a six-hour drive from the Johannesburg area, via N3, which takes you through extensive farmlands, until it meanders through the Drakensburg range of mountains, before descending towards the city of Pietermaritzburg, and finally, to the sandy beaches of Durban. KZN is home to the proud Zulu people, whose most famous native son was the nineteenth century legendary King Shaka Zulu, whose military prowess and aggression mirrored Napoleon Bonaparte's. His fearless fighters with their assegais, defeated the invading armies of the mighty British Empire in several battles, before succumbing to the more superior firepower of the gun.

Even today, prominent Zulu men like President Jacob Zuma, aren't afraid of shedding their business suits in favor of leopard skins and showing off their legs in traditional indaba and marriage ceremonies. The city of Durban also boasts one of the largest concentrations of Indians outside India. It's no wonder, that some of Mahatma Gandhi's ashes were spread here after his assassination during his quest for Indian independence from the British in 1948. Many Indians such as Ahmed Kathrada, and Mac Maharaj, stood by their black brethren in the fight against apartheid, and even shared the same premises on Robben Island including, admittedly, the world's most famous prisoner, Nelson Rolihlahla Mandela. It was Ahmed Kathrada, who stealthily hid Mandela's memoirs, chapter by chapter, and later released the manuscripts to fellow in-mate Maharaj, who then smuggled it to London culminating into the publication of Mandela's best-selling autobiography, "A Long Walk to Freedom".

The drive to Durban also refreshed my memories as we drove past signs pointing towards places like Ndosheni, Umzimkulu, and Pietermaritzburg that I had read about in Alan Paton's Cry the Beloved Country. The book was a must read during the anti-apartheid era, as it exposed, perhaps, more than any other, the follies of the apartheid regime in South Africa. One's presence in South Africa also reveals how intricate the race relations are between blacks, whites, Indians and a hodge-podge of other minorities. It is quite normal, for instance, to see a white construction supervisor driving a tiny pick-up truck, known as a "buckie", loaded with black workers in the back. Once on site, the same white man may be seen shouting out orders in one or more of South Africa's eleven official languages. Among the most widely spoken are Zulu, Xhosa, Afrikaans, English, Tswana and Sotho. To watch some programs on the South African Broadcasting Corporation network, is to immerse yourself in a multi-cultural experience, as conversation sometimes switches from one dialect to another on the same program.

The apartheid regime had tried to exploit this diversity by highlighting the differences, rather than the commonalities between these ethnicities. It had created the so-called "nations-within-a-nation", called "Bantustans", purely based on ethnicity. These were clearly unviable nations, which no other country, apart from South Africa, recognized. This concept was borrowed and refined from the European colonial rule's "divide-and-rule", which pitted one group against another, by quietly touting the virtues and superiority of one against the other, all the while waiting to become the arbiter once tempers began to flare among the protagonists. The Bantustans were characterized by the installation of a puppet king, paramount chief, or prime minister, whose worldly interests were ensured by the regime, so long as he sang its tune. On the fringes, were the ordinary black people, who had been deprived of their citizenship of South Africa, because they now had "their own country", but would be needed by the mighty South African mining sector which still needed their labor in order to continually satisfy the world's voracious appetite for precious metals, primarily, gold and diamonds.

Some remnants of the divide and rule policies have held sway in former colonies, and have manifested themselves in internecine violence in one form or another, some of it gruesome, like the Rwandan genocide, Burundi's infamous pogroms under Michel Micombero, the Biafran civil war and subsequent north-south clashes in Nigeria, and a host of other on-and-off conflicts on the continent such as the two-decade long Lord's Resistance Army in northern Uganda, under the reclusive Joseph Kony.

Eviction from the so-called "black spots", a euphemism for indigenous blacks occupying good land coveted by the white establishment near large cities like Johannesburg, Pretoria, Bloemfontein etc, was usually swift and brutal. It took the form of a late night knock on the door by armed police, ordering the residents to pack up their belongings and load them on waiting trucks for an unknown destination. This final destination most often turned out to be a desolate piece of bone-dry patched territory far-removed from the urban metropolitan life and its services to which the victims were accustomed. Devoid of any kind of meaningful services, this ensured that there would always be a dependency for survival, which the white employers exploited to pay pitiful wages for the cheap labor.

The result of these draconian measures was to squeeze the eighty percent black majority on to twenty percent of the nation's mostly unproductive land, while the twenty percent white population sit on eighty percent of the arable land. Attempts to ameliorate this imbalance since the end of apartheid through the policy of "willing seller-willing buyer", have only yielded miniscule results, as the white owners inflate prices of the land they own, making it almost impossible for the poorly-funded government land acquisition program to make any headway. A Zimbabwe style of forced eviction would also be disastrous for the African Continent's largest economy, mainly by the shear number of participants involved, compared to their much smaller northern neighbor. Those advocating a Zimbabwe style of land redistribution, such as the militant Youth leader, Julius Malema, have had to be pressured into silence, for fear of inciting a wider group of the dispossessed.

As a result, eighteen years after shedding the vestiges of the apartheid regime, that supervisor in the buckie, will, in all likelihood, return home to a mansion in one of the posh Pretoria neighborhoods such as Groenkloof or Waterkloof, attended to by a black maid, while his well-manicured lawn is also taken care of by a black gardener. The black workers, will, on the other hand, board a crowded mini-bus taxi to a township like Mamelodi, or beyond, to wash off the dust on a lonely water-tap, outside their tin shacks, lit by a single electric bulb, the only visible sign of "trickledown" economics that has impacted their lives since getting to Promised Land.

In spite of the giant steps taken by the ruling African National Congress (ANC), which celebrates one hundred years of its existence, this year (2012), South Africa remains a bastion of a highly unequal society, harboring perhaps, one of the highest percentages of the landless citizens in Africa, if not the world. The gap created by oppressive policies spread over nearly four centuries cannot be erased overnight, and will take a concerted effort from both the rulers and the governed, perpetrators and victims alike, to bridge this gap and create a more egalitarian society.

Early morning on December 31, 2007, our two kids, not known for being early risers, were, this time, up and ready by 5.00 am in the morning. I was determined to push the envelope, and drive the entire stretch of around 1312 kilometers (815 miles), between Pretoria and Cape Town in one day. Most drivers partition this trip into two days, but, as the kids would soon be returning to their respective colleges in the US after the brief Christmas holiday season, time was of the essence, leaving us with no option. My wife and I had picked enough snacks from the Pick'n Pay on Lynwood Road in Menlow Park, near where we stayed, knowing very well that this would minimize the number of stops for food along the route. Still shaking some sleep from our eyes, we packed ourselves in the little Toyota Corolla sedan, filled the fuel tank to the brim, and soon merged into the early morning Johannesburg traffic on N1.

Passing Alexandra Township, the yellow lights illuminated this well-lit stretch of the highway, as we sped further south, leaving a silhouette of Sandton and Jo'burg skylines in the background. By the time the summer sun came out fully, we had already crossed the Gauteng/Free State line, cruising towards the provincial capital of Bloemfontein. We didn't have any time to stop in the city, but only viewed it from the roadside as we sped by, noting, like all things South African, the stack contrast between the black and white divide as demarcated by the city's residential neighborhoods. This is akin to the rich (white)/poor (black) neighborhoods separated by railroad tracks in southern states such as Alabama and Mississippi.

We passed the road to Kimberly, a city located in the Northern Cape, and famed for its diamond mining past, that adorned it with the monumental Giant Hole. Cecil Rhodes, for whom the Rhodes scholarships are named, made his fortune here, and De Beers, the world's largest gem distributor, got its humble beginnings in this town. Diamonds were discovered there in the early 1870's, and by the time the rush was over around 1914, over twenty million tons of earth had been excavated, leaving a giant crater measuring 214 meters deep, with a perimeter of 1.6 kilometers, an effort that yielded 2722 kilograms of a girl's best friend.

The terrain began to change into the inhospitable rocky and dry veld of the Karroo, a huge expanse of territory that is part of the extensive Kalahari Desert. We took every chance along the way, to fill our tank, as there are few gas stations located along this vast wasteland. One can go for up to two hundred miles without coming across a gas station, or a store for provisions. One can only imagine what would happen, if by some mishap, the car developed trouble in this unforgiving wilderness.

Towards sundown, we began descending into the Western Cape, navigating our way through the wine-producing region north of Cape Town. The air became a little more tranquil, although the sea ensures that summer temperatures are accompanied with some degree of humidity. We had miscalculated on one issue. Cape Town hosts a carnival around New Year's Day, which practically chokes off most of the downtown areas, rendering access to some areas nearly impossible. I had been behind the wheel for nearly fourteen hours of non-stop driving, and we were thoroughly exhausted. The last thing we needed was an interruption that would make us leave the car nearly one mile from our hotel, and maneuver through the rowdy carnival crowd with our luggage.

At some point, my wife and daughter, who were walking ahead of us, disappeared into the crowd, leaving my son and I to fend off the curious youths who looked threateningly bent on relieving us of part of what we carried. After two hours of painstaking meandering, we caught up with my wife and daughter at the hotel, located near the South African Parliament in downtown Cape Town. A warm shower relaxed my body, sending me to sleep like a well-fed baby. In the morning, we joined other hotel guests in the expansive dining room, and enjoyed a luxurious breakfast of fresh juices, scrambled eggs, and tasty sausages for which South Africa registers very highly in my book.

After breakfast, we jumped on a tour bus which took us to many historical landmarks in the Mother city, as Cape Town is referred to. The highlight for the day was getting to the top of Table Mountain via the Cable car. Table Mountain, so-named because it has a flat top, offers an incredible panoramic view of the city of Cape Town and its immediate surroundings, including an eagle view of Robben Island, which was Nelson Mandela's domicile for seventeen out of his twenty seven years of incarceration. Tourists are allowed to remain on top of the mountain for a specific period, as the mountain experiences various weather patterns in a single day, some very windy and severe. The South African Park Service has done a wonderful job, sparing no efforts in labeling just about every object on top of this mountain, to ensure that all curious minds will be catered for. We wandered around as much as possible, taking in views of the city of Cape Town from as many angles as we could. Nearly three hours later, after combing practically every square inch of territory up there, and with winds beginning to gather dangerous speeds, we were called upon to get into the cable car for the descent.

It was late in the afternoon when we returned to our hotel. We decided to relax the rest of the day, as we prepared for an even more adventurous event scheduled for the following day. I placed an order for a few refreshments to be brought to our room, and the waiter who delivered them told me he was once a driver to the Congolese President Denis Sassou-Nguesso. An interesting conversation ensued between us, I, struggling with my French, while he barely made himself understood in English. Afterwards, my wife and I buzzed the kids in their rooms to join us for a leisurely exploratory walk around the neighborhood before returning to the hotel for dinner, and retiring for the night.

The following day, we had a sumptuous breakfast at the hotel, drove to the Victoria & Albert Harbor on the water front, found parking for our car, and proceeded to the Nelson Mandela wharf, from where we embarked on a vessel headed for Robben Island. The island, South Africa's version of Alcatraz, is located about twelve miles off the mainland, and takes about half an hour to get to. The day we sailed, the sea was calm, and visibility very clear. Two large ships, one of them a container ship, were anchored nearby, probably waiting their turn to enter Cape Town Harbor and off-load. Most of the passengers on the vessel we took were tourists, as anxious to get to the famed isle as we were.

Upon arrival, the passengers on the tour boat, numbering about two hundred, were broken into small groups of around twenty, and each group then assigned a guide. Our guide was a relatively young man by the name of Thulane Mabaso, himself once an inmate on the island. He first narrated the history of the island, beginning with its use as a leper colony, before being transformed into a prison for hardcore criminals. He took us to the most significant landmarks, including the infamous limestone quarry, where Nelson Mandela and other ANC luminaries like Goben Mbeki, Walter Sisulu etc, spent endless days chipping at stones with jack hammers, while at the same time, discussing and planning the course that would later shape the politics of today's South Africa.

Another significant landmark we saw was the Robert Sobukwe house. Robert Mangaliso Sobukwe was the leader of the Pan Africanist Congress party, a radical off-shoot of the African National Congress, which sought a more violent approach to the end of the apartheid system. It was, while its members were demonstrating at a police station near the township of Sharpeville in present day Gauteng Province, on March 21, 1960, that the South African police opened fire on the crowd, killing 69 unarmed protestors, an incident that would reverberate across the whole world, and infamously dubbed "the Sharpeville Massacre".

Sobukwe was among the ten leaders tried and convicted during the Rivonia Trials of 1964, which resulted in life sentences imposed on Mandela and others, for acts purportedly meant to overthrow the apartheid government. While on Robben Island, Sobukwe, presumably considered more radical than other fellow prisoners, was kept in solitary confinement in the little house which still stands today.

Mabaso conducted our group through the entire gamut of

conditions which the prisoners faced, including the segregated menu that allowed Indians and Coloreds more meat than their black counterparts, although the blacks were expected to work longer hours. We even visited the compound outside the cell block, where Mandela took to gardening, growing tomatoes and cucumbers which he used to donate to his jailers. This same garden was later used by Ahmed Kathrada, to hide the manuscript, chapter by chapter, of Mandela's best-selling Autobiography, A Long Walk to Freedom, which he penned by candlelight, usually after the guards turned the lights off for the night.

At the end of the official three-hour tour, we were allowed an extra hour to wander around on our own, exploring the nooks and crannies of this ragged island. The island appears to lie in a rain shadow, rendering it arid and unsuitable for vegetation typical of the Cape area. A few trees imported from Australia have been planted and seem to flourish better. We even saw two penguins in the bushes near the prison grounds. South African penguins are smaller than their Antarctica cousins, and long-adapted to warmer climates.

Later in the afternoon, we all gathered at the quay to board the boat for our return trip to Cape Town. The weather down here can change from summer-like to winter in a matter of a few hours. What had appeared like calm waters on our way to the Island had developed into 10 to 15-foot waves that swung the 30-foot vessel in dangerous fashion. We had been told that sometimes the sea gets so rough, that scheduled trips are cancelled. The winds gathered gale speeds, bringing a lot of moisture aboard, and leaving everyone on the upper deck soggy wet. Those who couldn't stand the breezy conditions run and took shelter in the covered lower deck. A few diehards, including myself, decided to stay put. The vessel labored on for what seemed like an eternity, although we could vividly see our destination amidst our misty eyes.

Finally, the Captain guided the vessel back into the calm waters of Victoria and Albert Harbor. Everyone was anxious to disembark and walk on solid ground again. The V & A offers all manner of eateries and shopping arcades. We picked our choices and then gathered on an empty table, to enjoy the food as we savored some free performances.

The following day was the last we intended to spend in the Mother City. We had a choice between visiting the wine-producing region around Stellenbosch, Penguin Bay, or Cape Agulhas. We opted for the latter. This is the southernmost point on the African continent, located 150 kilometers south-east of Cape Town. Beyond this, the next land mass is Antarctica, about 3000 miles away. The drive to Cape Agulhas offers the traveler, beautiful vistas of pristine Atlantic Ocean beaches, ragged cliffs, and, if one chooses, a refueling stop in the clean and attractive coastal town of Hermanus, most famous for its views of large schools of whales. Cape Agulhas also marks the artificial division between the Indian Ocean to the east, and the Atlantic Ocean to the west, as determined by the International Hydrographic Organization. The Portuguese first named it Cabo das Agulhas (Needle Point), when they first arrived there over five centuries ago, perhaps due to the ragged nature of the off-shore rocks near its approach. It is also referred to as the graveyard for ships, many shipwrecks having occurred here over the centuries.

Returning to Cape Town by 8.30 pm that night, I had the satisfied warm feeling of an explorer, having crossed the entire African continent from Algiers to Cape Agulhas in one single holiday trip. The next day, we ate breakfast hurriedly, so that by 7.30 am, we were checking out of the hotel, and ready for the long trek back to Pretoria. This time, we decided to take the Garden Route, although it's a little longer. We took a few shots of Table Mountain flanked by Devil's Peak on the left, and Lion's Head on the right, as we sped past Khayelitsha, the sprawling black township on the outskirts of Cape Town. The township is an indelible reminder of the evils of apartheid, and how greatly unequal black and white communities in South Africa will remain for the foreseeable future. We cruised east towards the city of Heidelberg, passing through without stopping, and continued towards Mossel Bay on N2 which runs along the Indian Ocean coastline towards the city of George. We turned north on a local road instead of going all the way to the city. This beautiful coastal city is a bastion of Afrikaanerdom, and was home to the recalcitrant late President Pik Botha, nicknamed "The crocodile" due to his stubbornness.

Soon, we rejoined N12 at Oudtshoom as we continued north towards Klaarstroom. By 4.00 pm, we had reached the city of Vereeniging, where we stopped at an Engen station for gas, and to stretch our legs before resuming our harrowing trip. My wife snapped photos of the old but colorful church with a long steeple as we headed towards the exit to rejoin N1, the main thorough-fare back to Johannesburg. We didn't get back to Pretoria until around 2.00 am in the morning, exhausted in every sense of the word. But our son was scheduled to leave for the US later that evening, so our options had been limited.

Twenty Seven

IN JANUARY 2011, I returned to Uganda to check on my ailing mother. Although her hip replacement operation the previous year had gone well, daily in-takes of pain killers on her already weakened body, continued to take a toll on her. Matters had been made worse, when my young brother Tony, had been stricken with a form of nervous paralysis which required a complicated operation. The old lady, in her agony, couldn't digest the news about Tony very well, and believed that he had died, and that we had concealed the fact from her. Neither Tony, nor his mother were in a position to travel and dispel this rumor, so for a long time, we struggled to try convincing my mother, that "Uncle Tony", as most kids in the family called him, was alive, though not exactly kicking.

It's always a thrill to go back "home", though at times this is laced with a sense of nostalgia. The country that was once one of the few envied on the African continent, has not lived up to its full potential. As its golden independence jubilee approached in October 2012, one could hardly find a noteworthy event or achievement that was really worth celebrating. It seems as though every opportunity that has availed itself to improve the people's lives has been squandered by regime after regime, seemingly leaving each successive generation worse off than its predecessor. As a result, people have since abandoned the hope of seeing a responsible and caring government whose raison d'etre is to serve and promote the interests of its people.

I arrived in the country a week before a presidential election, which, by all accounts, has always been a very tense period. Tense, because the current regime in power, the National Resistance Movement, has seen its image change from hero to villain, over the last quarter century they have held power. The nation, which has been governed by eight regimes, some, like Idi Amin's, extremely brutal, has not seen a peaceful power transfer since it got its independence from Britain on October 9, 1962. When it ascended into power in 1986, after a long and protracted guerilla war lasting five years, the war-weary citizens welcomed the NRM as the messiah that would deliver the country to the Promised Land, and restore the country back to what Winston Churchill had called "The Pearl of Africa". A quarter century later, the same regime that once promised democracy, peace and prosperity, had, instead, entrenched itself, staging rigged sham elections once every five years, to hoodwink the outside world about its democratic credentials, while a few top cadres enjoyed obscene wealth as the bulk of the population languished in abject poverty.

It was, therefore, not a surprise to find Kampala city, the capital, dotted with people in military gear, ready for combat, as if the country had, overnight, turned into a war zone. The previous election in 2006 had been conducted under extremely volatile conditions, after Mr. Museveni, having bribed the legislators in parliament to abolish the presidential term limits, allowing him to run indefinitely, had to fend off the surging popularity of his erstwhile nemesis, Dr. Kiiza Besigye, who had been exiled in South Africa. The president, never one to run out of tricks, had realized that repetition of 2006, would not only sink his reputation even among his dwindling supporters, but might even make him a candidate for later interrogation at the international Criminal Court at the Hague, once he relinquished power. Rather than visiting violence on his opponents this time, the regime opted for a softer, albeit more effective approach. Two weeks prior to the elections, the regime pressed the Bank of Uganda to release 600 billion shillings ($300 million) from the general fund, which they used to finance the elections, completely outside the budgetary process. Every conceivable enemy of the regime, both within the party, and outside, was given some sort of pacifier. Meanwhile, opposing parties like FDC, DP and UPC, who had counted on the brutality of the regime to alienate the population, were caught flat-footed when the anticipated violence failed to materialize. By the time the results of the elections were delivered by the president's hand-picked chairman of the Electoral Commission on February 28, 2011, the president, who the naysayers had predicted would lose on first ballot, had garnered 68% of the vote, leaving all the opposition parties to share the remaining 32% among them.

However, the opposition was not just about to absorb all these gimmicks without a fight. During the last two elections, (2001 & 2006), in which the main opposition contestant, Dr. Besigye had suspiciously lost to Mr. Museveni, the loser had taken his case to the Superior Court, and twice, he had lost on mere technicalities. Since then, he had vowed never to take his case back to the courts controlled by Mr. Museveni, but rather, to the court of public opinion, where the judgment might be in form of protests on the streets.

Beaming with confidence after an election result that surprised everyone, and stunned his opponents, Mr. Museveni took lightly the opposition threats of making the country ungovernable, threatening to crush anyone who would disrupt the peace and tranquility prevailing after an election devoid of violence. He had counted on the massive presence of the deployed military to instill fear in the would-be rioters. However, it was his turn to be caught flat-footed, as the charged opposition changed their usual tactics of going it alone, and instead involved the masses through a campaign they dubbed "walk to work", or simply, W2W. First, he instructed Police Chief Lt-Gen Kale Kayihura to focus on the main opposition antagonists, namely Dr. Kiiza-Besigye of FDC, Olara Otunnu, of UPC, and Nobert Mao of DP. By restricting the movements of these three, the president wrongly thought, that their absence on the street would cause the entire operation to lose momentum.

However, things didn't happen according to this script. Instead, with inflation raging at about 30%, causing food prices to be beyond reach for the majority of the citizens, and the Uganda shilling losing value, making traders jittery, the W2W soon took up a life of its own. The police did their best to restrict the movement of the masses, by mostly concentrating their ire on the opposition leaders, while at times engaging the riotous crowds in street battles. Dr. Besigye, the leader of the main opposition party, known as the Forum for Democratic Change (FDC), who had ran for the third time as Mr. Museveni's main opponent, took the brunt of the blows.

On April 29 2011, Dr. Besigye's car was intercepted at the Mulago Hospital round-about by a group of security operatives, composed of mainstream police, the army, and other offshoots of the security apparatus that dot the city, sometimes disguised as civilians. One young man going by the names of Gilbert Bwana Arinaitwe, of the Rapid Response unit based at Kireka, a suburb of Kampala City, distinguished himself with his brutality towards the retired Colonel, and one-time personal physician to the president. As the cameras rolled on, Arinaitwe, in civilian attire, drew his pistol, and used the butt to break the glass on the passenger side of Dr. Besigye's car, where the opposition leader was seated. In his zeal to further impress his bosses, the young man reached in his pocket, and pulled out a canister of pepper-spray, which he went on to empty into the doctor's eyes, almost totally blinding him. The incident was captured in real time, by some shocked observers, who soon posted it on You-Tube to the wider global audience, where it still resides as clear evidence of the regime's violation of human rights, should the International Criminal Court at The Hague ever need it.

But brutality is nothing new to this country, that the ebullient former British Prime Minister, Sir Winston Churchill called the "Pearl of Africa". In fact, the history of present day Uganda is rooted in violence and mayhem, exacted by various regimes, mostly on its own people. Recent serialization of the history of Uganda, by The Monitor Newspaper, as part of the nation's Independence Golden Jubilee shades more light on the country's tumultuous past.

The quest, by explorers like John Hanning Speke, and Henry Morton Stanley, to find the source of the Mighty River Nile, had sparked a lot of interest in Western Europe and the Americas, to learn about the interior of the African continent. Some of the stories they sent back contradicted the commonly held view of Africa as a land of carnivorous savages. Until then, there had been many fabricated and un-substantiated stories regarding the land and its occupants. They relied on such books as Joseph Conrad's Heart of Darkness, and used it as a broad brush to paint an unflattering picture of the continent. Unlike Arab sea-farers, who had established a presence on the East African coast in places like Mombasa, Dar-es-Salaam and the Islands of Zanzibar and Pemba, even trading with the interior for ivory and slaves, European powers of the time did not enjoy such experiences.

It was from this angle, which viewed Africa as devoid of form and organization that, Imperial Britain and other European powers, sought to conquer and acquire territories during the scramble for Africa. By and large, most of the explorers such as David Livingstone, John Speke, James Grant, and later, missionaries like Fr. Lourdel, Mackay and Tucker, penetrated the interior of the East African hinterland by way of the eastern route. This was partly because the Arabs who had established contacts with the coastal areas of East Africa for nearly a millennium, had already mapped out some established routes to the interior.

Once the explorers arrived in the interior, they were surprised to find that some of the most powerful kingdoms in the area, such as Buganda and Bunyoro-Kitara, had sophisticated levels of organization, headed by a king, with a prime minister, and a standing army. Kabaka Mutesa I, who had already dealt with Muslim traders, welcomed the new strangers with a mixture of caution and suspicion, partly to provide him with a buffer against Muslim intentions. By 1875, Henry Morton Stanley had even convinced the monarch to write what may be deemed the most significant letter from Buganda, in which he professed his "friendship to the white man", and invited more to visit his kingdom. Within three months of publishing this letter in the London Daily Telegraph, the Church Missionary Society (CMS), had recruited eight pioneer missionaries that would soon be on their way to change the course of history for the nation. Mutesa I had chosen friendship with Stanley, as insurance against the looming power of his arch-rival, Omukama Kabalega, whose forces occasionally invaded Buganda territory.

Kabalega, on the other hand, treated the arrival of Samuel Baker, who was then Governor of Equatoria Province (part of current South Sudan), and accompanied by a contingency of 1700 Egyptian troops armed to the teeth, with a great deal of suspicion. His suspicion soon proved correct, when Baker raised the Egyptian flag and declared the territory annexed to Egypt. The young Kabalega, who had only been king of Bunyoro for a few years, and fearing further loss of territory after the cessation of Toro earlier in the 1830's, put up a spirited fight against the invading forces, despite their superior weaponry, driving them out of Bunyoro, until Baker established a fort at Patiko in neighboring Acholi.

Baker did not take this serious humiliation kindly, and used his prolific writing in the British press, to paint an ugly picture of Kabalega as a manipulating coward, which picture would later turn all colonial administrators of Uganda against the Banyoro, including inflicting on them, some of the worst human rights atrocities on record.

Meantime, in Buganda, at the tender age of 16, Kabaka Mwanga had just taken over the reins of power after the death of his father Kabaka Mutesa I in 1884. Coincidentally, in the same year, European colonial powers gathered in Berlin, Germany, to decide how to divide and gobble up among themselves, the uncharted territories of the so-called "Dark" continent. The young monarch soon, found himself caught up amidst the foreign forces representing those competing colonial powers. When his father wrote his famous letter professing that he wanted "to be friends with the white man", nothing could have foretold him that this single act would mark the end of the glory of Buganda. Therefore, by the time Mwanga inherited the throne, the writing was already clearly on the wall.

First, he faced opposition from the Moslems, who were the strongest and most organized among the foreign religious faiths planting their roots in his kingdom. Mwanga had refused to be circumcised and become a Muslim. But rather than succumb to the whims of any single group, the king decided to play each against the other, hoping that in so-doing, he would stay above the fray. For instance, when the muslims turned the heat against him, he invited the Catholics, who, under Father Lourdel (better known as Father Mapera), had taken refuge in Mwanza, in present day nothernTanzania.

However, the Kabaka's love affair with them didn't last long when he realized that they'd fallen back to their old ways of alienating his subjects from him by converting them to Christianity. The climax came when Kabaka Mwanga ordered his now converted pages to renounce their new faith, and instead devote their loyalty to serving him. When they ignored his orders, it infuriated him so much that he soon gave orders for them to be burned alive. A total of 45 Christians were burnt in two places on Namugongo Hill, located about 8 miles from his Lubiri (palace) at Mengo. 22 of these were Catholic, with another 23 of them Protestant. The two spots where the pages were murdered have since been declared "Martyr's shrines, with annual commemorations every June 3rd attracting a world-wide audience of the religious faithful.

Despite their seemingly insurmountable differences, the persecution of the Christians, including the killing of Protestant Bishop James Hannington in 1885, temporarily united both the Catholics and Protestants against Kabaka Mwanga, maneuvering together until they dethroned him. The king had, by now no allies left. The Muslims had shunned him for refusing to convert to Islam, the Christians for executing their flock, while the traditionalists blamed the smallpox ravaging the kingdom at the time, on his abandoning the traditional beliefs.

But the most significant forces that would overwhelm him had been fostered in 1884, at the Berlin Conference, where European powers had congregated to apportion and distribute the African continent amongst themselves. By alienating his erstwhile allies, the Kabaka ensured that these forces would soon be ambling for a piece of his territory. Mwanga had been replaced by his brother Kiweewa, but when he, too, refused to undergo the knife, the Muslims, the most powerful foreign group at the time, dumped him after only forty days. By alienating the different religious faiths, which ultimately represented the various powers competing for territory in Africa at the time, the Kabaka had set himself up for manipulation that would later occur, using his subjects against him.

Not content to simply cede power to the Christians, the Muslims had managed to convert Kabaka Mwanga's other brother, Kalema to Islam, and installed him to the throne. However, in doing so, they had underestimated Mwanga's resolve to regain his throne, which he did by cutting a sweet deal with the Catholics, whose leadership had retreated to Mwanza, in present-day northern Tanzania. This new alliance was soon tested as Kalema sought help from Bunyoro's Omukama Kabalega, who was more than eager to oust his arch-rival in Bunganda, and install a puppet of his own.

By 1889, Mwanga was once again toppled from his throne, this time for good. He tried desperately to regain his throne by mobilizing his men from Bulingugwe Island, located in Lake Victoria, but the arrival of Captain Frederick Lugard that same year, accompanied by a retinue of Egyptian and Sudanese troops, armed with the superior Maxim gun, altered the power equation for good, in favor of Colonial Britain. Under duress from Captain Lugard, Mwanga signed an agreement that ceded power to the Imperial British East African Company over control of Buganda, paving the way to British rule in Uganda. Sir Gerald Portal, the first British Governor of Uganda was soon dispatched to the country, and raised the Union Jack over Mengo, the seat of the Kabaka on April 1, 1893.

For continuing their resistance against British colonial rule, Kabaka Mwanga, and Omukama Kabalega were captured in the swamps of Lake Kyoga in 1899, after betrayal by Langi and Bakedi allies, and exiled to the Indian Ocean Island of the Seychelles, where Mwanga died in 1903 at the tender age of 35.

Twenty Eight

I RETURNED TO Uganda in February 2011, just when the presidential election campaigns were reaching a crescendo. The usual perennial participants, namely, the long-serving incumbent Yoweri Museveni of the National Resistance Movement, (NRM), was at it again, against his nemesis, and erstwhile personal physician, Dr. Kiiza Besigye of the Opposition Forum for Democratic Change (FDC). The scenario was set to duplicate the events of 2006, replete with partisan military and police presence, creating outbursts of street violence each time there was some political rally. This time around, however, the presidential aspirants had been joined by two other colorful characters, Mr. Olara Otunnu, of the Uganda People's Congress, (UPC), and Mr. Nobert Mao of the Democratic Party (DP), the nation's oldest party. Although UPC and DP had displayed rather subpar performance in the last election, adherents to them still harbored the hope that their new presidents would re-invigorate them with new energy, and make them players on the national scene once again.

Mr. Otunnu had been in self-exile for the twenty-five years that the NRM regime had been in power, having been Foreign Minister during the Okello-Lutwa regime which was militarily overthrown by the NRM. He had also previously served as the country's UN Ambassador in New York, and later, as an Under Secretary for Children's Affairs at the same institution. With that kind of resume, backed by an Oxford and Harvard education, a lot of people thought his presence would tip the dynamics of the race. But the demographics of Uganda Mr. Otunnu had left behind in the mid-80's, had changed so dramatically, that when he finally made his way back, hardly anybody could recognize him. Moreover, most members of UPC, the party he aspired to represent, gave him a cold shoulder, going as far as accusing him of being part of the regime that overthrew party founder, and former president Milton Obote (R.I.P). His constituency, by and large, remained the non-voting members of the diaspora, whose voices, the regime in Kampala loathed, although it loved the workers' remittances that kept it afloat in good and bad time alike.

Any casual observer could not have failed to notice the heavy presence of security forces, in Kampala, who had been given a "shoot-to-kill" mandate by their commander-in-chief, supposedly, to prevent any election-related violence. Election Day, February 17th 2011, my niece Grace had invited me to have lunch at their new house off Masaka Road, which I had not had the occasion to see. But first, she wanted to cast her ballot before proceeding home. I welcomed the idea, knowing that it would allow me the opportunity to gauge the voting process as a non-participating observer. On the way to her home, I couldn't help noticing the hundreds of security personnel on the streets, standing in twos, dressed in full camouflage gear, weapons at the ready, with perhaps, 100 feet separating each pair.

Upon reaching her voting precinct on Buddo Road, I stayed in the car with Grace's two kids and another nephew, while she joined the voting line at the Primary School, where she had registered to vote a few months back. We could see her in line from where the car was parked. When she finally reached the Returning officers, they checked their list, or at least they pretended to do so, and a few minutes later, told her that her name wasn't on their register.

"But I live in this neighborhood, and I did register here in person, how can my name not be here?" she protested.

One of the officials advised her to proceed to the next precinct at Buddo to check. A number of other people were being told the same thing. Frustrated, Grace left without casting her vote, and we proceeded to her home to enjoy the lunch her domestic help had been preparing while she was away. Suspicion was that, for every voter sent away without casting the ballot, two were checked as having voted for the incumbent.

The heavy presence of soldiers had placed the entire population on tenterhooks, expecting a repeat of 2006, during which maximum force was used against the opposition, including, the use of the infamous "Black Mamba", who broke the sanctity of the Court of Appeal (equivalent of the US Supreme Court), to re-arrest members of the opposition, after they had been granted bail. This strategy, however, had not worked out well for the regime, and only brought it isolation and criticism from many quarters, including the donor community, from which it still relied for close to 40% of its annual budget. The regime figured that it was time to change this image, even if this meant raiding the treasury, to manipulate the electoral process by paying off anyone who might raise their voice.

By the time the elections were conducted in the 3rd week of February, the expected doom scenario of violence had not happened, and everyone was caught flat-footed as the final results of the elections were read out by the Chairman of the Electoral Commission, Dr. Badru Kiggundu. Not only did the results give Mr. Museveni a large margin, of 68%, against 26% for his closest rival, Dr. Besigye, but the results also showed him winning in traditionally hostile constituencies in the north of the country, now fielding their native sons, Olara Otunnu and Nobert Mao. Had the country resigned to fate and chosen Museveni, knowing very well that his army would cause mayhem if he wasn't chosen, or had he simply bought the election with the Ush 600 billion that State House had requested as supplementary budget only three weeks before the elections. Most conventional wisdom pointed towards the latter.

The stage was set for the kind of confrontation which had eluded the country during the election. As expected, all the presidential candidates who had stood against Mr. Museveni, denounced the results as fraudulent, and refused to recognize the final results as legitimate. To some extent, these groups shared the blame, as they had accepted to participate in the process, after their pleas to reform the electoral process had been totally ignored by the regime. For one month following the election exercise, the opposition toiled with the next move, but remained afraid to confront the impenetrable lines of security without a real cause to rally behind. They only taunted the regime, but Museveni was used to this, and ignored them, occasionally adding insult to injury by boasting about his newly found mandate.

But, by April, food and fuel prices were soaring, hitting family budgets like Mike Tyson's left hook. The Ush 600 billion suddenly injected into the economy during the electoral process, in combination with such natural phenomena as drought, had jolted prices of goods and services in a very short time. People's cries for the government to reduce taxes on petroleum products and ease transportation costs, as had been done in neighboring countries, were met with a resounding no, bordering on insensitivity to the plight of the same people the president had, not too long ago, begged for a vote. Then, some creative minds in the opposition concocted a scheme they dubbed "walk-to-work", or W2W. The idea appeared simple enough, leave your vehicles at home, don't even take a taxi or a bus, but just walk to work. After all, the majority of the population already walks to work on a daily basis, simply because they have no vehicles of their own, or they can't afford the commuting fare in the kamunyes (minibuses) that plow the city.

The first two days, the regime sat on the fence and watched, as thousands of people took to the streets on foot. The government dismissed this as a ploy by the opposition, hoping it would not attract many people, and that it would dissipate soon. But it didn't. By the end of the first week, the transportation sector was feeling the pinch, as most vehicles were idle. Adding salt to the wound, was the fact that the crowds began to chant pro-opposition slogans, and carrying their symbols too. This became quite a mouthful for Mr. Museveni to swallow, and he swang into action. He instructed Police Chief Major General (now Lt. Gen) Kale Kayihura, to crack down on these activities, and prevent a bad situation from getting worse. Problem was, the activities had spilled over into other towns upcountry, and the regime didn't have enough men and women in police uniform to handle the situation. The first few days, the police tried the standard crowd-control techniques, to no avail.

Then, in a process he alone controls, Mr. Museveni called in the army, arguing that this was a matter of national security. However, the military's raison d'etre is, universally, to fight and neutralize the enemy by applying maximum force. But in this case, who was the enemy? Wasn't this classic Will Rogers telling his audience, that "I found the enemy, and it is us?" Sure enough the troops came in brandishing their AK 47s, and soon the world began to watch images of bleeding pedestrians, whose only crime was an attempt to use their muscles to get to work. These street fights went on unabated for almost a month, mostly targeting the leaders of the major opposition parties, but particularly the Forum for Democratic Change (FDC), headed by Dr. Besigye. The situation climaxed when an over-zealous young man named Gilbert Arineitwe Bwana, attached to one of the shadowy paramilitary groups called Rapid Response Unit, got involved. Mr. Museveni has, over the two-and-half decades of his stay in power, created anywhere from four to six such outfits, including the infamous "Kiboko Squad", composed of rag-tag invalids, whose job is to set upon demonstration crowds in the city, while the police stand by and watch, pretending to be overwhelmed by the crowds. Some of the groups like the Presidential Guard Brigade (PGB), headed by Museveni's son Brigadier Muhoozi Keinerugaba, have enormous fire power, essentially making it "an army within the army".

It took the intervention of some foreign diplomats to plead with the NRM government, to allow Dr. Besigye , who was nearly blinded by the pepper spray, to travel to Nairobi, Kenya, for treatment. Two weeks later, Dr. Besigye made a triumphant return to the country, ironically on the day that President Museveni was supposed to be sworn in for the 4th term (or 6th if you count the first ten years of unelected Movement rule). Throngs of cheering citizens lined up the main Kampala-Entebbe thoroughfare, blocking traffic on the only road that leads to the nation's only international airport. Any attempt by the police to disperse the crowds, was swatted by highly-charged supporters who taunted them by chanting opposition slogans. It took nearly ten hours for Dr. Besigye's motorcade to cover the 35 kilometers between Entebbe and Kampala, a distance which normally lasts less than an hour.

Meanwhile, at the Kololo Independence Grounds, the cheering crowds were much thinner than usual, with a somewhat belligerent Museveni spitting fire over the so-called un-patriotic opposition leaders, who had taken a unanimous decision to boycott the occasion. Later as the day's events were winding down, some of the chauffer-driven vehicles, carrying invited guests, including heads of states (almost all African), were pelted with stones along Entebbe Road, on their way to a state dinner, much to the chagrin of the tough-talking host. But the battle didn't end there. The next three or four weeks were consumed with sometimes gruesome pictures that went viral on social media such as You Tube, Face Book and Twitter, as police unleashed water cannons, body-itching liquids, or even live bullets on riotous crowds.

These actions were roundly condemned in the international press, but Mr. Museveni continued to dismiss these verbal actions with a wave of his hand. He has long satisfied himself that, unless he commits a real massacre on the population, the west can never send in the Marines, or a Swart team to drive him out of power for only a few body counts, considered the collateral damage of routine crowd control. Besides, he has cushioned himself by presenting himself as the bulwark fortification against terrorism in the Great Lakes region of Africa. He has successfully done that by sending the largest contingent of men and women in uniform to Somalia, under the guise of AMISOM, the United Nations/African Union mission to stabilize Somalia. And as long as Mr. Museveni fights a proxy war on behalf of western powers, his checkered record of democracy and human rights violation can be put on the back banner.

Presidents Museveni of Uganda, Paul Kagame of Rwanda, and the late Prime Minister Meles Zenawi of Ethiopia, once referred to as "a new breed of African leaders" during the Bill Clinton Administration, had since lost their luster, especially on the domestic front, due to their high-handedness in dealing with internal opposition. However, in spite of the tribulations inflicted on their opponents, the west has not abandoned them, a la Qaddafi, Mubarak, or lately Bashar al-Assad of Syria. But there is no guarantee that this couldn't happen in future, once they've outlived their usefulness.

The Ugandan president who shot his way to power twenty six years ago, benefitted tremendously from the disenchantment the country had had with brutal regimes such as that of Idi Amin, followed by the equally unpopular second Obote regime. His nearly daily condemnations of the past leaders, whom he often painted in such derogatory terms as "swine" or worse, initially ingratiated him to the public. However, as the regime finally took full charge of the country, after defeating internal dissent from such groups as the Holly Spirit Movement of Alice Lakwena, Force Obote Back Again (FOBA), and the most formidable of *all, the Lord's Resistance Army (LRA) of reclusive Joseph Kony, the long suffering people* have yet to reap considerable tangible benefits.

Instead, they see a regime bent on perpetuating its stay through a combination of carrot and stick, weighing in more heavily on the side of the stick. For a country that boasted of a clean and seemingly incorruptible civil service at the time of independence, 50 years ago, the people now look on, with disdain, as the country competes with such countries as Nigeria, for the label of "most corrupt" on the Transparency International index.

Military expenditures, considered "classified", in Uganda, have long surpassed outlays on social programs such as health and education, which are more vital for uplifting the economic welfare of any society. The 2011 purchase of 6 Sukhoi SU-30 fighter jets at a whopping $740 million dollars, when the country was raging with galloping inflation due to high food and fuel prices, showed where the president's priorities lie. Cajoled by his own ruling party members recently, over a proposal suggesting he should cut a miserly Ush 39 billion (about US$15 million), from Defense and channel the funds to the crippled health sector, he retorted,

"You want me to reduce the soldiers' allowances so they can overthrow me?"

But, as bad as corruption is deplorable, nothing has worsened the country's conditions as the erosion of the institutional framework that existed before the current NRM regime took charge. Be it the court system, parliament, or the educational institutions, all these have been degraded to the point where the president has remained the only arbiter in situations as minute as dealing with a chicken thief, or as important a decision as who the major players should be in the country's nascent oil industry. In the case of the court system, the regime has, occasionally, interfered at will, to protect its interests as it deemed it fit, as it did when the infamous "Black Mambas" invaded the High Court and re-arrested opposition leaders who had just been granted bail by the same court.

For Parliament, supposedly, the second pillar of a tri-branched government, this institution has become a charade of praise-singers for the executive branch, due to the lop-sidedness of its composition as a result of influence-peddling, and bribery on the side of the regime. In one of the most infamous incidents in 2005, the president passed on a cash envelope containing Ush 5 million (about US$2,500 at the time), to each member of the majority NRM members of parliament, to amend the Ugandan constitution and drop Article 105, which removed presidential term limits, thus paving the way for what has, since, been called, "the life presidency project". It has become commonplace, for the president to take positions contrary to those of parliament, and then doggedly pursue them behind closed doors, till he changes the outcome to his liking. This has, by and large, left the legislative branch mostly functioning as a "rubber stamp" for the executive branch, calling into place, the efficacy of having the three branches of government.

Since no major investment activity can escape the scrutiny of the president, who seems to have a penchant for favoring foreign, as opposed to domestic indigenous investors, most major decisions are either made at State House, Entebbe, or better still, at the president's up-country home at Rwakitura in Kiruhura District, where he appears more relaxed. These kinds of activities have tended to sideline the decision- makers in such moribund institutions as the Uganda Investment Authority, created to be "a one-stop shop" for all investment activities. With a population of 34 million packed in a country the size of Wyoming (236,000 square kilometers), and galloping at about 3.6% a year, one of the fastest rates in the world, the country is hamstrung by a leadership bent on self-preservation, rather than creating a modern economy that would propel the country forward and uplift the standards of the bulging young population.

The prospects of an oil bonanza associated with the recently discovered oil in the Albertine-Graben section of the western rift valley, have already shown the usual traits of an "oil curse". The regime's secrecy, regarding the Production and Sharing Agreements,

(PSA), initially with Tullow and Heritage Oil companies, and more recent farming agreements with French firm Total, and Chinese firm CNOOC have not been encouraging, to say the least. The constant bickering between the executive branch and the legislative, over contentious issues relating to bribery and kickbacks, even before the first barrel of oil is pumped from the ground, has left a bad taste in the mouth of those who had hoped for early production revenue to rejuvenate the country's economy.

Further complicating the situation for Uganda's nascent oil Industry has been discoveries of sizeable oil deposits in the Lake Turkana area of Kenya, and vast natural gas finds in the Mtwara region of Tanzania, extending into Mozambique. Uganda's insistence on processing its crude by building a refinery makes it a very expensive operation for a country already disadvantaged naturally by being land-locked. It would, therefore, not surprise anyone if, Kenya, with its shrewd pro-business approach, and more developed infrastructure, got its oil out of the ground, and onto the market faster than Uganda.

To avoid the pitfalls of the oil curse, Uganda, which advertises itself as "Gifted by Nature", needs to adopt a multi-pronged approach to development, and boost production in other sectors such as agriculture, mining and manufacturing parallel to the oil sector. As a finite resource, oil revenues should be invested productively, especially in improving vital areas such as health, education and infrastructure, which have long term benefits. With more focus and tenacity, the country known as the Source of River Nile, in which the mighty river flows for hundreds of miles, could easily become an exporter of hydro-electric power to some neighboring countries. Despite all the natural advantages the country possesses, it has failed to develop a product that is uniquely Ugandan. The country needs a niche to distinguish itself from the rest of the pack. Couldn't the charlatans in the Ministry of Tourism, at least fight back against the Hawaiian hula dance by showing off Baganda women performing the Nankasa beat?

Twenty Nine

BY THE BEGINNING of 2012, it was getting clear that my mother's health was continuing to deteriorate. Oftentimes, she would be well one week, only to be rushed to hospital the following week. During this time, her mind would wonder off, to the extent that at times, she wouldn't recognize some of the people around her. The next week, she would turn around and almost appear normal again, only to repeat that cycle again. It was an extremely frustrating time for both my sister and I, living half a world away, and mostly relying on a caretaker to update us on her condition almost on a daily basis. In mid-January, I mobilized my wife, and our son, to rush to Uganda and see her while she at least retained some semblance of her mental faculties.

I had paid a last minute visit to my father in April 2004, at the time he was on his death bed. However, due to the urgency and logistics of such an abrupt trip, I had not been able to take my two kids to say farewell to their grandpa. After staying for two weeks, with his condition remaining unchanged, the relatives had encouraged me to come back to the US, and resume my work, saying that I had done all that was humanly possible for the old man, and that the rest was in the hands of God. On April 6th, 2004, I reluctantly boarded a KLM flight via Amsterdam and Detroit. By my reckoning, Mzee Tobi passed away at about the time the plane touched the tarmac in Detroit. Arriving at Washington's Dulles

International Airport, I got the somber message from my wife and sister's faces as I emerged from International Arrivals lounge. Nature had pulled the rug from under my feet, robbing me of the opportunity to be home when my father was laid to rest.

The high travel expenses involved prevented the family from making frequent visits. Mostly, it was I alone who visited my parents, often coming up with all kinds of excuses about why the rest of the family didn't travel with me. There was a genuine sense that they missed interacting with their grand children, the same way they were doing with the other grand children who lived in Uganda, and visited more often. But such is the plight of every immigrant, who, for one reason or another, finds himself or herself unable to ferry their brood home to play with a grandma or grandpa, whose dialect they can't even understand.

Our son, now a young adult in his mid-20's, enjoyed the experience of being re-united with his grandmother. He also seemed to hold a special place in my parents' life, being the only grandchild in my extended family, who carries my father's full names. I didn't want to live the double guilt of failing to connect these two generations before the old folks passed on. We spent nearly a week at my ancestral home of Kabura in Rukungiri District, and then returned to Kampala for a few more days. By the time we left, my mother was in a relatively good condition, although she had initially had problems recognizing me the night we arrived there.

Born in 1922, in Buhunga, a small village near Rutooma Parish along Rukungiri-Ishaka Road, her parents, Nyakugita and Rosa died before she was a teenager, forcing her and her young sister Aunt Anna Maria, (R.I.P), to move in and take residence with their elder sister, Esteri who was already married. No educational facilities were available in the area at that time, least of all for a girl. However, she managed to get a little exposure to some reading and writing through catechism classes offered by the newly established church at Nyakibale. She met and married my father in

1942. My eldest brother Matia, was born in 1943, followed thereafter, by eight of us, in all, six brothers and two sisters, stretching
over a twenty year period. Except for temporary illnesses, such
as a bout of malaria here and there, my parents enjoyed good
health. But for my mother, all that changed in 1996, after a major
fall in our backyard, a fall that left her with a broken hip.

I had left my job at the World Bank, with a purpose of setting up on my own, and spent some time, busily working out the
logistics of getting started in a system that seemed intractable as
a business environment. By all accounts, the country was not yet
ready for prime time. Then one evening, while at Uncle Matia's
home, an old friend of the family, Kalori, a prominent businessman who operated a fleet of buses, stopped by. He started by
asking us why nobody had rushed home to bring Mother to one
of the hospitals in Kampala. Except for Cel-Tel Communications
Co, which was still a start-up in the country, there were no other
mobile phone providers at the time. Upon inquiring a little more
from Kalori, we learned that Mother had broken her hip a few
days back, and had been admitted at Nyakibale Hospital, the only
functioning facility in Rukungiri District at the time.

My brother Tony and I rushed there on the double the following morning. We intended to make the two hundred-twenty
mile trip and back the same day, everything permitting. When
we got home, we were shocked to see the condition she was
in. She had fractured her femur bone near the top, and was in
excruciating pain, after Nyakibale Hospital doctors dismissed her,
recommending that she be taken to Mulago Hospital Orthopedic
and Trauma Center. Unfortunately, that message had not been
communicated to us in time. Instead, they had transported her
back home, as they awaited our arrival. We quickly arranged for
a doctor from Nyakibale to come home and inject her with a
painkiller, which would give her temporary relief as we sped back
to Kampala at full throttle.

Stretching a mattress on the folded back seats of my Peugeot station wagon, we gently lifted and placed her on the mattress, then got Paulina, our cousin, to sit behind with her, to ensure that the broken leg would remain in place. But even with the pain-killer, my mother was groaning with pain all the way, every five miles or so, asking us whether or not we were anywhere close to Mulago Hospital. It's quite a humbling experience for anybody to see their parents cry. We finally got her to the Emergency Ward at Mulago Hospital at around 8.00 pm, but we were told the ortho-pedic doctors wouldn't be available until the following day. They gave her more painkillers, and we just had to wait it out.

Early the following morning, with some help from doctors we knew at Mulago, we located Dr. Edward Naddumba, the head of Orthopedics at Mulago, who saw her, and assigned the case to Dr. Rodney Belcher, an American doctor, previously teaching medicine at Georgetown University, and at the time, training ortho-pedic surgeons at Mulago Hospital. Within one week, my mother had hip replacement surgery, performed by Drs. Naddumba and Belcher. But two days after the operation, while my mother was still recuperating in the hospital, a tragic event happened. On March 11, 1996, as Dr. Belcher was attempting to open his new Nissan Hatchback in the parking lot just outside the Orthopedic Center, two young men approached him and demanded the keys from him. When he hesitated for a brief moment, one of the men, who carried a loaded AK47, shot him twice in the chest, and the two drove away in his car, leaving him in a pool of blood. The police who investigated the case, and even apprehended the culprits, simply referred to the incident as an unfortunate case of car-jacking gone bad. The slain doctor was from the Washington DC suburb of Arlington. My family received this tragic news with tremendous sadness, considering that barely one week earlier, he had given my mother a new lease on life. Mzee Tobi, who had all along remained at our upcountry home, came to pay a visit after the operation. I watched both my parents shed "tears of joy" as they embraced, perhaps, believing, and justifiably so, that a miracle had just happened to keep my mom alive.

Although the operation had been done successfully, the doctors had recommended that my mother should engage in some kind of regular physical therapy, which would eventually help the weakened muscles around the hip to develop and regain their natural strength. Initially, she practiced walking around the house with the aid of crutches. But exercise had never been her cup of tea. So, as time went by, she took to sitting down in her chair most of the day, occasionally getting up with a little help, and taking a few steps to the front porch, and then back to her seat. As a result of sitting for long hours, she started accumulating fluids in her legs, problems that made it increasingly more difficult for her to get up and walk. Paranoia about walking eventually set in, a fear that she might fall again. Unfortunately, her nightmare came true again in 2007, while she tried to take a few steps. As she fell to the ground, the artificial joint implant got dislocated, cracking the bone on which it sat, once again, bombarding her with that earlier excruciating pain she had felt the first time, nearly a decade earlier.

This time around, however, I was not in Uganda to run to her rescue, and some of my brothers who had helped in the first accident, had since been called by their maker. My sister and I, upon learning about the fall, scrambled to find an ambulance that would transport her from her home to a hospital in Kampala, some two hundred miles away. Once that was done, we had to go through her orthopedic surgeon, to import a new hip implant from South Africa, since none were readily available in Uganda. Finally, another operation was successfully performed at Rubaga Hospital. As much as physical therapy was once again recommended, we knew this wasn't going to be a viable option. Instead, we got her a wheelchair and a walker with wheels, the kind typically used by the elderly in the US. This too, can be problematic in an environment devoid of level pavement. But, as former Defense Secretary Donald Rumsfeld once put it, "You go to war with the army you have, not the army you want". Or, as one African proverb goes, "Since you can't bend the wind, you bend the sail".

My mom's health held on after the second operation, but it was not so great. Oftentimes, we'd get false alarms from the caretaker, and then we would either call in a doctor from nearby Rukungiri town, or arrange for her to be taken in for checkups. This process went on and off unabated for close to four years. Sensing that she may not maintain this condition for much longer, I organized for my wife and I to take our son with us and visit while she could at least still recognize some people. By this time, she was beginning to display some signs of mild dementia. Some days she would wake up, take her seat in the usual place, and eat her meals cheerfully, occasionally injecting a word or two in the conversation. But on her bad days, she was reluctant to leave her bed, and even when she did, she just sat there with a sullen face, staring, seemingly at the ceiling, with neither interest in the people around her, nor the food or drink they offered her.

We left Uganda in the second week of March, 2012, and had barely settled back in the US, when we got an S.O.S call alerting us that my mom had been admitted at Nyakibale Hospital in serious condition. Her frequent visits had acquainted us with the medical personnel there, so we placed some calls to a few of them to find out what was the problem. She had slipped into a comma, and for about three days, doctors had relentlessly tried to bring her back without success. Meantime, we bit the bullet and held our breath. We contemplated transporting her back to Kampala, but the doctors ruled that out, given her very delicate condition. Then on the fourth day, she miraculously opened her eyes again, and after a good rest, was able to talk without the impaired speech of people who go through a stroke. We were naturally very relieved. My sister made immediate arrangements to go see her and nurse her for a few weeks.

It appears, the good Lord had allowed us to say our goodbyes, for that would be the last time we'd see her alive. During the second week of July 2012, we got another distress call from the caretaker, telling us that mom had once again been admitted at the hospital in a much weakened state. My sister, as a trained medical professional, always wanted specifics about the vital records. This time around, the signs indicated such low pressure as could only happen if someone had lost vast quantities of blood. She insisted that they give her a blood transfusion immediately, without any further delay. They also hooked her on oxygen to aid her breathing, since her lungs appeared to be full of fluids. By now, she was in a comma, unable to open her eyes. As test after test was conducted, it began to appear that her end was getting ever closer. As one thing was corrected, another would show signs of failing.

For three weeks, we were on tenterhooks, making daily calls on the hour for updates of the situation. The doctors at the hospital did all they could to keep her alive in an upcountry hospital with bare-bone facilities. The first few days following the transfusion, some of the vital signs like blood cell counts showed considerable improvements, giving us a sense of optimism. But her lungs remained a major concern. If she could not be made to breathe on her own, then her quality of life was, for all intents and purposes, practically over. My sister and I began to deliberate over the unthinkable. How long, for instance, were we prepared to keep her on a life-support system? And which one of us would eventually authorize the doctors to pull the plug?

We did not have to answer any of the painstaking questions. On July 30th 2012, upon my insistence, my niece Grace left Kampala to go spend some last moments with her grandma. I had instructed her to call me as soon as she reached the hospital, no matter what hour. Grace is a composed mother of four, who also happens to be my parents' oldest female grandchild. Every family has a kid that commands more trust than the rest. In my family, Grace is that kid. In most cases, if she gives you her word, you can take that to the bank. As soon as she arrived at the hospital, she called me and said,

"Uncle, you need to buy a ticket and come at once, there's no life left in her". I knew better not to argue with her. It was about ten O'clock in the morning over there (2.00 a.m EST). I had not been able to catch any sleep all night, perhaps in anticipation. Another hour or so elapsed, as many thoughts and scenarios run through my mind. Then at 2.38 a.m, another call came through, this time from Gloria, one of Grace's sisters. She too, was at the hospital, and is a medic at Mulago Hospital. She didn't mince words.

"Uncle", she said, "Grandma just passed on a few minutes ago" She was naturally distraught, and I took a few minutes to console her. I had an urgent mission to accomplish, one that couldn't wait. Fortunately, I had alerted management at my work on the impending possibility of my mom's passing, and they had all given me the green light to leave whenever I felt it was appropriate. The day was a Monday, right at the peak of the summer travel season. My wife decided that she would accompany me on the long trip, quite a welcome relief, considering what I had endured alone on previous trips of a similar nature. We set a target for the following day, and went about searching for same-day tickets. These are by far the most expensive. By the time we went to bed that evening, we had booked two tickets on KLM traveling from Dulles to Entebbe, via Detroit Amsterdam and Kigali.

When we got to Dulles Airport the following day, one airline official made us stand in the KLM line for so long, until they realized we should have been in the Delta line, due to their intricate co-share arrangement. We missed the Detroit flight, and instead got booked on a direct KLM flight to Amsterdam. The rest of the connections remained the same. Arriving in Kampala on Wednesday evening, we rested that night and left for upcountry on Thursday. Thanks to my other niece Madina, and her generous husband Johnson, a vehicle and a driver were put at our disposal to take us upcountry. Most other arrangements were already in place when we got home. There was a sea of people who had come from near and far, to pay tribute to the matriarch of the family. Funerals in Africa are not a private affair, restricted only to close-knit family members. By our estimate, there were at least in excess of seven hundred people on Friday when we finally laid the old lady to rest in a colorful ceremony. The Baganda say, "Amaze omulimu gwe" meaning she has accomplished her task on earth.

We stayed behind a couple of days after the funeral to tie up some loose ends. With both parents now gone, my natural bond with the country has become looser, although I still have many relatives spread all over the place. But I'll always cherish the love and principles they instilled in me. Nobody else can duplicate that, and no amount of money can ever buy it.

As I posed by my parents' graves lying next to each other, before leaving, I was reminded of Chief Seattle's words,

"The earth does not belong to us, we belong to it. Whatever befalls the earth befalls the sons and daughters of the earth. We did not weave the web of life, but we are merely strands in it. Whatever we do to the web, we do to ourselves".

Thirty

THE US ELECTION is a two-year grueling exercise that climaxes as a clash of the titans. It's not a task for the faint-hearted. To succeed in the undertaking, one must have a lot of stamina, backed by immense resources, allowing a candidate to crisscross and persuade people of all shades in this vast nation, stretching over several time zones, to vote for his or her philosophy. The American people are among the most difficult to please. With the nation's foundation rooted on the basis of individual liberty, choice and equality, some people pursue these principles to a fault.

I had left Uganda during the unforgettable reign of terror of Idi Amin, and therefore, if anybody could appreciate the price of freedom, that person had to be me. I had watched many presidential campaigns, beginning with 1980, when Ronald Reagan sought to unseat the then incumbent President Jimmy Carter. Although I have never declared any party affiliation, over the years one eventually gets aligned one way or another. During the first two decades of my stay, most of which I spent at the World Bank, I couldn't vote, because I had not yet acquired US citizenship. However, after leaving the Bank, I changed my status, and have, since been exercising my civic duty, choosing Congressmen, Senators, Governors, and, the ultimate prize, the US President.

Barack Obama's declaration of his intention to run for the

presidency of the US in 2008 captivated me more than any I had watched in this country. Although he was not the first black candidate to run (Congresswoman Shirley Chisholm and the Rev. Jesse L, Jackson had run before him), he was the only one given a remote chance of being considered as a serious candidate for the most powerful job in the world. If he prevailed, this would entirely change the course of history, not only in the US, but the world over. It would almost certainly, be the first time in recent history of the world that a black man would be at the helm of a power-crazy world that has been dominated mainly by white people.

For the African American community, and other people of color, there is no better role model than having one of their own sitting at the pinnacle of power.

But beyond this aspect, one has to consider the odds stacked against him to appreciate the hurdles he needed to overcome to win the ultimate prize. For a young colored boy abandoned at a pre-teen age by a Kenyan father on student visa, the chances of his ever making it to the Congress of the United States appeared quite remote. Yet, here was the same young man, with no apparent big sponsor, still cutting his teeth in his first term senate seat, daring to stand on the steps of the Illinois Capitol Building in Springfield that Abraham Lincoln stood on seeking the same office. Although America has taken giant steps to overcome racism and bigotry over the years since Lincoln's emancipation of slavery, there are still plenty of people in this great country, who labeled such an action as Obama's, simply heresy. To such people, the black man is, forever condemned to remain subservient to the white race. Viewed from this angle, therefore, Obama treaded on sacred ground and some oracle needed to be called in to cleanse the tarnished site.

On his first attempt, some people say, Obama was accorded a sympathetic hearing, mostly from a white community, bent on atoning for all things sinister visited on the black race since the beginning of time. While this might have had some truth to it, why didn't they extend the same courtesy to his predecessors, Chisholm and Jackson? The answer to this is that, unlike the black candidates before him, he didn't contest based on the sense of entitlement, born out of the civil rights movement. Moreover, with a Columbia and Harvard resume, he struck even his worst detractors as more polished and knowledgeable than those before him. In short, he was a well-rounded candidate who happened to be black. His biracialism was both a blessing and a curse at the same time. Within the black community, there is a certain degree of suspicion about biracial products, viewed as likely to emphasize their white side in order to gain access to services and facilities they would not otherwise get. This concept was exploited to maximum advantage in apartheid South Africa, where the coloreds identified more with the Afrikaans than with their more oppressed black brethren.

To the white community, on the other hand, a biracial candidate appears more acceptable, as someone in the neutral zone. These are not issues many people are willing to sing about in the town square, but, which, as one judge said, when asked if he could define pornography, "I may not be able to define it, but you know it when you see it". Even then, given his social standing as a junior Senator from Illinois, nobody expected him to marshal enough resources to compete effectively against his white counterparts, especially a household name like Hillary Clinton, a New York Senator in her own right, and former First Lady of a popular president like Bill Clinton. And herein is where the Obama genius began to manifest itself. Since he clearly couldn't compete for funds from the big guns on Wall Street, why not beat his competitors by collecting more pocket change on Main Street?

It didn't hurt that he'd forsaken the former for the latter, when he had a choice of picking careers after completing his Harvard Law School course. The rough and tumble life he experienced as a Community Organizer in the low income neighborhoods of Chicago's Southside allowed him the encounter with more of the down-trodden members of society, that would eventually form a very reliable base. These are not necessarily members of any particular racial group. Nevertheless, they share a lot of common traits that tend to unite them towards a common destiny. They are the teachers, valued for their services, but always underpaid. They also include the police and firefighters, eking out a living under risky circumstances. Don't forget the trash collectors, always punctual to pick up someone else's, trash leaving them no time to pick their own, and finally, all those Wal-Mart moms who wake up every day to ring the checkout counter machines, for customers, but can ill-afford to pay for their own items. These are not the so-called "welfare queens" Reagan referred to, but America's working poor, always one paycheck away from catastrophe.

Most of these people constitute the bulk of what Mitt Romney, the president's challenger during his second term election campaign, designated as the infamous 47% of the population who would vote for the president because they expect some "free stuff". This group would also embrace students in college, or about to enter, being saddled and crushed with student loan debt, with few prospects of landing a well-paying job upon graduation.

Candidate Obama first tapped into this pool of voters using the latest internet technology. Through a combination of e-mail, text, twitter and Facebook, the Obama-For-America organization mobilized these diversified groups, kept them abreast with campaign literature, while asking them to commit tiny amounts as little as $5, but on a more frequent basis. The numbers soon grew like a wild fire, boosted, especially by Generation Xers, who felt that joining the organization was chic. With the numbers swelling by the minute, the $5-$25 frequent contributions soon added up to real money, trouncing those of the old school who relied on a few big contributors to max out with the $2500 individual amount allowed by the law. By the time Obama's opponents realized what had hit them, it was too late to reverse the trend, and the lanky Senator with a funny name was ready for prime time, unencumbered by the nuances of lack of finances.

The Obama phenomenon became a fad that proved too strong for Hillary to overcome, despite her all-too-familiar name recognition. Selling himself in the "Change You Can Believe In" wrapper, Mr. Obama played offence in Hillary's end zone with no time-outs left for her. After a grueling primary season, the campaign ended with Obama being nominated as the Democrat's flag-bearer after some acrimonious debates.

The young Senator was then pitied against Republican Senator John McCain of Arizona who had earlier, won his party's nomination. Like Hillary, Senator McCain was a household name. A Vietnam War hero who spent five years under captivity by the enemy, he was everything Obama was not. His father and grandfather were Admirals in the US Navy, and besides being backed by the old Republican Money juggernaut, McCain himself had married into old money, a heiress of the brewing industry.

Yet, in spite of all these disadvantages, Obama's more appealing message of hope and change prevailed. First, McCain showed poor judgment by selecting a bimbo named Sarah Palin, whose only contribution to the ticket appeared to be her folksy talking style and a pretty face. Obama more than compensated for this by picking Good Old Joe Biden.

Joe was an old hand in the Senate and schooled in the intricate ways of Washington, having served in the US Senate since 1972. He too, could be folksy, but with substance. Senator McCain ended up giving lackluster debate performance during the presidential debates he held with Obama. In the end, Obama's fundraising strategy also overwhelmed McCain's funding advantages, allowing Senator Obama to sail home triumphantly. By the end of Election night on November 3, 2008, for the first time in the history of the American Republic, the White House would be occupied by a non-white man. Obama had defied every theory in the book. But could he repeat the experience four years later?

President Barack Obama's re-election campaign was

supposed to be a hard road to travel from the moment he pro-
nounced himself on his intention to run. What, with the nation's
unemployment rate hovering around 8%, and in some places,
much higher. The only other time in recent memory that an incumbent president was returned with such numbers, was when
Franklin D. Roosevelt was re-elected in 1936 with the unemployment rate standing at a whopping 17% following the Great
Depression. But then again, no other president had inherited such
a weak economy since FDR. The rule of thumb had, until the
presidential election of 2012, been that no incumbent would be
returned to the White House with an economy in such a shape.
President Obama's initial campaign message of blaming the economy's poor performance on his predecessor, George W. Bush,
wasn't resonating very well with the general public, who felt that
with nearly four years under his belt, the policies he instituted
should have reversed the situation. The president had began his
first term with an ambitious program meant to reverse the massive
financial meltdown and job losses averaging up to 800,000 jobs
per month. To do this, he had convinced Congress whose two
chambers (House of Representatives and the Senate) were at the
time, controlled by Democrats, to approve the Economic Stimulus
Package in February 2009, to the tune of $787 billion.

However, given the state of the economy at the time, this
huge borrowing from the treasury would add to the already spiral-
ing federal budget deficit. Republicans opposed this move from
the beginning, and it would later form the basis of the GOP's election platform for their flag-bearer's campaign 2012. Meanwhile,
Republicans began selling Mitt Romney, the presumed Republican
nominee as the whiz kid of the business establishment, who was
the only one with the magic wand that could rescue the ailing
US economy. But during the Republican primaries held earlier
in the year, Mr. Romney had failed to convince the right-wing
faction of his party, that he had the right conservative mettle to
earn their vote. In fact, his two toughest competitors during the

primary, former Senator Rick Santorum of Pennsylvania, and former Speaker of the House, Newt Gingrich of Georgia, had inflicted so much damage on Mitt, that Obama's campaign strategists adopted some of the literature in their playbook.

The Democratic and Republican candidates couldn't have been more different. Obama, born in 1961, was a product of a biracial relationship between an African student from Kenya, who had landed at the University of Hawaii in the early 1960's , benefitting from scholarships the US extended to African countries as they prepared for their independence. The senior Obama had met the future president's mother, Ann Dunham Stanley then 18 years old, at the University of Hawaii, married her in a hurry, before abandoning her and the baby, soon after, as he embarked on a Ph D. course at Harvard University. The young Obama, who was later bundled up to follow his mother to Jakarta, Indonesia, after she re-married a citizen of that Asian archipelago, would not be re-united with his father again until he was ten years old, even then, for a very brief moment.

Mostly raised by his maternal Grandparents, and a relentlessly determined mother, but one who was more often desperately short of cash, Obama's path to success was improbable at best. Defying the old cliché of "Go west young man", Obama kept going east, first landing at Occidental College in Los Angeles, California, where, his initial pre-occupation appeared to be finding his own identity. Two years later, Barack Obama went further east, transferring to Columbia University in the Big Apple, whose tough neighborhoods would chart the course of his first career as Community Organizer in the "Project Housing" of Chicago's South Side. Leaving the bustling streets of Chicago for Harvard Law School, he would later return to the windy city to cut his teeth in politics, first as a State Senator, then later as an Illinois Senator.

The nation first got a glimpse of his oratory in 2004, when he delivered the Key Note Address during Senator John Kerry's democratic nomination for that year's presidential election against then incumbent George W. Bush. The World was awed by the lanky wide-eared electrifying speaker "with a funny name", who implored his fellow citizens, not to box themselves in little cocoons by defining themselves as "Irish Americans", Jewish Americans, "African Americans", "Republicans", or "Democrats", but rather project themselves in the wider context as Americans.

Willard Mitt Romney, the 2012 Republican candidate for the US presidency, was a product of privilege. His father, George, was an auto company executive, before becoming the 43rd Governor of the state of Michigan in the 1960's. He later made an unsuccessful bid for the White House before exiting the public arena. Born on March 12, 1947, Mitt spent his formative years in Bloomfield Michigan, later enrolling at Stanford University, which he left after two years, to participate as a missionary in France, for his Mormon Church. Returning to the US two years later, he completed his bachelor's degree at Brigham Young University in Salt Lake City, Utah. He went on to pursue a JD/MBA at Harvard Business School, which he completed in 1975. He first cut his teeth in the field of Management Consulting at Bain Company starting in 1977, later forming Equity Firm Bain Capital for which he became chief executive officer.

But Bain Capital was a predatory company in the mold of the so-called irrational exuberance era of the 1980s, as portrayed in the movie "Wall Street", with Michael Douglas as the ubiquitous Gordon Gekko. With Mitt Romney at the helm, Bain Capital gobbled up failing companies, intending to turn them around and sell them off for a handsome profit. With the help of Junk Bond shenanigans like Michael Milken, financing such ventures was often just a phone call away for well-known takeover archetypes like Carl Icahn. The end results were, however, not always what the target companies desired. Oftentimes, the management as well as "non-essential" employees in the target companies were quickly shown the door, usually followed by some form of asset-stripping to create a lean and mean company.

Because the new companies were highly financially lever-aged, if the newly trimmed company's products did not sell well enough to generate enough revenue to service the mountain of debt, the new owners like Bain Capital, quickly put the compa-nies on the chopping block, in order to recoup their investment before the debt holders themselves came calling with an auction-eer's gavel. To streamline production, some units were eliminated and set up in far-flung places like China, Malaysia, or Mexico, leaving former US employees holding empty bags, with neither pension nor healthcare benefits.

Mr. Romney, who had hoped to sell himself to the American voters as a white knight with a wealth of experience to turn around companies, had underestimated the Obama campaign's ability to tie Bain Capital's ruthless reputation like an albatross around his neck. The protracted Republican primaries had extended into the summer, sucking enormous energy from Mr. Romney, and leaving Mr. Obama, who had no challenger for the Democratic nomina-tion, to have an early start on chipping away at Mr. Romney's advantages. He soon found himself on the defensive, against an onslaught that painted him as a cold-hearted profiteer who took over companies and ruined people's lives with reckless aban-don. It didn't help his cause any bit when, after the Republican Convention in Miami, Florida, Mitt Romney made a U-turn in his campaign, and started moving towards the center, away from the extreme right conservative positions he had taken during the primaries.

Then, Mitt dropped the bombshell, which turned out to be the game changer. While addressing a group of wealthy do-nors, he was caught on videotape, referring to nearly half of the American voters (47%), as those who rely on the government "for free stuff". It didn't matter to him that, most of these were hard-working Americans like veterans of foreign wars, police officers, teachers, Wal-Mart moms and all those people who toil daily, but do not earn enough to afford a decent lifestyle. Once this video surfaced, curtsey of Mother Jones News organization, it reinforced the portrait the Democrats had already painted of him as a heartless spoiled brat, born with a silver spoon in his mouth. For a man, whose wealth is estimated in the neighborhood of $250 million and whose only released tax return showed that he had paid income tax at a rate of 13%, lower than Billionaire Warren Buffett's secretary, his reference to the 47% as those who pay no taxes, rubbed salt in many peoples' open wounds.

Republicans had also counted on their fundraising prowess over Democrats to overwhelm the Obama campaign. Little did they know that Obama's campaign network, first created for his campaign in 2008, which he used successfully against Hillary Clinton, was still in place, and with little greasing of the wheels, could be re-ignited to give Mitt a run for his money. While Mitt relied on the big guns to bundle up large donors who could max out on the individual contribution of $2500, the Obama campaign matched this with their democratic capitalism that relied on small donors of $200 or less, but spread out much wider among the voters. In the end, with a more consistent message than Mitt's flip-flops, no amount of money could sway enough voters in Mitt's way. Despite mainstream polling which indicated that the president maintained overwhelming advantages over his well-heeled opponent, some conservative pollsters such as Rasmussen and Karl Rove's American Crossroads, continued tweaking their numbers, to present their billionaire sponsors, like the Kohl Brothers, a picture that appeared favorable to their candidate.

By Tuesday, November 6th, 2012, America woke up exhausted by the seemingly endless campaigns, and ready to put an end to the circus. The saga was captured best by a YouTube video of a six-year old girl from Florida, which went viral. Asked by her mother why she was crying incessantly, she simply replied,

"I am tired of watching Mitt Romney and Barack Obama".

The state of Virginia, whose voting record had been with

Republicans since last backing Lyndon B Johnson in 1964, had broken for Barack Obama in 2008, but was very much on the watch list of swing states like Ohio, Iowa, Wisconsin, Colorado, Florida, and North Carolina. Although the south-western corridor of the state, comprising cities like Roanoke, Bristol and Lynchburg are solidly in the GOP camp, the northern Virginia suburbs of Washington DC, consisting of the affluent, and influential counties of Arlington, Fairfax, Loudon, Prince William, and the cities of Alexandria, and Falls Church, have, over the past thirty years or so, become the 800-pound gorilla in the state. With its multi-ethnic composition and high income power, the northern Virginia region has become the bellwether for the entire state. Almost half the resident population in the region constitutes recent immigrants, most born outside the US. Also, since a lot of socio-demographic studies have shown that new immigrants tend to identify more closely with Democrats than with the GOP, one of the consequences of the growing power of northern Virginia has been to slowly transform the state from a red to a blue state. So, as we sat home, glued to the TV screens watching the returns on Election night, we could not be swayed by the early picture that showed Mitt Romney doing well in the state just because the south and southwest were the first to report. We knew clearly, that this would be reversed, whenever Northern Virginia's numbers started trickling in. President Obama ended up trouncing Mitt Romney in the state, 51% to 49%. By eleven o'clock, Mitt Romney's fate was sealed with the loss of eight out of the nine swing states, with exception of North Carolina. Chicago's home boy was back on the saddle, marking the end of the most acrimonious presidential campaign seasons in recent memory.

Despite Mr. Obama's victory, however, the euphoria of "Hope, and Change you can believe in", are yet to be fulfilled for most of his core supporters, let alone for the nation and the world at large. Many groups, including his strongest core base, the African Americans, have not fared well during his administration. In fact, as a group, their economic condition as measured by most indicators, including asset accumulation, college graduation, home ownership, unemployment, etc, have somewhat worsened. But they've not been alone in this, except that, since in most cases, their wellbeing is often worse off than their white and Asian counterparts, any negative disruption in the economy is bound to have a larger impact on the group.

On the flip side, the president's signature policies such as Obamacare, and student loan program restructuring, would give more benefits to groups like these at the bottom of the economic ladder, compared to the more well-off citizens. Although it's too early to assess the impact of these policies, which are as yet to be fully implemented, in the end, they may turn out to be the greatest gift he will leave behind for posterity.

For Africa, whose euphoria and expectations were raised several notches by the election of the first black president with roots not far removed from the same continent, the 1st term was a great disappointment. President Obama, whose only visit to sub-Saharan Africa, was to Ghana (2nd term visit in June 2013, included Senegal, South Africa & Tanzania), has at times appeared disconnected from, or at least minimally engaged in the region's affairs. One would have, at the very least expected the president to have made a symbolic gesture by visiting Kenya, his paternal ancestors' home. Domestic budget shortfalls notwithstanding, his African policy is devoid of such major initiatives as Agoa and PEPFAR, launched by his two immediate predecessors, Bill Clinton and George W. Bush. Having failed to hit the iron while it was hot, it's unlikely that, whatever initiative Mr. Obama prescribes for the Continent in his second term would be greeted with a lot of fanfare.

Thirty One

THE CHINESE ARE coming! That's the cry heard in every capital city on the African Continent. And come, they have. In a little less than ten years, China's annual investments in Africa, have outstripped the volume of development aid (both bi-lateral and multi-lateral) that has, hitherto, flowed into the continent annually. The reasons for this new shift revolve around two main issues. The Chinese want a steady source of raw materials for their galloping economy, while the Africans want trade and aid on terms that are less stringent than western conglomerates and donors have always delivered. Until only recently, international trade with Africa was controlled from a few European capitals such as London, Paris, Brussels, and for the Portuguese-speaking countries, Lisbon. The so-called colonial bond between the colonies and the colonizers had held most African countries hostage, almost to the exclusion of other meaningful players. That marriage of convenience seems to have been fatally punctured with the emergence of a new suitor wearing a Beijing mask. Afro-pessimism, which was the hallmark of a by-gone era, seems to be slowly yielding to a wave of optimism about the continent. Even the Economist Magazine, which once dubbed Africa as "the hopeless continent", has lately jumped on the bandwagon of optimists.

This about-turn on Africa isn't without some merit. For start-ers, while most of the world's economies plunged into a deep recession, the continent seems to have weathered the storm, relatively unscathed, and, currently, about six out of the ten fastest-growing economies are African. Growing economies have produced a sizeable middle-class, whose boldness has challenged the notion that Africa always has to remain at the bottom of the totem pole, no matter what effort.

The new middle class has also come with their own demands, both from their leaders and their benefactors, pushing the idea of "trade, not aid". This will imply a major policy shift for traditional aid agencies like USAID, if they intend to continue their activities on the continent. The new message appears to be, that "Africa, is no longer a continent for the taking", just there to supply raw materials for others to manufacture goods, that they could make for themselves.

The rush to Africa is not limited to the Chinese, although, by the laws of large numbers, they appear to be everywhere. From Indians, Brazilians, Russians and Americans, everyone, it seems, wants in on the new "African gold rush".

From Angola to Zambia, and every country in between, Chinese technocrats are quickly replacing their western counterparts, as they come in droves to implement projects recently signed between some Chinese company and an African government. Smitten with incredibly corrupt governments, the Chinese, themselves, no strangers to the art, have become "partners in crime", with regimes that have been willing to sacrifice transparency at the altar of fast development aid. While western aid is not totally immune from underhand methods, the bulk of it has almost always been negotiated with clearly identifiable government technocrats, and is rarely disbursed in large amounts so quickly, without stringent conditions. Chinese aid on the other hand, appears to flow in very fast, usually on a handshake with the big man, or someone acting on his behalf, and whose personal needs are often taken care of long before the aid itself gets in the pipeline.

Although the casual observer may quickly discern several Chinese-funded projects being implemented in most countries across the Continent, the jury is still out, regarding the efficacy of these projects towards addressing the common weaknesses afflicting the economies. For instance, while multi-lateral aid from organizations such as the World Bank, the IMF, or the African Development Bank have tended to weave in a technical transfer element, Chinese companies not only import their own equipment from China, they also bring in hordes of Chinese workers (some sources say, a number of these may be unpaid prisoners) as well. While this approach might speed up the process of implementation, it conveys very little, if any technology transfer, and creates very few employment opportunities for the recipient countries. Moreover, other issues such as environmental impact are rarely seriously addressed, since the chief negotiators of the projects are by no means, experts in such fields.

Take the example of fish factories set up around Lake Victoria. Before the industry was opened to outsiders during economic liberalization in the 1980s, Ugandan lakes maintained a balanced supply of fish, because the local fishermen operated under a regulation that banned the use of small open hole nets. But, in an attempt to diversify exports, the government opened the industry to investors (mostly Chinese and Koreans), who arrived with half-a-mile narrow-hole nets, which trapped virtually anything in their way. At first, the fish exports rose by leaps and bounds. However, soon the local fishermen with dug-out canoes found out that they needed to go further and further in the lakes' interior to get the same catch they used to obtain near the shores. Gradually, that too, could not yield much, as fish stocks got depleted. Generations of fishing families became redundant, and were also forced to supplement their diets, since all they could afford now was "mgongo wazi" (fish bones), the fillet being processed and exported by the factories. Some of the Chinese factories have since closed their doors due to lack of enough fish supplies to keep them running.

Another area in which China is impacting the African continent is through the purchase of endangered animal products, such as rhino horns, and elephant tasks. Globally, Africa is known as the land of safaris and big-game hunting. But, unless African governments redouble their efforts to contain the current level of poaching to satisfy China's appetite for animal trophies, the claim to being home of big game will soon turn into a hollow statement. The new affluence in China has increased the demand for such hard-to-find objects as ivory and rhino horns. As more Chinese have poured onto the continent, some as workers, others as investors, most have doubled up as traders as well. This trade has carried them further into the interior, where poor communities have been lured by small amounts of cash to go out and slaughter the largest bull elephants with meter-long tasks. Lately, crates containing tons of illegal tusks have surfaced in Hong Kong and other Chinese cities, destined towards carvers' workshops.

The impact of the poaching is immediately felt in the tourism sector, as herds of elephants, buffalo and rhinos, which have long been the major attractions to foreign visitors, have been dwindling each year. The animals themselves, sensing danger from their close contact with human beings, have adopted a defensive mechanism that drives them further into the interior, leaving an occasional elephant or buffalo, to be viewed along the road. Fewer herds attract smaller numbers of tourists, bringing less revenue to the country in the long run. The new trophies extend beyond ivory to such other endangered species as rare birds, reptiles, hardwoods and minerals such as Columbite tantalite (coltan). It is, in fact, minerals like gold, diamonds, and coltan which continue fueling wars in God-forsaken places like Goma in the eastern Democratic Republic of Congo (DRC), as featured in the Box Office hit movie "Blood Diamonds", starring Leonardo DiCaprio. Coltan has particularly taken on significance with the escalating use of the cell-phone, of which it supplies a major component.

Now that Uganda has struck commercially exploitable quantities of oil in the western part of the country known as the Albertine Graben, many global players are clamoring to line up and be part of the action. The Irish company Tullow Oil, which initially broke ground in 2005, has since teamed up with giants Total of France, and China National Offshore Oil Corporation (CNOOC), to tap into the latter companies' financial muscle and hasten the pace of production upstream. However, the president's insistence that the oil companies build a refinery in the country in order to spread the oil benefits beyond the mere export of crude, may come with additional costs, bundled with unintended consequences. With no proper civic education regarding the benefits and evils of the oil sector, the Banyoro communities of Bulisa and Bugungu near the concentration of the oil wells, and likely future home of the mini-refinery, will discover, to their dismay, that they should have waved large posters bearing the letters "NIMBY" (Not In My Back Yard), instead of begging the government to locate the refinery there. Ask the Ogoni people of the Nigerian oil delta about this oil curse.

But water pollution and environmental damage aren't all that the so-called black gold will affect. For instance, the oil deposits are scattered in a region that includes Nwoya and Amuru Districts in Acholi, that's partly home to the indomitable Kabalega National Park. The drilling and traffic associated with the oil industry will ultimately disrupt the free movements of the park animals, to the extent that some may have to be re-located to other parks to save them. If the nation is to maximize the benefits from the oil industry, the country's economic managers need to take a holistic approach that looks at the economy in totality.

With a few exceptions, African countries have, over the last decade, taken a few strides in the right direction to address the economic malaise which afflicted them during the lost decades of the 70's and 80's. Economic growth and foreign direct investment (FDI), are no longer the preserve of a handful of countries such as South Africa, and oil exporters like Nigeria, Angola and Gabon. The liberalization of economies, which did away with fixed exchange rates, bloated government parastatals, and foreign exchange rationing, allowing private ownership, has resulted in massive infusions of capital in selected sectors, lifting economic growth and employment. More funds have flowed in as equity by way of the nascent capital markets that have sprung up in many countries around the continent.

Although the continent's export base is still primarily in raw material form, many countries are making efforts to diversify into manufacturing, away from a mono-commodity such as coffee or cocoa, and tap into other sources. The continent's brain-drain that saw hordes of professionals flock to western countries during the period of economic low tide, are proving to be a boon to the region, as billions of dollars in workers' remittances are sent back. During the hey-days of the European and US economies in the middle of the last decade, remittances to sub-Saharan Africa topped $40 billion according to World Bank estimates. This figure was higher than the net flow of official development aid to these countries. However, the deep financial crisis in western countries has since trimmed this to around $31 billion by 2012. Lately also, there have been a few cases of reverse migration, as entrepreneurially-minded professionals, with a sense of patriotism, head back to make fortunes in their home countries. This trend is likely to grow, if economic reforms continue taking hold, making Africa a more attractive destination to do business.

Technological breakthroughs, especially in telecommunications via cell phones and the internet, have allowed the continent to get closer to the rest of the world, partially compensating for the lack of physical infrastructure that has long been the major hindrance to doing business in the region. On the basis of head count alone, companies like MTN, Airtel and Celtel, have more customers on the African continent than exist in the US. Even the physical infrastructure bottlenecks such as roads and railways are beginning to be systematically tackled. That's where the Chinese have beaten the west, with symbolic edifices of hydroelectric dams, multi-lane highways, and giant stadiums, usually in exchange for harnessing resources such as oil, minerals, timber, etc. Thus, a number of countries such as Kenya and Ethiopia, neighbors since the beginning of time, will soon be linked by a super highway between Nairobi and Addis Ababa. Similar large scale projects, such as an oil pipeline from South Sudan, to the Kenyan port of Lamu, and extending the railway from Kasese in western Uganda to the Congolese city of Kisangani are currently on the drawing board, although some may take decades to realize. The Chinese government's command structure has been favored by African countries in such projects, because it allows for faster implementation. On the geopolitical front, China is also devoid of the colonial baggage which afflicts the west, hence less prone to the suspicion about its intentions to meddle in the affairs of these countries. But those who hold such subliminal views of an impending aggressive China would be advised to have an audience with the Dalai Lama, who would educate them about the Tibetan experience. It took western colonialist a long time to establish their patterns of behavior in their colonies, and my guess is the Chinese won't be too far behind. As the Baganda say, 'Gakyali mabaga", or, "It's still open season".

A new energy frontier has been opened in Africa over the last five years or so, with country after country either striking commercial reserves of oil or natural gas. Apart from the well-established players like Nigeria, Libya, Algeria, Angola, Gabon and Equatorial Guinea, new producers such as Ghana and South Sudan, have come on board, with yet others like Uganda, Kenya and Ethiopia clamoring to join the club. Tanzania has so far identified about 33 trillion cubic feet of natural gas, while Mozambique, with help from Italy's ENI oil giant, has discovered around 68 trillion cubic feet, equivalent to 12 billion barrels of oil. Should all the East African countries manage to start exploiting the oil and gas potential that is slowly emerging, the region might re-focus the west's attention grudgingly away from the perpetually volatile Middle East. This, however, might be where the rubber meets the road. The Chinese, who are already digging their heels in the region, grabbing whatever share of resources they can lay their hands on, are unlikely to sit back and watch, as the west re-establish themselves in the region to exploit the very same re-sources. A clash of the titans is therefore inevitable at some point in the future.

The US has already fired the first salvo by establishing the US Africa Command (US Africom), a military establishment head-quartered at Kelly Barracks in Stuttgart-Moehringen, Germany. Its role is to coordinate operations of the US Army, Air Force, and Marines with any military activity on the African Continent, including preventing the spread, and if necessary, pre-empting activities of such terrorist groups as Al Qaeda. An offshoot of this command structure is the Joint Task Force for the Horn of Africa, headquartered at Camp Lemonnier, Djibouti. While these efforts may sound well-intentioned, one cannot help interpreting them as flash points that say, "Big brother is watching you".

Events that began with the Arab Spring in 2011 have shown that western countries are not just about to take a back seat and watch their erstwhile colonies switch loyalties. As I write this, the French Army is engulfed in a war that pities Islamic extremists in the north against the Malian government in Bamako. French intervention also removed the regime of Laurent Gbagbo in Cote d'Ivoire, while heavy collaboration between the French and British bombardment softened the ground in Libya, before NATO offi-cially went in to put out the fire that swept out Colonel Qaddafi in the process. President Obama may be the man who initially cam-paigned on an anti-war platform, and even picked up a Nobel Peace Prize along the way, but he has since dropped more drones on the territories of Pakistan, Afghanistan and Yemen than all his predecessors combined.

Thirty Two

AFRICA IS A continent in transition like all the others before it. It has experienced teething problems along the way, the worst of which have, in my opinion, been self-inflicted,... caused by regimes that entrench themselves way past their sale-by-date mandate. It is ironic, that, the region that produced Nelson Mandela, who took on the reins of power for only one four-year term, after being incarcerated for 27 years, is the same one, where leaders frequently tamper with national constitutions to remove term limits, in order to extend their regimes indefinitely. The ramifications from this are many. Among these, is a serious crisis of leadership, arising from the fact that the self-anointed leaders, eventually wish to bequeath the throne to their offspring, irrespective of the brood's capacity to execute the duties of chief executive. The D R Congo's intractable problems may partly be blamed on this phenomenon.

Uganda may slowly be sliding into that mold. Recent uttering about a coup d'etat, first by the Minister of defense, followed by the President, and finally echoed by the Chief of Defense Forces, left the country rather jittery about the real purpose. One cannot help but note, that similar words in the past, from members of the opposition parties, or the military, have been deemed treasonable, landing the culprits in civil courts, or court martial, if uttered by enlisted members of the military. Astoundingly, the ruling party, NRM, and its affiliate, the UPDF, display the impunity of constantly reminding the governed how they live by a different set of rules. However, this time around, the deliberate message about the possibility of a coup, has taken up a life of its own.

Some observers have gone so far as suggesting that, the president, after 27 years of uninterrupted rule, may be seeking a way out, without being humiliated the Ben Ali or Hosni Mubarak style. Not used to being heckled and challenged, the president reigned supreme for nearly a quarter of a century. But of late, he's been battered by members of his own party since being re-elected in a sham election in February 2011. The president, who looks utterly exhausted in his rancher's hat, may have realized that his time has finally come, and turned to the army, the only saving grace he still effectively controls. This route would surprise very few, as further speculation is that it's through a military coup, that his son, now a Brigadier, and in charge of the presidential protection unit would emerge to ascend the throne. Muhoozi, the first son, aged 39, joined the UPDF in 1999 at the junior rank of lieutenant. In the thirteen years he's been there, he has been fast-tracked to the officer corps by sending him to elite military colleges such as the Royal Military Academy at Sandhurst in the UK, and the US Army Garrison at Fort Leavenworth, Kansas in the US. An attempt to bestow upon him the rank of Major by a visiting Col Muammar Qaddafi, then a regular guest of Museveni's state house, did not augur well with the public, and was quickly abandoned. Much older battle hardened officers who fought alongside his father in the early 1980's, are still languishing at lower ranks.

Lately, General David Sejusa (formerly known as Tinyefuza), added to this imbroglio by touching on the forbidden topic of President Museveni's succession, which he dubbed "the Muhoozi Project". If anybody would know about the existence of such a scheme, General Sejusa should be that man. Until rushing into self-imposed exile in late April 2013, he was the Coordinator of Uganda's Intelligence agencies, giving him a unique vantage point over such issues. According to a statement he released in a missive to the Daily Monitor Newspaper, he wanted the Director of Internal Security Organization (ISO), to investigate a purported plot to eliminate senior military officers such as himself, opposed to the so-called "Muhoozi Project. The project is meant to have the President's son succeed him when he finally decides to relinquish power, perhaps as early as 2016, when his current term ends.

Naturally, this was followed by denial after denial, mainly from the president's courtiers, although the president heightened the speculation by keeping mum about the issue for a long time, in the hope that it would die a natural death. However, the actions that the president has taken since General Sejusa's exile, including replacing the Chief of Defense Forces, and reshuffling his cabinet, lends credence to the old saying, "there's no smoke without fire".

Nevertheless, such grand schemes concocted in the leader's head to preserve his immortality, rarely succeed. Oftentimes, by the time they are supposed to be implemented, the riotous populations will have seized the grand palaces, including the occupants, overwhelming, and subjecting them to the same justice that the leader rained on them while in power. There is ample evidence that the re-awakening of the proletariat is already in the formative stages in the country. First, until recently, the president could count on the NRM caucus in parliament, where they outnumber the opposition party members by a factor of nearly 4 to 1, to hand him legislative victory that appeared to rubber-stamp the executive's proposals.

The president, who, for so long, has adroitly played the role of sole arbiter, by dangling the legendary sword of Damocles among his would-be ambitious challengers, both civilian and military alike, is slowly learning that there are limits even to an astute gambler. By virtually pulling the strings in every aspect that governs the ruling party, and by extension, the country's governance, the president managed to dominate the political space much longer than anybody could have anticipated.

The 9th parliament seems to have discovered his Achilles heel, and began charting a different course. A group of young Turks, appalled by the excessive corruption committed by either higher echelons of the regime or its associates, and the impunity with which corruption cases are dismissed by courts, even when the evidence is crystal clear, started voting overwhelmingly in support of opposition discourses. Efforts to rain them in by the president have not yielded positive results. Instead, their boldness has turned them into heroes in the eyes of a desperate public, who for so long watched the same misdeeds helplessly. Then, as never before, the general public has been emboldened to speak without fear, through all kinds of media fora. Under these circumstances, the atmosphere has turned into a malaise of sorts, in which people tend to speak in whispers, not sure who might be listening. Despite all the condemnation, the regime soldiers on shamelessly. In any case, as the Baganda say, "Okukokolima kwa wankoko tekutta kamunye", or simply, the angry protests of mother chicken are no armor against a hungry hawk.

Unfortunately, the country has been through this route before, first during former President Obote's Martial Law period, known locally as "bisela bya kabenge", then through Amin's reign of terror, and back to Obote II's "Panda Gali". Although the atrocities committed by the UPDF and the militarized police pale in comparison to earlier regimes, the fact that they are being registered, and undeniably so, is something every peace-loving citizen should loathe. No country deserves to go through atrocities of this type even once.

Africa's future will have to be determined by its people's willingness to sacrifice in order to create institutions that do away with the current circus of one-man shows. Institutions are the incubators for independent-mindedness. The continent must re-orient its education away from the colonial structure, whose objective was to create a pyramid, with a few administrative elites at the top, while relegating the majority to a substandard culture of non-thinkers. For a continent that lags behind all others in infrastructure, the civil engineers for roads, railways and bridges, electricians, gemologists etc, must be homegrown if any substantial progress is to be made. Without institutions, leadership by individuals, no matter how charismatic or how long they stay, cannot ensure continuity, and will condemn these countries on a vicious path of taking one step forward, and two steps back. No solutions imported totally from outside will ever transform a country to achieve the desired results. Thus the constant cries extolling the big powers such as the US, UK or France, to come to the rescue will always be an exercise in futility, if not to compliment already on-going efforts at home.

The long-entrenched leaders in Africa can borrow a leaf from Pope Benedict XVI, who, in early February 2013, saw it fit to abdicate his leadership of the world's 1.2 billion Catholics citing his advanced age, and physical inability to cope with the grueling demands of the position. This incident, the first of its kind in 600 years, where conventional wisdom was that a pontiff's term is for life, will allow the conservative church to do some soul-searching. TV images showing Pope John Paul II's frailty challenged the wisdom of retaining a clearly physically incapacitated incumbent as head of Christendom's largest prize. Although the Pontiff's real reasons for resignation may never be known, there are many stories regarding a power struggle inside the Vatican. Add to these the fact that his papacy was dominated by issues surrounding sex scandals by the clergy at all levels, and the rigidity of the ultra conservative church leaders against today's hot button issues such as abortion, celibacy and the elevation of women into the church's top echelons.

To watch Octogenarian "Uncle Bob" of Zimbabwe struggling to convince a generation of his compatriots, most of them born during his rule, that he is, still, the only wise man around to steer the country out of its economic doldrums, is a pathetic spectacle.

The African Union's peer review, constituted to rid the continent of such evils as dictatorships, and malcontents like Joseph Kony, should also be courageous enough to remind "perpetual revolutionary democrats", that there is a time to rule, and a time to exit the stage.

For me, the resignation of the Pope creates a once-in-a-lifetime opportunity to throw in my hat as the driver of the Pope mobile for Pope Francis I, although his first act of shunning the papal limo gave me some goosebumps, and doubts about quitting my day job. But, you see, this job is like no other. Imagine starting your job every day with a blessing from the Holly Father! Among other perks, you'll probably never need to renew your driver's license, as no sane member of the carabinieri would dare stop you. For that matter, even if you had a glass or two of Martini & Rossi, celebrating after seeing that famous white smoke over the Sistine Chapel's chimney, you'd still escape the sobriety test from the Swiss Guards.

Finally, watching the recently concluded elections in Kenya, gave me a lot of hope about the African potential to democratize its system. Kenya, whose last murky exercise in 2007 plunged the country into the post-election mayhem that resulted into the death of over 1300 people, while hundreds of thousands more were displaced from their homes by internecine violence, appeared to have learned well from that tragedy. On the surface, the presidential candidate field was over-populated by no less than eight candidates, although the real focus was on the two antagonists, namely, Uhuru Kenyatta of the Jubilee Coalition, and his nemesis, Raila Odinga heading the CORD ticket. The two titans rode on name recognition, derived from their famous fathers. Uhuru, is the son of the late Mzee Jomo Kenyatta, Baba Taifa, or father of present day Independent Kenya. Raila Odinga, the nation's Prime Minister over the last five years, is the son of the late Jaramogi Oginga Odinga, who served as President Jomo Kenyatta's Vice President from 1963, until the two had a fall out in 1966.

The rivalry between Uhuru and Raila, can therefore be dubbed intergenerational. Although Africa's era of the "Big Man" may be peaking, trans-generational power succession is very much alive and well. From the foiled attempts to install their off-springs by Qaddafi and Mubarak in North Africa, cases abound with those whose broods have succeeded them. Immediate examples include Eyadema of Togo, Bongo of Gabon, Kabila of D.R. Congo, Khama of Botswana, and now, president Uhuru Kenyatta of Kenya . Then there are those like Museveni of Uganda, whose son, now a brigadier in the country's army, appears to be an understudy for papa's job.

Kenya's ability to maneuver around the electoral process without being mired into the violence that plagued the nation in 2008 appears to have sprung from the new constitution promulgated in 2010, and deep reforms, particularly enacted in the judiciary, which strengthened the independence of institutions such as the Independent Electoral and Borders Commission (IEBC). Kenya, by and large, still remains an ethnocentric society with power and resources dominated by whichever ethnic group happens to control State House. Thus, the Uhuru-Ruto Jubilee Coalition benefited from the all-powerful Kikuyu, who have produced three out of the four presidents who have ruled the nation since independence in 1963. Mr. William Ruto, is a powerful politician from the Kalenjin ethnic group, which, during Daniel arap Moi's 24-year rule, had displaced more numerically superior groups such as the Luhya and Luo, to assume second place after the Kikuyu in Kenya's pecking order.

Drawing on the vast resources his father, Mzee Jomo Kenyatta bequeathed him, and the blessings of the other two presidents that followed his dad, Moi and Kibaki, Uhuru was , from the word go, the anointed establishment candidate. By contrast, the Raila-Musyoka CORD coalition, though representing two of the big five ethnic groups in the country, the Luhya and Luo, were in the second tier by default. Although, both Raila Odinga and

Kalonzo Musyoka are political heavy-weights in their own right, their merger lacked the resources and cache associated with the Kenyatta name.

The International Criminal Court's (ICC) indictment of the Jubilee Coalition's duo, for crimes against humanity, in connection with the 2008 ethnic riots that took the lives of over 1000 people, and displaced thousands more, appeared to have strengthened, rather than weakened the position of Team Uhuruto. Given the ICC's track record of seemingly picking on African leaders for prosecution at The Hague, Kenyans rallied around the flag in defiance of Moreno Ocampo's ICC's action against the six men indicted. However, going by the rate at which the prosecution is losing its star witnesses, who recant their earlier statements, it still remains to be seen, if Ocampo's replacement, Ms. Fatou Bensouda from the Gambia will pursue the charges against Uhuru and Ruto with the same zeal.